Women and War in South Africa

Women and War in South Africa

Jacklyn Cock

The Pilgrim Press
Cleveland, Ohio

HOUSTON PUBLIC LIBRARY

Originally published by Oxford University Press, Cape Town, South Africa, as
Colonels and Cadres: War and Gender in South Africa. © 1991 by Jacklyn Cock

Pilgrim Press edition published 1993
The Pilgrim Press, Cleveland, Ohio 44115

Printed in the United States of America

The paper used in this publication is acid free and meets the minimum requirements
of American National Standard for Information Sciences-Permanence of Paper for
Printed Library Materials, ANSI Z39.48-1984

98 97 96 95 94 93   5 4 3 2 1

Library of Congress Cataloging-in-Publication Data

Cock, Jacklyn.
    [Colonels & cadres]
    Women and war in South Africa / Jacklyn Cock. — Pilgrim Press ed.
        p.   cm.
    Originally published: Colonels & cadres. Cape Town : Oxford University Press,
1991.
    Includes bibliographical references (p.) and index.
    ISBN 0-8298-0966-X (acid-free)
    1. South Africa—Politics and government—1978-1989. 2. Women and war—
South Africa. 3. Women and the military—South Africa. 4. Women—South
Africa—Interviews. I. Title.
    [DT1963.C63 1993]
    968.06'3—dc20   93-16270
                                                              CIP

Contents

Acknowledgements

The ideas on which this book is based were first aired at an African Studies Institute seminar at the University of the Witwatersrand in 1987. I am extremely grateful to everyone who responded to that seminar paper and gave me useful criticisms and encouragement. In particular I would like to thank Laurie Nathan, April Carter, Moira Maconachie, William Cobbett, and Charles van Onselen for the detailed comments they made at that time. I would also like to thank Eddie Webster and Frene Ginwala for their support and encouragement, and Penny Nyren for her editing. I am indebted to the many people who helped to arrange access to the diverse South Africans whose experiences and understandings are recorded in this book. My largest debt is to my informants, for having given up their time to be interviewed, and for sharing their ideas with me. I have learned a great deal from all of them.

Johannesburg
December 1990

Introduction

'Jane' and 'Ellen' are both forceful, independent women who wield power and authority in their working lives. Both emerged from interviews as extremely principled people who define themselves as patriots and whose daily actions are informed and inspired by their particular commitments to notions of 'peace' and 'justice'. Both came from working class families and had known poverty in their youth. Both are also mothers, and have found it difficult to balance caring for their children with the demands of their jobs. Both have relied largely on their own parents, particularly their mothers, to assist with child care, especially when their children were young. Both have experienced difficulties in their relationships with men and have gone through divorce. Both came across as extremely competent, strong and self-directed women. Neither describes herself as a 'feminist' – in fact they are both critical of feminism – but both are strongly committed to 'women's rights'. Both women feel strongly about this issue, and speak with some anger about the discrimination they have had to struggle against at work.

'Jane' is one of only ten women colonels in the South African Defence Force (SADF). 'Ellen' is a member of Umkhonto we Sizwe (MK), the armed wing of the African National Congress. As such they belong to opposing armies, in a conflict that both of them defined as a 'war'.

Were we – South Africans living through the decade of the eighties – at war? For a time I put this question to everyone I came across – in the classroom, at meetings, at parties – and was surprised at the vehemence and indignation of their answers. People who replied in both the positive and the negative prefaced their remarks with 'Of course ...' The certainty and diversity of the answers made me want to explore this question in a more systematic way.

The notion of 'war' conjures up images of battle-scarred fields and levelled buildings; trenches, bullets, bombs exploding ... I only once heard a bomb explode during this period; it had been placed outside the Johannesburg headquarters of an SADF unit, the Witwatersrand Command. Three people were killed and 90 injured. Years later in Lusaka I spoke to the extraordinary young man who is widely believed to be responsible for this action. He defined himself as a soldier engaged in fighting a 'people's war'. What motivated people like him was another question that interested me. Why – given that most people's impulse for self-preservation is so strong – do individuals fight wars? In conversation with widely differing people in Lusaka, Harare and all parts of South Africa over the past few years, I have heard various individual motivations, usually expressed in ideological terms. People go to war as 'nationalists' and 'patriots'. But they do so in their gender identities as 'men' and 'women'. I have come to believe that understanding war involves examining the military and its power in society. Understanding the military involves examining gender relations – in particular the way masculinity and femininity are defined. The military mobilizes gender identities, and in periods of war this process is sharpened.

The central argument of this book is that South Africa in the decade of the eighties was a society at war, and that individuals' experience of this war was shaped by gender relations. Of course people's experiences were also coloured by a variety of other social factors such as ideology, race, class and ethnic identity. But gender is a crucial and neglected dimension.

The connection between war and gender has been made before – most eloquently by Virginia Woolf in *Three Guineas*. But it has not been demonstrated. In this book the relation between war and gender is explored in a specific society and period – South Africa in the 1980s. It documents the actual experience and understandings of very different South Africans, ranging from colonels in the SADF to cadres in Umkhonto we Sizwe (MK).The book is intended as a contribution towards reconciliation. We need to address the past in order to redress the future. War is the crucible of the 'new' South Africa. This book provides a backdrop to understanding the present, by voicing some of the experiences and understandings which different South Africans carry with them into what will hopefully be a democratic, non-racial and non-sexist future.

The first chapter is called 'Inside South Africa's twilight war'. (The phrase was used by Captain Dirk Coetzee of the state's 'death squads'.) This chapter focuses on the different experiences and perceptions of violent conflict in the decade of the 1980s. It demonstrates that the SADF was a crucial agency of political violence in this period.

Chapter two is a discussion of the politics of gender in South Africa, focusing on power relations between men and women. The chapter shows how men and women have different access to power and resources in South African society; it looks at the different meanings given to masculinity and femininity, and at how different gender identities –

the notion of men as 'the protectors' and women as 'the protected' – were mobilized for war.

The next five chapters go on to examine the experiences and understandings of five very different groups of people:

• the 'protectors'

These are members of the SADF who were active in what one informant termed 'an atrocious war' in Namibia, as well as in Angola and the townships. Drawing on interview material, the chapter describes the 'protectors'' various experiences and understandings of 'atrocities', and demonstrates how the SADF uses the concept of masculinity in military training and in combat.

• the 'protected'

Many soldiers go to war to defend an image of social order, of 'home and hearth', in which women are central. This chapter focuses on the paradox in the increasing incorporation of women into war and the SADF, both directly (14 per cent of the Permanent Force are now women), and indirectly through work in munitions factories, support organizations, and so on.

• the resisters

This focuses on two organizations which played very different roles in the resistance to state militarization in the eighties – MK and the End Conscription Campaign (ECC). The SADF and MK reflect all the myriad differences between a conventional and a guerrilla army. However, it is shown that women in both armies have been the subjects of similar processes of incorporation and exclusion. The chapter shows how gender identities shape resistance; how the concept of 'resistance' must be expanded to understand women's roles; and how the politics of gender was used against both radical men (castigated as 'effeminate') and women (dismissed as 'social failures') to discredit them and denigrate their commitment.

• the feminists and the militarists

Does equal rights mean equal responsibilities? Should equal responsibilities include military service for women? Should such military service include combat roles? These questions are logically at the cutting edge of contemporary feminism. This chapter explores some of the different answers and understandings of feminism and militarism that emerged from interviews with South African women, including women soldiers in both the SADF and MK.

● the victims

This demonstrates that all South Africans were damaged by the political violence of the eighties – albeit in very different ways. Through a discussion of 'the militarization of childhood' it is argued that the worst-affected victims are our youth.

Each chapter includes a profile, and draws on interview material to give colour and immediacy to the issues. The profiles attempt to move the reader beyond simplistic divisions and to unsettle the conventional racial and gender stereotypes. Given that the research for this book was done between 1986 and 1990 – before the unbanning of the ANC – some of the interviews were extremely difficult to obtain. The main source of material for the book was 120 structured 'pearl fishing' interviews. This is how Hannah Arendt describes her approach: 'One dives in not knowing quite what one will come up with.' The important thing is to remain open to one's informants, to see where they come from and to follow them – not to impose a prefabricated formula over their diverse and often paradoxical accounts. These accounts are reported verbatim as much as possible, so as to allow the very diverse voices to be heard clearly and directly.

In different ways all the voices from the interviews illustrate the link between war and gender. War is a gendering activity. It both uses and maintains the ideological construction of gender in the definitions of 'masculinity' and 'femininity'. Women are widely cast in the role of 'the protected' and 'the defended', often excluded from military service, and almost always – whether in conventional armies such as the SADF or guerrilla armies such as MK – excluded from direct combat. Dividing the protector from the protected, defender from defended, is crucial to both sexism and militarism. Thus, in the final analysis, changing gender relations is one of the essential tasks for reducing the risks of war in the future.

1

Inside South Africa's twilight war

'We in South Africa have a war going on. Those who have not realized it are foolish.'
(Rev. Frank Chikane, from address given in 1986)

Different understandings

Was South Africa in the 1980s involved in a war? For most people 'war' involves widespread, violent conflict. But in South Africa much of the violence was hidden. It was hidden in the sense that many acts of political violence were performed in secret by anonymous agents. One such agent, Captain Dirk Coetzee of the South African state's 'death squads', thus referred to it as 'a twilight war'. Much of the violent conflict was also hidden in the sense that it occurred in the black townships which are cordoned off – geographically and socially – from the suburbs in which most white South Africans live.

Commenting on the bomb explosion in August 1988 at the Hyde Park Corner in Johannesburg, Member of Parliament Harry Schwartz said,

> This blast, in one of the country's richest shopping centres, brings the war to the northern suburbs. It also brings home to the people in our upper echelons the reality of South Africa and makes us conscious that we live in a society which is terrorized.
> *(Quoted in the* Sunday Star *14.8.1988)*

This quotation highlights a number of key questions: Were African National Congress (ANC) bombings acts of terrorism, or were they part of a war of liberation? Did the violent conflict in South Africa in the 1980s indeed constitute a 'war'? What were the main forms and agencies of violence in this conflict? These are crucial questions which evoked very different answers among the South Africans interviewed for this book.[1]

According to an Afrikaans-speaking woman who is a Nationalist Party M.P.,

> In the 1984-6 period there was a revolution. Revolution and war are different. A war is full-scale, like in South West Africa and Rhodesia. We haven't had it in white areas. Only in a few black townships. And the violence all stopped when the instigators were removed. The instigators were children who were rebellious and trying to prove they were grown up. They're frustrated because they don't understand and there's no one to explain things to them .... Many groups of people among the coloureds, Indians and blacks are anxious to develop themselves. But they don't know where to start. The real enemy is communism .... It's basically an East-West conflict that we have here. It's toning down because communism has proved it can't work. But communism still tries to take over the world. They work through weak spots. That's why they work through blacks ... so, it appears to be a black-white conflict in South Africa. But it's not. There's lots of goodwill. The blacks are really very grateful.
> *(Informant 1)*

A similar view was expressed by the only woman member of the President's Council:

> No, there isn't a war on. I lived through World War Two in Britain and I know what war is like. But we had a revolution in the mid-1980s, and it failed. The ANC thought they'd come to power that way. We don't know a lot of what happened in the townships at that time. A lot has been suppressed. The ANC don't want to share power; they're only interested in a take-over. Fortunately not all black people are like that. South Africa is no more violent than any western society. A lot of our violence comes from the ANC. But South Africa is not a distinctively violent world. Anyway, I don't think about it. I get on with what I have to do.
> *(Informant 25)*

The first woman to achieve the rank of brigadier in the SADF said,

> No, there's no question of a war in South Africa. The bombings inside are terrorism, not a war.
> *(Informant 14)*

Other white informants seemed uncertain:

I'm not really sure, but yes, I think we're at war against the ANC. I don't know much about them, but what I know, I don't like. Their leaders can't be quoted, so they must be saying really dreadful things.
(Informant 10)

A small number of white informants were more emphatic. A white grandmother about to emigrate to Australia said,

Yes, there's a war about maintaining white power. The government is fighting anyone in opposition – any opposition at all, either liberal or radical. South Africa is a terrorist state. The government maintains power through the police and the army. They use terrorist methods in order to scare people. They frighten people into submission.
(Informant 8)

A young white woman who had been imprisoned for four years for supporting the ANC said,

Yes, there's a war in South Africa. The government is fighting the disenfranchised majority. The role of the SADF is to keep the Nationalist Party in government, to keep it in power.
(Informant 12)

Another white woman, who had left South Africa in 1980 to join the ANC, said,

Yes, our struggle in South Africa is a war. It's a matter of scale really. If you look at the scale of militarization, and the scale of armed force used against the people. And resistance is increasingly violent. The armed struggle is increasingly important.
(Informant 6)

A woman prisoner awaiting trial on charges of treason said,

The period 1984-9 was a war, in a sense a war of a special type. It's a civil war – citizen against citizen. It's a just war – of a colonized majority against a dictatorial minority colonial power. It's a non-conventional war – with the one side having a conventional army and police force which is pitted against a guerrilla army supported by the masses, armed with whatever weapons are available to them, such as stones and pangas.
(Informant 49)

However, perceptions such as these from white informants were un-usual. In contrast, every single black informant interviewed described the conflict as a war. One of the three women members of the ANC's National Executive Committee (NEC) said,

> Yes, there's a war raging in our country. For the black majority it's a war for survival. The black townships are like concentration camps. Black children are shooting targets for trigger-happy soldiers. Black children dig the dustbins for food. Even children are herded into cells.
> *(Informant 2)*

These different interpretations of the situation clearly require explanation. They reflect the splintered nature of South African society, which separates black people from white and results in very fractured and distorted perceptions.

Violence and terrorism

The phrase 'political violence' is used here to mean acts of human destruction that impact on power relations in society. 'Terrorism' is used to mean a strategy of political violence that involves systematic acts of destruction aimed at altering or maintaining power relations through spreading extreme fear. Terrorism is usually defined as political violence exercised by one's opponents.[2] Other definitions are anchored in a distinction between military and civilian personnel. For example:

> Terrorism is acts of intimidation, injuring unarmed, presumably innocent civilians.
> *(Said, 1988: 50)*

> Terrorism is political violence directed against non-combatants.
> *(Craig Williamson interviewed on* Network, SABC-TV, *11.9.88)*

The notion of 'non-combatants' and 'civilians' rests upon a precise demarcation of the battlefield, which is difficult to draw in revolutionary situations. Terrorism is also said to operate outside international law and definitions of human rights:

> Terrorists kill and maim defenceless men, women and children, [while freedom fighters] seek to adhere to international law and civilized standards of conduct.
> *(George Bush, cited in* The Weekly Mail *13.1.1989)*

In this sense terrorism is anarchic and devoid of moral content. It is the amorality and unpredictability of terrorism that distinguish it from 'guerrilla warfare'.

> In its assumption that the use of armed force against state power is a logical extension of existing political objectives, guerrilla warfare exhibits a far greater degree of predictability and political morality than terrorism.
>
> *(Rich, 1984: 70)*

Violence and war

The ANC has presented its strategy of 'armed struggle' as a form of guerrilla warfare. It has been described as

> the most quixotic guerrilla organization of modern times. Its leadership endorses violence, but with manifest reluctance and an aversion to terrorist tactics.
>
> *(Davis, 1987: 203)*

'Armed struggle' is said to be one phase of a much wider strategy of political mobilization, culminating in the notion of 'people's war' which the ANC adopted at its Kabwe Conference in 1985. The ANC leadership has often argued that this 'people's war' is informed by moral considerations. Firstly in relation to the purpose of the war:

> We are fighting a war of liberation against the apartheid regime and against colonialism of a very special type. We have continuously restrained the oppressed people from allowing themselves to be put into a position where they will find themselves fighting a racial war.
>
> *(Jacob Zuma giving evidence on commission in London, quoted in* The Star *7.10.1988)*

Furthermore, the leadership has repeatedly affirmed that the methods to be employed in this 'war of liberation' must be informed by moral restraints which prohibit attacks on civilian targets:

> The National Executive Committee (NEC) hereby underscores that it is contrary to our policy to select targets whose sole objective is to strike at civilians. Our morality as revolutionaries dictates that we respect the values underpinning the humane conduct of war.
>
> *(NEC statement quoted by Kasrils giving evidence on commission in London, quoted in the* New Nation *6.10.1988)*

President Tambo has signed a protocol of the Geneva Convention binding the ANC to 'humanitarian conduct of the war' and to avoiding attacks on civilian targets. This is said to be the first time a guerrilla group has ever done so (Davis, 1987: 122).

Moral considerations are sometimes cited by members of the ANC's military wing, MK, to underline their status as 'soldiers' as opposed to 'terrorists':

> I am a soldier trained to shoot other soldiers. I was trained in guns, the weapons of soldiers.
> *(Interview with prisoner awaiting trial, 1988, Informant 52)*

Asked whether he would place a bomb in a shopping centre and risk killing civilians if ordered to do so, this informant replied,

> The ANC would not give such an order. They told us we should not hurt civilians.
> *(Ibid.)*

Nevertheless the bombing of civilian or 'soft' targets occurred on an increasing scale in 1988, as did attacks on military and police targets. In one treason trial, Brigadier Hermanus Stadler, quoted in *The Star* on 2.8.1988, maintained that the ANC cannot be regarded as being at war with the South African government. Instead the government was facing a 'revolutionary onslaught'. In another treason trial Brigadier Stadler said that South Africa was at war in Angola, but that inside South Africa only acts of terror took place. He said,

> The security police regarded these acts of terror as criminal actions and not actions of war. Unrest does not make a war. There is a definite difference between terror and war.
> *(Quoted in* The Star *29.11.1988)*

In a different court case in the same year – 1988 – the state did describe itself as at war. Lieutenant General Jan van Loggerenberg, former Chief of Staff Operations and now Chief of the Air Force, said in an affidavit that the SADF was on a 'war footing'. In this case the state's argument was that the SADF was beyond the reach of the courts and outside the law. In this application the End Conscription Campaign (ECC) brought a Supreme Court action against the SADF to restrain it from illegally harassing the organization (*The Weekly Mail* 2.9.1988). Clearly one of the sites of struggle in South Africa in the eighties was the definition of the struggle itself.

The concept of 'war' is not simple (Scruton, 1987; Shaw, 1988). While Hannah Arendt's definition of war as 'the massification of violence' implies a straightforward relation between the two phenomena, it is clear that the conflict in South Africa does not easily fit into other conventional definitions. For example,

Warfare is socially organized physical coercion against a similarly socially organized opponent.
(Kaldor, 1982: 263)

War is an open armed conflict in which: regular, uniformed forces are engaged, on at least one side; the fighters and the fighting are organized centrally to some extent; and there is some continuity between armed clashes.
(Kidron and Smith, 1983: 6)

MK and the SADF are not 'similarly socially organized opponents'. Nor was there 'continuity between armed clashes'. Much of the violent confrontation was episodic in nature.[3]

In this book war is viewed along a continuum of violent conflict. It is defined as intense, widespread conflict that involves organized, collective, socially-sanctioned violence. Throughout its history South Africa has known several different types of wars: pre-colonial wars between different African polities fought before European conquest; imperial World Wars One and Two; protracted colonial wars of conquest; and wars of independence. Many MK cadres understand themselves to be fighting a war of independence against 'colonialism of a special type'. The Anglo-Boer war was an anti-imperialist guerrilla war. Many of the ancestors of SADF soldiers fought in the Anglo-Boer war against what they understood to be a particularly oppressive form of colonial rule. These different experiences and understandings of wars of resistance are a powerful force in the present.

In the eighties both the SADF and MK developed an inclusive concept of 'total war' – war which involved the entire population. This was variously described as 'people's war' by the ANC, or 'total strategy' by the SADF. From about 1975, SADF personnel referred to a 'total onslaught' against the South African state. The state's response of 'total strategy' provided the basis for legitimizing an increasing military involvement in all spheres of decision-making. In this sense total strategy was the launching pad for the militarization of South

African society. Militarization – the mobilization of resources for war – occurred at political, economic and ideological levels.[4] This process was paralleled by increasing resistance to the apartheid state. The outcome was that South Africa in the eighties was engaged in a low-level civil war in which the SADF and MK were important – though not the sole – agencies in a spiralling pattern of violent conflict.

Agencies of violence

During 1984-6 violence escalated in many of South Africa's black townships. The immediate trigger event was the implementation of the tricameral parliament system, which came into force in September 1984 and incorporated 'coloureds' and Indians, but exluded Africans altogether. The SADF was sent into a number of townships, ostensibly to contain this violence. During 1985 alone, 35 000 troops were used in townships throughout the country. In October 1984, army units joined the police patrolling Soweto. This was followed by Operation Palmiet, in which 7 000 soldiers sealed off the township of Sebokeng, carrying out house-to-house searches and making at least 350 arrests. This represented a strategic shift away from a reliance on the police force alone to maintain what the state called 'law and order'.

Since that time the SADF has been used increasingly in internal repression to maintain minority rule and the apartheid system. It has been deployed in many areas of black life, such as health, housing, labour, and education. The army has been employed to evict rent defaulters in an effort to break the rent boycott, and has occupied classrooms in attempts to break the schools boycott. In August 1985, 800 children, some only seven years old, were arrested after a curfew was declared forcing Sowetan children to stay inside classrooms during school hours. In 1986 this was enforced by the occupation of black schools by white soldiers, and there were stories of children even having a military escort to visit the lavatory. The SADF has been deployed to guard polling booths, to go into health clinics to identify those injured in demonstrations, to maintain beach apartheid, in forced removals, monitoring demonstrations, suppressing resistance to homeland independence, organizing student registration at Turfloop University, and strike-breaking.

There is a good deal of evidence of SADF violence during the 1984-6 period, directed against township residents generally, and young people in particular. The Detainees' Parents' Support Committee reported a pattern which involved soldiers picking black children off the streets at random and holding them for several hours in military vehicles or in remote areas of the veld. The children describe being beaten with fists and rifle butts, and even being subjected to electric shock treatment. During this period the SADF often acted together with the South African Police (SAP). The activities of the two were indistinguishable to many township residents, as they fused in a pattern of indiscriminate violence:

> Today's army is lions. They hate a person. If one of the police or army come towards you, you are so scared. You know that the first thing they may do is beat you up and then shoot you.
> *(Crossroads squatter, in* Out of Step, *May 1987)*

It was the arbitrary and indiscriminate nature of the violence that intensified the spread of extreme fear:

> In our streets, one day it's all right. The next day, you can cross the street when a Casspir (police vehicle) comes round the corner, and you'll die. It's like Beirut.
> *(Soweto resident, quoted in the* Sunday Star, *8.9.1985)*

The degree to which the SADF and SAP were linked in suppressing black resistance during this period is an important indicator both of the level of violent conflict in South African society and of the role of the SADF within that conflict. This role changed during 1986, as surrogate forces in the form of vigilantes and municipal constables came to be agents of violence and fear. Vigilantes first emerged in 1985 as organized and conservative groups acting violently against anti-apartheid forces. Their violent actions were markedly to the advantage of the South African state. However,

> it is virtually impossible to establish the actual links between vigilantes and the state, more so under the emergency restrictions which effectively permit vigilante activity to go unreported. Nevertheless, there is growing evidence which suggests tacit and active approval by the state for vigilante groups.
> *(Levin, 1987: 26)*

Such evidence relates to widespread areas, such as Crossroads, Kwanobuhle, and Queenstown, as over the next few years vigilante attacks on progressive community organizations and leaders became common across the country. Vigilante groups disorganized and destabilized such organizations and individuals. Whether the police actively sanctioned and supported the vigilantes, whether they were incapable of curbing vigilante activities, or were merely reluctant to do so, made little difference to the end results (Haysom, 1989).

The violent actions of the vigilante group, the *Witdoeke,* in Cross-roads are well known, and their open support from the police is well documented (Cole, 1987). Another case study which illustrates how vigilantes operated violently without legal consequences is the community of Leandra, a black township on the East Rand. Residents had been involved in a grassroots campaign to prevent their forced removal. This enjoyed such popular support that the authorities were forced to negotiate with one of the residents' association leaders, Chief Mayise. Vigilante attacks culminated in a mob assault on Chief Mayise's house in January 1986, during which he was hacked to death. To date no one has been prosecuted for his killing.

The reliance on vigilantes as a disorganizing force represented a shift away from a reliance on the SADF and SAP to suppress black resistance. However, it is crucial to appreciate that this shift was part of a military strategy – a strategy of counter-insurgency, in which the military had a covert, co-ordinating role (McCuen, 1966; Saul, 1987).

The vigilante phenomenon illustrates two key elements of this strategy – the neutralization of opponents and the use of surrogate forces. However, the use of surrogate forces also extended to new forms of policing. Two major additions were made to the police force in 1986, at the height of the uprising against the apartheid state. Sixteen thousand *kitskonstabels* (special constables) and municipal policemen were added to the force.

> These hastily trained black policemen were deployed in large groups in all areas where resistance was strong. From the beginning they used excessive violence. Their brutality created an atmosphere of fear that was not only aimed at activists, but at intimidating entire communities. The behaviour of the new police is characterized by an arrogant disregard for the law.
> *(CIIR, 1988: 13-14)*

A township resident described them as follows:

> They are the dogs of the SAP, doing all their hunting and watching.
> *(Ibid. 19)*

In some communities the new police forces established what the Catholic Institute for International Relations publication describes as a 'reign of terror'. The violence involved both systematic torture and beatings. For example Mr VB of Duncan Village (the African township near East London) was bundled into a van driven by municipal policemen:

> 'I was taken into a building where I was instructed to lie on my stomach. Three policemen wielding metal bars then struck me on the back. When they hit me, I tried to jump up. I grabbed one of them and pleaded with him to help me, as I did not know where the firearm was. Another one then grabbed me by the throat and choked me. I lost consciousness. When I woke up I was lying beneath a tap with water running over me.' After more interrogation Mr VB was burned with cigarettes on the arm and foot.
> *(Ibid. 61)*

Clearly the effect of this kind of violence was to spread extreme fear. This fear became more and more widespread due to its arbitrary pattern and the fact that it was directed not only against anti-apartheid activists, but also against ordinary township residents.

> One day I came home late from work. It was 6.30 p.m. A taxi stopped near my house and a woman got out. She was carrying a lot of parcels and as she passed my house some 'greenflies' (municipal police) stopped her. They just started beating her with sjamboks. She cried out to them, 'What have I done? I have come from work.' They gave no reply. The 'greenflies' saw that I was watching this and they told me to go into my house. The woman had dropped her parcels and her groceries were lying all over the street .... you just can't send your children to the shop after half-past six any more. It seems that is how they want to control the townships. They want the people off the streets.
> *(Duncan Village resident, quoted in ibid.: 53)*

This indiscriminate violence generating widespread fear was also reported from Bhongolethu, a black township outside Oudtshoorn:

> A feeling of constant fear of assault by the constables was widespread.
> *(Ibid. 37)*

It was also reported by Van Eyk, who wrote of a 'campaign of terror' waged by black policemen against township residents in Valhalla Park and Elsies River:

We heard detailed eye-witness accounts from ordinary people: men, women and children being sjambokked viciously for no other reason than their being outside their homes; of a young woman seriously wounded by buckshot while trying to get into her own yard, of a boy shot dead at point-blank range.
(Van Eyk, 1989: 19-20)

When the fear of arbitrary imprisonment was added to a fear of assault, the effect was to freeze anti-apartheid activity. A municipal policeman interviewed in the Eastern Cape is reported to have said,

... now everyone is afraid of going to jail without any reason, no one is causing trouble.
(CIIR, 1988: 1)

During 1984-6 many black South African townships were re-constituted as 'zones of terror' (Walzer, 1987). Within these areas relationships were structured around violence and fear. It is important to remember that the violence and fear was largely confined to these areas. Outside the townships, power relations followed the conventional rules of authority for most people not involved in anti-apartheid activities.

However, the SADF, the SAP, vigilantes, municipal policemen, and *kitskonstabels* were not the only agencies of violence and fear during this period. Pietermaritzburg was described as 'the battleground in a war' (Von Holdt, 1988: 16). The 'war' has been fought between supporters of two different political groups – Inkatha and the ANC – and there has been much destruction of life and property. In 1988 alone, 680 people were killed, 3 000 homes destroyed and 30 000 people displaced (Cock, 1989). Both sides have been implicated in many violent acts, and it is clear that both groups have considerable grassroots support. However, there have been numerous affidavits filed in court applications suggesting SAP support for Inkatha vigilantes. Despite the affidavits filed against Inkatha office-bearers – alleging arson, assault, and murder – and despite the granting of court interdicts against such office-bearers, very few of the respondents have been arrested or charged. Buthelezi now speaks of a 'black civil war', but the state also has to take some responsibility for the banning and restricting of organizations and individuals, which made peace negotiations impossible.

There were two main agencies of 'resistance violence' in South Africa in the 1980s. First, it has been estimated that the ANC had between 8 000 and 10 000 trained guerrillas in its Umkhonto we Sizwe (Spear of the Nation) structure (*City Press* 12.1.1986; Davis, 1987; Lodge, 1983). Much ANC guerrilla violence has been directed against military and collaborationist targets. These have included some elaborate and spectacular missions, such as the bombings at the Sasol oil-from-coal plant, the rocket attack on Voortrekkerhoogte base, and the explosions at the Koeberg nuclear complex in 1982.

The second agency of resistance or counter-violence was the 'comrades' – largely unemployed township youth. The 'comrades' have tried to neutralize state control of the townships, and have perpetrated some cruel acts of political violence in the name of the liberation struggle. These acts have included the burning and stoning to death of suspected informers and 'collaborators'. There were many 'necklace murders' in the 1980s, and some of the perpetrators were imprisoned on Death Row.

One such was Paul Tefo Setlaba, a member of the Colesberg Youth Organization, who was sentenced to death on 10 December 1986 for his role in the burning to death of a woman who broke the Colesberg consumer boycott. Setlaba was reported as having undergone a 'personality change after his friend was shot by police during political unrest in July, 1985' (Black Sash, 1989: 20). Setlaba was detained under the emergency regulations for five months in 1986. Apparently this detention affected him a great deal.

> It was when he needed to support his girlfriend, who was carrying his child, and he couldn't go to look for work.
> *(Black Sash, 1989: 20)*

In his judgment in Setlaba's case, Mr Justice Kannemeyer said that in September 1985 a consumer boycott was being observed by the black community in Colesberg. On 21 September Mrs Julia Dilato bought some meat from a butchery in defiance of the boycott. When she took the meat back to the township, she was stopped by the 'comrades', who were enforcing the boycott. The meat was thrown to the ground and stamped on. Mrs Dilato reported this incident to the police and thereafter she was considered to be an *impimpi* (informer). On 24 September her house was stoned, and on 2 October she was set upon by a group of people on her way to work. Petrol was poured over her, she was set alight and burned to death. Setlaba was sentenced to death for his role in this killing.

This horrifying incident highlights a number of important themes. Firstly, it points to the violent and punitive action taken in some townships to enforce political compliance. Such action was common during the 1985 consumer boycott of white-owned shops. Many of the victims of these tactics were African women who were subjected to cruel treatment. For instance a case was reported of a woman who went into town and bought fresh meat and was made to eat it raw. Another was made to swallow a whole bottle of cooking oil (Cock, 1987: 139). Secondly, the Setlaba case illustrates a worrying aspect of state violence. The trial, which took place in Graaff-Reinet, lasted only three days, which has deepened doubts among many legal people about the legal process involved in the death penalty.

An increasing number of death penalties involve political offences. According to official figures, a total of 101 people have been sentenced to death for 'unrest-related incidents' since 1985. Among the Black Sash's small sample of people presently on Death Row, almost half (47 per cent) were found guilty in cases widely regarded as politically-related. Some of those hanged have been members of the ANC's military wing, Umkhonto we Sizwe, and there have been pleas that they should be treated as prisoners of war under the Geneva Convention.

One of this category presently on Death Row is the Messina trialist and MK guerrilla, Mthetheleli Mncube. He told the court that he had acted as a soldier. When he was captured by the SADF soldiers, he expected to be treated as a prisoner of war. Instead he was stripped, put in the back of a truck, and the dead bodies of his shot comrades were piled on top of him. When he was transferred to another open truck shortly afterwards, he broke the shoe-laces with which his hands were tied, grabbed a rifle lying near him on the back of the truck and fired into the cabin, killing two policemen. He said any soldier would have done this in the circumstances (Black Sash, 1989: 30). Both Messina trialists said that when they left the country their original intention had been to join the ANC to further their education. Both had changed their plans after commando raids on neighbouring African countries which they believed were staged by the SADF. Mncube was in Matola, in Mozambique, in 1981, when ANC men staying near him were killed in such a raid.

Another case in which the imposition of the death penalty was considered was that of the 'Bethal trial', when Ebrahim, Dladla, and Maseko were sentenced to long terms of imprisonment. Ishmael Ebrahim's story is a case study which highlights some of the main forms of political violence prevalent in South Africa in the eighties.

A case study: Ishmael Ebrahim

Ebrahim, one of the most senior members of the ANC to go on trial in recent years, was sentenced in January 1989 to 20 years' imprisonment. He had been active in anti-apartheid politics since his early teens. He participated in the defiance campaigns of the 1950s, and was a delegate to the Congress of the People at Kliptown in 1955, at which the historic Freedom Charter was adopted. At this time his political orientation was determinedly non-violent, and he was a great admirer of Gandhi. The Sharpeville Massacre in 1960, when 69 peaceful protesters were shot dead by police, and the banning of the ANC were key influences on him. His commitment was to 'the establishment of a free democratic society', but

> the banning of the ANC removed our hopes of achieving this through peaceful non-violent means. A chapter closed in our history. We decided to fight rather than surrender. We decided to meet the repressive violence of the state with the revolutionary violence of the people.
> *(Court statement quoted by Orkin, 1989)*

It was at that point that Ebrahim joined MK. He was first convicted in 1964, when he was found guilty on three counts of sabotage:

> I was arrested in 1963, detained, and tortured, and finally tried and sentenced to 15 years' imprisonment.

This he served on Robben Island. After his release, he was banned and heavily restricted:

> I was under constant police harassment and found it difficult to live a normal life. In 1980 I left South Africa illegally and went into exile.

In 1986 he was allegedly abducted from Swaziland by South African state agents:

> I was kidnapped from a foreign state by the South African security forces. At that point I was carrying an Indian passport, issued to me by the government of India. The lack of any judicial restraint has given the security forces of apartheid a free hand to continue their abductions with impunity. The violation of the borders of a neighbouring state, of its independence and sovereignty, is itself a great offence against international law, and has in the past resulted in countries going to war. Kidnapping people and forcibly bringing them across the border fences into South Africa is an act of state terrorism.

Ebrahim said his abduction took place only four days after the murder of a close friend, allegedly by South African Police, and the kidnapping of a Swiss couple, a Swazi woman, and a registered South African refugee from Swaziland. He asked,

> Are these abductions and murder not acts of state terrorism? We in the ANC never advocated a policy of murdering or abducting South African personnel abroad. Yet it is now the accepted policy of the South African security forces to assassinate and abduct opponents of the apartheid regime in foreign lands.

Ebrahim said his abduction was followed by police torture through the use of electronic sound 'to the point where I nearly lost my mind'. He told the court that the use of violence was

> a painful necessity .... But there was no other way out. One hated the racist system and knew it was violent, and found oneself forced to use force.

As a member of the ANC, he said he supported all four pillars of the struggle:

> One of them, the armed struggle, inevitably involves violence and, in its ambit, includes white farmers on the borders, because they have become part and parcel of the defence machinery.

The judge said he did not impose the death sentence because no one had been killed by the landmines placed in these border areas.

The Ebrahim case illustrates a number of different kinds of state violence.[5] For many of the people interviewed for this book, the scale of this state violence defined the conflict of the eighties as a 'war'.

Forms of state violence

Capital punishment

This form of state violence involves a bizarre combination of both covert and overt violence, in that while the legal process is public, the identity of the executioner and the process of execution are secret. This secrecy was underlined following an incident at Pretoria Central Prison when tear-gas was used to force four men out of their cell to the place of execution. A member of parliament asked the Minister of Justice the following questions:

- How long do condemned prisoners have to wait after arriving at the gallows before being executed?
- Are condemned prisoners sedated?
- How often is it necessary to use physical force or tear-gas to force condemned prisoners to the gallows?

The Minister said he did not want to answer the questions because the answers were 'too gruesome'.

Capital punishment has increased in recent years; over 1 000 people have been executed in South Africa since 1980.

Death squads, assassinations and disappearances

The murder and disappearance of at least 50 prominent anti-apartheid activists in South Africa in the 1980s, and the fact that their killers and kidnappers have not been brought to court, provoked speculation that there were 'death squads' operating in the country. These were a familiar feature of some Latin American states such as Columbia, El Salvador, Guatemala and Peru. They are a means of obscuring the responsibility of the terrorist state for the violent acts it commits.

The assassinations began with the parcel bomb which killed Abraham Tiro in Botswana in 1974, and include the attacks on Joe Gqabi (gunned down in his Harare home in 1980), Ruth First, and others. However, in 1988 Moss suggested that:

> ... in the last few months action against opponents of apartheid – in particular ANC members – appears to have changed from random slaughter to a sustained campaign; from individual covert hits to generalized policy – a policy that would dovetail almost exactly with the statement: 'Wherever the ANC is, we will eliminate it.' (A statement made by Magnus Malan on 19 February 1988.) Every twelve days since the beginning of the year there has been at least one armed attack on an ANC member living outside South Africa. *(Moss, 1988: 25)*

It is widely believed that the victims were killed by state agents acting in terms of the state's counter-revolutionary strategy as expressed by Major-General C.J. Lloyd when he said,

> Sometimes you have to take out the revolutionaries, if they are controlling the people.
> *(Quoted in the* Christian Science Monitor *11.5.1988)*

Until the end of 1989 it was not possible to establish with any certainty whether particular forms of state violence, such as death squads, were operating under the formal direction of state agents or with their informal sanction. However, in November of that year, the Afrikaans alternative newspaper *Vrye Weekblad* published a lengthy interview with Dirk Coetzee, who held a police medal for faithful service. He said,

> I was the commander of the South African Police's death squad ... I was in the heart of the whore. My men and I had to murder political and security opponents of the police and the government ... I myself am guilty of, or at least an accomplice to, several murders.

One of these was the brutal killing of Griffiths Mxenge. In October 1989, a prisoner on death row, Nofomela, had made a sworn statement that he was a member of the police assassination squad which had murdered Mxenge.

Investigations of these allegations by Nofomela and Coetzee resulted in the uncovering of a secret organization involved in political violence against the opponents of apartheid that was formally constituted as a unit of the SADF, the Civil Co-operation Bureau (CCB). This was formed in 1986 and, according to the Chief of Staff of the Army, who gave evidence to the Harms Commission, its primary offensive function was to disrupt the activities of the ANC, the South African Communist Party (SACP), and the Pan-African Congress (PAC). Judge Harms was told that in 1989 the CCB was involved in 200 projects. These projects varied from the terrifying (such as the suspected murder of David Webster and Anton Lubowski) to the grotesque (such as 'Project Apie', which involved nailing a monkey foetus to the wall of Archbishop Desmond Tutu's official residence).

Legal police killings

Police shootings have made South Africa notorious since 1961, when 69 African protestors against the pass system were shot by police in what came to be widely known as the Sharpeville Massacre. This was followed by the Soweto revolt, initiated on 16 June 1976, when around 10 000 students in Soweto protested against Bantu Education and met with police violence. Some sources put the death toll on that day at 25, while others placed it at nearer 100 (Hirson, 1979: 184). The Soweto protest became an uprising that lasted a year, during which some 700 African people were killed.

Police shootings have increased in South Africa in recent years. In 1987 more than 1 000 people were wounded or killed by the South African Police (Minister of Law and Order, Adrian Vlok, reported in the *Sunday Times* 3.4.1988).

Detention without trial

This way of 'neutralizing' political opponents is a familiar strategy of counter-insurgency and has been used in many different social contexts. In South Africa detention without trial has been lawful since the 1960s, but during the 1980s the numbers of people detained without trial increased very dramatically. Altogether an estimated 70 000 detentions have taken place since 1980. Many of these detentions involved extremely lengthy periods. For example, Chris Ngcobo was detained for two years from 15 June 1986. At that time he was an extremely popular and influential student leader at the University of the Witwatersrand. On the night of 15 June 1986 he was asleep in Room 263 of his student residence, when

> about 200 men covered by balaclavas and brandishing rifles surrounded Glyn Thomas dormitory in the middle of the night. They stormed the hallways of this residence for black students at the University of the Witwatersrand, forcing the monitor at gunpoint to open up rooms with his pass key. The security forces roused sleeping students, tore off their blankets and marched several of them, including Mr Ngcobo, into waiting vans.
> *(Christian Science Monitor 23.6.1988)*

The violent and frightening circumstances of Christopher Ngcobo's arrest are significant. He is one of some 200 people who spent over two years in detention. He was subsequently released, with severe restriction orders which made it impossible for him to continue studying.

The effectiveness of this form of state violence depends on the fear associated with detention without trial. This fear is well founded given that approximately 70 detainees have died while in custody – the most famous case being Steve Biko, in September 1977. Many detainees have been held in solitary confinement, which is an acknowledged form of torture. However, the forms of torture documented in South Africa extend further than isolation.

Torture

Torture is an important element in modern 'counter-revolutionary war'. Trinquier (one of the architects of the 'pacification' programme in the Casbah in Algiers) emphasized the necessity of this:

> Torture is not only considered as a means of obtaining information on clandestine networks, at any price, but also as a means for destroying every individual who is captured, as well as his or her sense of solidarity with an organization or a community.
> *(Trinquier, cited by Mattelart, 1979: 415)*

Thus torture is an effective instrument of social atomization, a function which may be more important than obtaining information.

Torture has been widely used in South Africa to achieve this. A study done at the University of Cape Town established that 85 per cent of a sample of 175 ex-detainees had suffered torture (Foster and Chandler, 1987). Among the forms of physical torture that have been detailed are assault, electric shock, suffocation, and immersion in cold water. Ebrahim reported being subjected to a continuous pattern of electronic sound which 'almost destroyed his nervous system' (Interview with key informant, January 1989). Women detainees have also been subjected to various forms of sexual abuse and humiliation (Russell, 1989b). All this is in addition to the torture of solitary confinement itself.

Arson and armed attacks

There have also been arson and bomb attacks on the homes of anti-apartheid activists and the headquarters of anti-apartheid organizations. Much of this violence has been attributed to the SADF. Evidence has emerged that the security department of the Johannesburg City Council operated its own 'hit squad', which had links to the CCB and military intelligence, and was basically an extension of the SADF. An ex-member told an investigation that

> We burnt down houses, intimidated people and broke arms and legs.

As Laurence writes,

> There were striking parallels between the City Council connection and the CCB nexus in the evidence of surveillance, harassment, and murder of anti-apartheid activists in the name of patriotism.
> *(Laurence 1990: 50)*

The scale of this state violence is such that it raises the question of whether or not South Africa in the eighties was a 'regime of terror', or a 'terrorist state', that maintained its authority largely by the spread of fear through an organized and sustained policy of violence. The phrase 'terrorist state' appears to involve a contradiction in terms: 'terrorism' is usually defined as illegitimate violence, and the source of legitimacy is conventionally defined as the state. However, Van der Vyver (1988: 70) argued that 'South Africa is now solidly in the grip of state terror violence'. Similarly Riordaan (1988: 4) described the state strategies of repression as 'state terrorism'.[6]

For all the black people interviewed for this book, the scale and nature of state violence defined the conflict as a war. A minority of politically-engaged whites shared this perception. As one white woman prisoner awaiting trial on charges of treason expressed it,

> The SADF's role over the whole decade of the 80s has been to defend a minority regime through unleashing its guns on the largely unarmed masses. It was a war ... a war in which the SADF was fighting for the apartheid state, for the continuation of colonialism of a special type, for the oppression of the majority. It was a war against progress, against democracy, against the majority of South Africans, against peace, against both black and white democrats.
>
> *(Informant 49)*

The fact that so many of the whites interviewed for this book failed to define the conflict as a war is partly a reflection of how little they were affected by it. There are similarities to French perceptions of the war in Algeria, which Horne (1977) has analysed as a 'savage war of peace'. No declaration of hostilities was ever made, and during most of the eight-year period the majority of French people lived unaffected by the 'war'. Another parallel is that the French government, like the South African state authorities, 'assiduously refused to recognize operations in Algeria as anything more than the "maintenance of order"' (Horne, 1977: 35).

A further factor explaining the gulf between white and black perceptions is that much of the violence was obscured by state censorship of the media.

> The result: the war being waged behind the myriad images of protest has gone unnoticed by vast numbers of South Africans and foreigners alike.
>
> *(Davis 1987: x)*

The SADF was a central actor in this war in South Africa in the 1980s. The SADF has always been used to maintain the apartheid regime and white minority rule. It has done so both inside and outside the country in an undeclared and brutal war. The SADF maintained a military occupation of Namibia and engaged in an undeclared war of destabilization against neighbouring states. This policy of destabilization has wrought havoc, destroying social and economic life, and causing widespread death and social dislocation. It is estimated that at least 1.5 million people have died as a direct or indirect result of Pretoria's undeclared wars of destabilization against neighbouring states, while the damage inflicted on the economies of regional states between 1980 and 1988 is estimated to be not less than R90 billion (Johnson and Martin, 1989). The effects of this policy of aggression and destabilization have been felt most intensely in Angola – which the SADF has repeatedly attacked since 1975 – and Mozambique – where the SADF has supported Renamo. The SADF has also attacked ANC targets in Lesotho, Swaziland, Botswana, Zambia, and Zimbabwe.

These attacks were justified by the apartheid regime and the military in terms of a 'total onslaught' against the country and its inhabitants. According to Defence Minister General Magnus Malan in 1977, this onslaught

> involves so many different fronts, unknown to the South African experience, that it has gained the telling but horrifying name of total war.

Many acts of violence and murder were perpetrated by the SADF in response to this understanding of 'total war'. Several members of the CCB justified their actions on the grounds that they were 'actions of war'. For example Carl 'Calla' Botha, giving evidence to the Harms Commission, said he had joined the special unit of the SADF, the CCB, for 'the adventure' and because the enemies of South Africa had launched an onslaught against the country during the 1980s and were trying to overthrow the government.

> I understood and believed there was a war raging inside South Africa and it was about the survival of moderate South Africans .... The African National Congress was involved and the normal action was not adequate.
> (The Star *4.4.1990; 5.4.1990*)

Similarly, former SAP captain Dirk Coetzee admitted to participation in murder, but said that at the time he justified such actions to himself as part of a 'just war' against South Africa's enemies (*Sunday Star* 29.4.1990). On another occasion he referred to 'the twilight war against terrorists and the onslaught against South Africa' (*The Star* 27.4.1990). Coetzee justified his actions in terms of patriotism. He told *Vrye Weekblad*:

> I did it for *Volk* and *Vaderland*, for my wife and children and father and mother. It was a dirty war ... I didn't see myself as a murderer or a car thief. I saw myself as a security policeman fighting the enemy.
> *(Cited by Laurence, 1990: 42)*

Slang van Zyl, former policeman and CCB member, was told by the CCB's managing director, Joe Verster, an SADF colonel, that the CCB's role was to wage a 'secret war' against the ANC – the enemy within the borders of South Africa. A local newspaper later arranged a meeting between van Zyl and one of the targets of assassination, Gavin Evans. Van Zyl invoked the familiar notions of 'war' and 'patriotism' to defend his actions:

> I am very proud to have been a member of the CCB. It was something we had to do to bring peace to South Africa. We did not start the physical war. You have to fight war with war.
> *(Ibid.: 34)*

This notion that South Africa was involved in a war is frequently invoked as a moral legitimation for violence. For example Dr Boy Geldenhuys, chairman of the joint parliamentary standing committee on security and chairman of the National Party's group on defence, said,

> In times of war – and there is no doubt we were in a state of undeclared war – our opponents did not play by the rules. To win the war the special forces had to use extraordinary measures ....
> *(Sunday Star 4.3.1990)*

In such an undeclared war the special forces have the right to 'eliminate terrorists before they have a chance to kill innocent people' (ibid.).

It is now widely acknowledged by a range of very different sources that South Africa was involved in a war. For example, announcing the second round of talks between the ANC and the government, the *Sunday Times* (5.8.1990) headlined:

The 30-year-old war between the ANC and the government will effectively be over by tomorrow night.

Not all the antagonists were voluntary participants in this war. As individuals, most SADF members were subject to coercion:

> Not all the national servicemen in the SADF fight with a strong ideological commitment, since they are conscripted. However the SADF does its best to indoctrinate national servicemen to see this as their role, and as a correct role.
> *(Informant 49)*

In this process of indoctrination the SADF mobilizes a particular conception of masculinity. This conception is derived from the way gender relations are structured in South African society.

Notes

1. The main sources of data for this study were semi-structured in-depth interviews. This research strategy was adopted in an attempt to avoid the tendency of questionnaires to fracture experience, when respondents are encouraged to reduce their experiences and understandings to fragments which can be captured in a question-and-answer format. The interviews were conducted in South Africa, Zimbabwe, Zambia, and England between 1986 and 1990.

    The question arises, 'How widespread are the different understandings?' Clearly the pool from which informants were drawn – South Africa – is an enormous one. No attempt was made to sample systematically from this pool. The sample is 'multi-dimensional' in the sense of trying to capture the different social characteristics such as age, class, race, education, occupation, residence, ideology, religion, ethnicity, marital status, and circumstances. The sample also attempted to include protagonists (people closely involved in the issue), for example soldiers in the SADF or MK. This is what Glaser and Strauss (1967) term 'theoretical sampling' – the idea being to include all categories and differences significant to the research aim. Nothing is said in this book about the typicality or representativeness of the views identified. In other words the data is *illustrative*; it is used to identify certain patterns, but says nothing about how widespread these patterns are.

2. Walther (1969: 4) points out that ever since the French Revolution, 'terrorist' has been an epithet to fasten on a political enemy. Most definitions are partisan and unsatisfactory: 'the disputes about a comprehensive, detailed definition of terrorism will continue for a long time ... and will make no notable contribution towards the understanding of terrorism' (Laqueur, 1987: 24).

3. According to Riordaan (1988: 2), there were 3 400 deaths from political violence in the four years between September 1984 and 1988. The South African Institute of Race Relations (SAIRR, 1988: 23) estimates that there were 2 987 deaths

from political violence between the outbreak of the violence in September 1984 and the end of 1987. According to the 1987 police report tabled in parliament, there were 10 129 cases of 'public violence' during 1986 and 1987 (SAIRR,1988: 22). Clearly there are difficulties involved in the construction of these figures, relating both to the reporting and the use of the labels 'political violence', 'public violence', 'incidents of unrest', and so forth (Tomaselli, 1988).

4. A distinction should be made between the military as a social institution (a set of social relationships organized around war and taking the shape of an armed force); militarism as an ideology (the key component of which is an acceptance of organized violence as a legitimate solution to conflict); and militarization as a social process that involves a mobilization of resources for war. These phenomena are closely related. Militarization involves both the spread of militarism as an ideology, and an expansion of the power and influence of the military as a social institution. See Cock (1989) for a more detailed discussion.

5. Much of this violence is obscured by public acceptance of official state violence. 'Violence by the state is strangely absent from most discussions of the problem of violence' (Archer and Gartner, 1978: 219). These authors point out that 'Public support for official violence is so pervasive that the definition of violence is itself affected. In a 1969 survey (in the USA) for example, 30 per cent of a national sample said that "police beating students" was *not* an act of violence, and an astonishing 57 per cent said that "police shooting looters" was *not* an act of violence .... The same survey asked respondents what violent events were of greatest concern to them. Even though the survey occurred during the Vietnam War, only 4 per cent of those interviewed mentioned war (ibid.: 221).

6. However, it is important to note that if the South African state did maintain its authority largely by the spread of fear through an organized and sustained policy of violence, this was not practised on a scale comparable to the situation in the South American countries that have been termed terrorist states.

2
The politics of gender in South Africa

The 'politics of gender' is about power relations between men and women. The focus on 'gender' rather than on women is important. It means a shift away from an exclusive emphasis on women's disadvantage and difference, to the organization of gender in all social structures and processes.[1] This implies that we must take account not only of the social construction of 'femininity' but also of how masculinity is constructed and inscribed in structures of power and domination. It also implies that we must take account of how men are disadvantaged by the predominant pattern of gender relations.

Olive Schreiner, the author of the first feminist book written in South Africa believed, along with Ibsen's Nora, that men suffered 'as much as women from the falseness of the relations'. The male role of 'protector' and 'defender' is an onerous one. Men die sooner than women. They suffer from blocked arteries as well as blocked emotions. The two are related. In many cultures definitions of masculinity require men to appear tough, dominant, aggressive, competitive, objective, controlling, achieving, and emotionally inexpressive. Jourard suggests that this definition of manliness may be 'lethal'.

> Manliness ... seems to carry with it a chronic burden of stress and energy expenditure which could be a factor related to man's relatively shorter life span.
> *(Jourard, 1971: 22)*

Despite this, gender relations operate mainly to privilege men and subordinate women.

However, gender is not the only social relation which shapes experience and determines access to power and resources. Much has been written of the triple oppression of black working-class women in South Africa, who are located at the intersection of the three lines along which privilege runs – gender, race, and class. Less has been written of the triple privilege of white, middle-class men. This group has a monopoly on power in South African society. In South Africa, as Eva Figes once said,

> power is like the disease of haemophilia. It is transmitted by females but is only manifest in males.
> *(Figes, 1970)*

There is only a small number of white women who have formal power and influence. There is one woman cabinet minister. The largest computer retailer, with a turnover of millions of rands, is a woman. There is one woman among the 130 judges on the bench of the Supreme Court; she has three daughters, the eldest of whom is a major in the SADF.[2] Some of this small group of women were interviewed for this study. They include a 75-year-old member of the President's Council, who is also the founder and director of a powerful women's organization. In 1989 this organization had about 20 000 members and 16 branches. She maintains that she has always exerted political power and influence over her long life:

> I've known all the heads of government since General Smuts. All the cabinet ministers I've known personally .... My achieving this power has been largely a matter of luck, being in the right place at the right time. However, probably the key was that I trained as a newspaper *man* [my emphasis] which was then a rarity for a woman .... Being a woman has helped me, because as a woman I have a special ability to relate to people and to make contacts .... I had no role models but I was the eldest child and my father encouraged me to be an achiever. Both my husbands [she has been married twice and has two sons] encouraged me to develop my own interests. My second husband did so, so that he could go off and play golf. He got me into public relations. He didn't want me to grow into a nattery old woman. I grew up in a man's world and I feel at home in a man's world .... My whole philosophy is not to work against power, but to work with it.

She describes her 'greatest achievement' as:

> my sons and grandsons. I'm very proud of them and of my relationship with them.
> *(Informant 25)*

A much younger woman, who is active in the business world, focused all her energies on achieving power. She did so from avery early age:

The demarcation between male and female roles is very strong in Afrikaans culture. But I was never encouraged to act like a typical little girl. My father always focused me on world events. I was brought up not to focus on the home, because we had servants, but rather on something creative. When I was young, it was important to me to achieve. Being the best student in the class was very important to me. I'm committed to knowledge and expertise as a power base ... I have learned to play with networks as an access to power .... Men are usually intimidated by me. It keeps them at a distance. But I don't want to get close to them. It's not functional. Men are sometimes patronizing, but I play along with that because it suits me ... I feel I've escaped marriage. Or rather, let me put it this way, all the men who've wanted to marry me would have confined me.
(Informant 3)

The male monopoly of power is illustrated by the fact that only recently – in 1989 – has South Africa acquired a woman Cabinet Minister, Dr Rina Venter, Minister of National Health and Population Development. There is no question of any compromise with her femininity.

She is a soft-spoken woman, the voice light and feminine and the blond hair always in a romantic curl over the forehead. You could well imagine her behind the *melktert* (milk tart) counter. But in politics you immediately sense in her the Voortrekker woman who crossed the Drakensberg mountains barefoot.
*(*Saturday Star *23.9.1989)*

In a brief survey of women candidates Pat Schwartz asked why there were so few women in parliament.

Female candidates had a simple answer: For women with young children and homes to run, the demands of a political career are almost intolerable.
*(*The Star *3.8.1989)*

Many women define their prime role as wife and mother, and it is their commitment to their domestic role that blocks their political participation:

The woman can't shut the door and forget that she has to look after her home and children.
(Conservative Party candidate in Worcester, Rinie du Toit, quoted in The Star *3.8.1989)*

There is also an absence of women from the leadership of the ANC and most organizations within the mass democratic movement. In 1989 the ANC had three women members in its National Executive Committee (NEC), and eight women as heads of missions in its diplomatic service. While the ANC delegation to the Pretoria talks included two women, the second round of talks in August 1990 consisted of ten men. At a more general level, there is a virtual absence of women's leadership in organizations in the civic, youth, student, and other sectors. The labour movement is male-dominated. Women leaders are largely absent from all levels of the trade unions, and from the Congress of South African Trade Unions (Cosatu). Baskin found that of the eighty-three office-bearers at national level in Cosatu's affiliates in 1988, only eight were women. This concentration of political power in male hands is not surprising. There is no tradition of gender equality in South African society. Gender is inscribed differently in different cultures, but in all South African cultural traditions gender roles are highly structured and unequal. The outcome is that women are often understood as 'the weaker sex' and always as needing to be protected and defended.

Gender ideologies

'Tradition' is often invoked to justify gender inequality. It is a pattern which is rooted deep in our history – indigenous as well as colonial. The European communities from which the white settlers came, as well as the indigenous societies of Southern Africa, were male-dominated and patriarchal. In pre-colonial Africa the majority of women were subordinated to male authority. Perhaps the most dramatic example of female subordination rituals was the *hlonipha* language of deference which an Nguni woman was expected to adopt in the home of her in-laws. Once married she was not allowed to utter any word containing a syllable that occurred in the names of her husband's relatives, extending back to great-grandparents. She was publically shamed if she ignored the rules.

There is also a Zulu tradition of female deference and subordination. At a recent meeting kwaZulu chief, Mzangani Ngcobo, said that if a Zulu man told his wife to fetch water and she did not, he must ask one more time. If she failed once again to fulfil her duty, then the man must hit her (*The Weekly Mail* 1.6.1990). Inkatha reflects a similar attitude in its 1987 *'Ubuntu-Bond: Good Citizenship'*, which states:

> In the family the man is the head. The woman knows she is not equal
> to her husband. She addresses the husband as 'father', and by so doing
> the children also get a good example of how to behave. A woman
> refrains from exchanging words with a man, and if she does, this
> reflects bad upbringing on her part.

Afrikaner culture is also extremely patriarchal. The Voortrekker tradition involves the theme of militant, patriotic womanhood. Stories of
courage and physical hardiness, of heroism and self-sacrifice abound.
Voortrekker women are spoken of as able to shoot with 'a heavy
ten-bore shotgun', handle the oxen, drive the wagon, and shoot for the
pot. At the same time the theme of passive female suffering evoked by
the images of the concentration camps of the Anglo-Boer War is also
common. It is a theme which has been harnessed by Afrikaner nationalism today.

   In both the African and the Afrikaner traditions there is an image of
the tough but submissive female. This is very different to the English
middle-class definition of femininity, which includes attributes of help-
lessness and delicacy. This is what Olive Schreiner termed 'the phenomenon of female parasitism': she speaks of women

> clad in fine raiment, the work of others' fingers, waited on and tended
> by the labour of others, fed on luxurious viands, the results of others'
> toil ... [seeking] by dissipation and amusements to fill up the inordi-
> nate blank left by the lack of productive activity.
> *(Schreiner, 1911: 98)*

The implication is that these class-bound definitions of femininity are
more coercive and restricting. These dominant-class women are, as
Mary Wollstonecraft expressed it,

> reduced to the status of birds confined to their cages with nothing to
> do but plume themselves and stalk with mock majesty from perch to
> perch.
> *(Wollstonecraft, 1967: 21)*

All of these diverse traditions have contributed to shaping the current
understandings of gender differences in South Africa. In all these
traditions the ideals of masculinity and femininity have been sharply
polarized. In all of them an ideology of domesticity is deeply inscribed
in the sense that being a wife and mother is viewed as the core of
women's role in society.[3] According to this polarized ideology of gender
roles, women are viewed as nurturing, caring, emotional, and receptive.

Men are linked to self-assertion, competition, aggression, rationality, and power-seeking. With the dominance of men over women has come the promotion of these 'masculine virtues' at the expense of the 'feminine'. The outcome is that women are often viewed as less competent than men. For example a recent survey found that 30 per cent of lawyers and 24 per cent of advertising executives believe that women are less capable of contributing to the overall goals of their company than men.

Women – in their roles as wives – are sometimes viewed as a form of property. For example an advertisement in a business magazine said:

'An investment in your wife could become your biggest asset. Business executives need their wives to contribute to their success. We will help your wife to have the poise and confidence to be able to rise to any occasion.'

The advertisement was for a course which included deportment, grooming, and home entertaining (*Financial Mail* 16.9.1983).

This is not an impractical view. The General Manager of one of South Africa's largest banks, the Trust Bank, believes that a wife's main function is as follows:

My wife must help me use my talents to the maximum. She must help to increase my business achievements, must better the quality of my life and make me happy ... a businessman has certain needs which only his wife could see to. One of the most important needs is love. But another important function is as an outlet of tension. That can be achieved through the right reception when the businessman comes home – a comfortable and calm atmosphere in the house .... A businessman expects his wife to be a good listener. Instead of him having to listen to her dozens of catastrophies and problems, she must be prepared to give him the opportunity to tell her of his problems. The wife also has to provide for her husband's health, relaxation and spiritual needs.
(Sunday Times *24.10.1982)*

All the people interviewed for this study maintained that men and women were very different. Women were generally viewed as more caring and nurturing than men, though there were exceptions.

Several informants' views were distorted by their perceptions of racial differences. According to a Nationalist Party M.P.,

... Women are more violent than men, particularly in the African culture. Winnie Mandela proves that women are more violent than men. In the white culture women are more concerned than men with peace and life, but the black culture is different. There the women instigate violence. The men don't really get going until the women get them going .... All the township violence was instigated by women.
(Informant 1)

This woman went on to talk about how important it was to her to maintain her femininity:

Men and women are very different. It's important for a girl to be pretty. Appearance is important. It's important to me to be feminine – it makes me feel normal.

This concern with feminity was also expressed by a very different woman, who is an MK cadre:

Yes, we're different to men. Our anatomical upkeep is not the same. We are not as strong physically. We can't lift a lorry. We should preserve our femininity. I enjoy clothes. When I was in the camps in Angola, wearing a khaki uniform and doing physical exercises I was very strong. But I sometimes used to look at myself in the mirror and wonder.
(Informant 5)

Other informants commented:

Women are gentler and softer, more concerned with big issues. It's not innate, but because men are more concerned with making a living.
(Informant 8)

Women hold onto their ideals more.Women are more caring than men. Women are also more efficient. They have to be, as household administrators. But we're all mothers, we all want peace. We have a natural empathy with each other. We can understand another woman's difficulties and problems.
(Informant 25)

A white businesswoman said:

Women are different from men. South African women have always used their femininity very constructively. They provide a different style of leadership; they are more intuitive. We used to have a very

male, hard type of society. Now a nurturing openness is coming to
the fore. If women can get on this bandwagon; if they can link
economic power with peace initiatives, we will make a difference.
(Informant 3)

A woman who is on the NEC of the ANC said:

Women are creative, intuitive, and inclusive. We mustn't copy men.
(Informant 2)

The same sentiments were expressed by a woman colonel in the SADF:

It is the task of women to give life and to preserve it.
(Informant 7)

These differences were variously attributed to biological or cultural
differences, but some informants found it difficult to separate them:

The differences between men and women have to be defined in terms
of biological and socially determined differences ... after centuries
of oppression it's dificult to distinguish between them. For example
the fact that a lot of women experience severe difficulties with, say,
a march through the bush, is because they have worn high-heeled
shoes since childhood, so they have distorted hips and spines, and
because they have seldom experienced stamina-taxing exercise,
rather than because we are weaklings.
(Informant 49)

Gender discrimination

Gender differences in access to power and resources in South Africa in
the decade of the eighties may be demonstrated at a number of different
levels, such as employment, the household, control of reproduction, the
law, education, and sexuality.

Employment

In South Africa, as in all industrialized societies today, an increasing
number of women work outside the home as well as within it. Employment rates have been increasing amongst women of all races since 1960,
and women now constitute about 40 per cent of the economically-active
population.

Women are generally employed in a fairly narrow range of occupations, which are subordinate to those of men in terms of pay, power, and

prestige. Women in South Africa earn on average approximately 70 per cent of men's earnings (Pillay, 1988). Black women work mainly in the service and agricultural sectors in the least skilled, lowest paid and most insecure jobs of all. Overall the employment pattern is extremely skewed. In 1983 women constituted 9.2 per cent of all doctors, 3.2 per cent of all architects, and 0.7 per cent of engineers (ibid.). Even in areas where women dominate, such as teaching (65.3 per cent), they occupy subordinate positions. In education in 1981 the ratio of male to female teachers was 0.4:1, but the ratio of male to female school principals was 3:1. In the administrative, executive, and managerial categories the ratio of male to female managing directors was 23:1 (ibid.: 282).

The 1985 census revealed that nearly three-quarters of the total female workforce is employed in three occupational categories: service, clerical, and sales and professional. Women also tend to be in particular kinds of jobs in each category. Three-quarters of all female service workers are domestic workers. Three-quarters of all professional women are either teachers or nurses (Maconachie, 1985). Maconachie shows that white women are over-represented in the higher status white-collar occupations. This partly reflects their greater access to schooling and further education.

The situation of the woman domestic worker illustrates much of the powerlessness of the black woman (Cock, 1980; Cock, 1989). Mrs Elizabeth Motaung is a domestic worker who was employed by the same family for 40 years. Her monthly wage in 1988 was only R30 in addition to food and a room. The only holidays she ever enjoyed were when the family took their annual leave, and then she was expected to continue living in the house. In 1988 she was dismissed on the grounds that she was too old to continue working. There was no pension or retrenchment pay (*The Star* 9.9.1989).

The vast majority (81.6 per cent) of all domestic workers are African women. Over two-thirds of all white South African households employ domestic workers. The average wage in 1989, including the value of food and accommodation, was R156 a month, according to official government statistics. Domestic workers are still not covered by the Labour Relations Act or the Basic Conditions of Employment Act. They are excluded from unemployment benefits and workmen's compensation. There is a growing awareness among domestic workers themselves of the need to organize to change these exploitative working conditions. This is illustrated by the growing strength of the South African Domestic Workers Union (SADWU) nationally. Marches were held throughout the country in 1990, and the march in Port Elizabeth drew 30 000 people.

The marchers demanded legal protection, as well as a minimum salary of R450 and an eight-hour working day. Domestic workers suffer particularly acutely from the inadequacy of crèches and the neglect of state child care provisions for Africans. In a national sample of urban African working women it was found that almost 40 per cent were leaving their children in the care of adult relatives, particularly grandmothers (Cock *et al.*, 1983). Young children are often sent away to remote rural areas. The pain of separation is amplified for the black women employed as nannies to care for the children of their employers, separated from their own children in the process.

South Africa has no national policy of leave for maternity or paternity at all, no national policy encouraging flexible working arrangements and part-time and shared jobs, and no national policy to provide child care for those who need it. Starting in the early eighties, the Commercial, Catering and Allied Workers Union of South Africa (CCAWUSA) began to fight for maternity rights, and won a number of agreements. Maternity rights have been taken up by a number of other unions, as have issues such as protection against hazardous working conditions for pregnant women, sexual harassment at work, and equal pay for jobs of equal value. While women are entitled to the same minimum pay as men under Wage Board and Industrial Council determinations, this does not ensure equality of pay or benefits.[4] In 1988 the definition of an unfair labour practice in the Labour Relations Act was amended to include 'unfair discrimination on the grounds of ... sex'. However, as has been emphasized, legislation alone does not remove discrimination (Budlender, 1990).

Sex discrimination goes beyond wages: there is often discrimination against women in recruitment, fringe benefits, and promotions. Some companies will not give women housing loans, expense accounts, medical aid, company cars, and other perks that are available to men. A married woman must belong to her husband's medical aid, even if that offered by her company is preferable. In addition, of the three million or so South Africans active in the informal sector, about 60 per cent are women.

Education

While women are generally disadvantaged in comparison to men, white women have greater access to education. Women tend to be fairly well represented up to Standard 8 in schools and then to be increasingly under-represented as men acquire higher qualifications (Maconachie,

1989). In particular, women have less access to a university education. Women form half of the adult population, but only a third of all adults with a bachelor's degree, a fifth of those with a master's degree, and only 17 per cent of those with a doctorate (Maconachie, 1985). The explanation of this pattern lies in a structure of constraints or 'sex bars' which exist in the home, the school, and the wider society, and which effectively limit women's access to educational opportunity (Cock,1980).

Control of reproduction

In South Africa both white and black women experience discrimination as regards control of reproduction. Contraception is theoretically available and free to all women, but this is far from the situation in reality, and women in the remote, rural areas are at a particular disadvantage. This applies especially to black women, and one health worker has estimated that 80 per cent of black women in rural areas are given Depo Provera as a form of contraception. Studies elsewhere in the world have shown clearly that this is a health risk.

Overall the utilization of contraception is low in South Africa. The same health worker claims that 60 per cent of women never use it. This partly reflects inadequate levels of health education. A recent headline in *The Sowetan* announced, 'Condoms are out. Jo'burg women want "sperms not rubber".' In a random survey many contended that condoms deprived them of the joy of sex. One woman said,

> I want sperms not rubber.

Another comment was,

> It should be flesh to flesh.

Another said,

> I only use plastic when it is raining. I do not think there is any rain when we are making love, and so there is no need for condoms or raincoats.

And another,

> Sperms have proteins and I need those proteins.

Sowetan men were also reported to be very resistant to condoms. One said,

> Sex is the fusion of two souls, and once there is a cushion in the form of a condom, the whole exercise loses meaning.

And another,

> It is like washing your hands while wearing gloves. I do not enjoy using the condom. And many women I have approached do not want it. Some will tell you that you must not 'take them cheap'. They think you are implying that they have diseases. I have met so much resistance that I realized there is no point in using condoms.

This last comment is unusual. Other quotations point to an important source of coercion in women's contraceptive choice – male resistance. A Human Sciences Research Council (HSRC) study claimed that 38 per cent of African men prefer a family of six to eight children, while a third will not allow their wives to use any kind of modern contraception. A large number of contemporary urban African men are antagonistic to contraception (Klugman, 1988).

Another source of resistance is political. For example it was reported that in 1986 young girls in Durban were told that African girls *had* to fall pregnant:

> every woman – married or not, at school or not – must be pregnant by February … to replace the black people killed in the struggle last year. An informant said, 'They have threatened to search our hand-bags for contraceptives'.
> *(City Press, 26.1.1986)*

A third source of coercion in women's contraceptive choice is in the opposite direction. I know of two cases where practising contraception was made a condition of women's employment. In one case women employed as seasonal agricultural workers were required to produce written evidence.

A result of these low levels of contraceptive utilization is the problem of abortion. The 1975 Abortion and Sterilization Act allows abortions to be performed following rape and incest, and in the case of foetal abnormality or when the mother's physical or mental health is threatened. Between mid-1988 and mid-1989 only 963 legal abortions were performed – 600 of which cited a risk to the mental health of the woman as the reason. A disproportionate number are done on white women because 'they know how to work the system' (Interview with key informant, 1989). Affluent women also have the option of going abroad. An estimated 2 000 a year fly to Europe to be operated on in clean, sophisticated clinics after routine counselling. The plane ticket and clinic fees total about R5 000 (*The Star* 9.5.1990). At the same time, illegal abortions are estimated to total 300 000 a year (Mr Chris Diamond of the Abortion Reform Action Group, quoted in *The Star* 30.10.1988). Many women undergo medical treatment because of a subsequent infection. Hospitals throughout the country deal with cases of gynaecological complications known to have been brought about by illegal abortions. This applies particularly to black women.

Clearly all women in South Africa are subject to constraints on their control over their own bodies and reproductive functions, but it is black women who are most severely constrained.

Sexual harrassment

Sexual harassment in one form or another is a real problem for many women. 'Love abuse' – varying from jokes and insults to acts of rape and jobs in exchange for sex – appears to be common in the workplace (Bird, 1985: 89). At the 1989 Cosatu Congress, the Transport and General Workers' Union tabled a resolution calling for 'tighter sexual discipline' within COSATU and its affiliates

> to counter the detrimental effect on the organization of male comrades engaging in 'unequal relationships' with newly recruited women members.

The resolution was not adopted.

Violence

Violence against women is increasing in South African society. At an academic conference, one practising psychologist estimated that 60 per cent of South African husbands beat their wives. He maintained that most cases were not reported because many families thought a certain amount of violence was 'normal', in the sense that it was deserved (*Sunday Star* 29.9.1985).

This violence peaks in the case of 'family murder', where wives (and often children) are killed. Between 1986 and 1988, 223 people died in family murders. Pretoria is thought to be the capital of the world for 'family murder', which is generally understood to be an Afrikaner phenomenon. At a conference on family murders, the head of the University of Pretoria's Psychology Department said that more than 70 per cent of the incidents were by Afrikaner parents. He drew a parallel between this pattern and apartheid; both were generated, he said, by an 'excessive sense of responsibility'. The violence reflected the Afrikaner's right of possession of his family, and overdeveloped sense of responsibility:

> With the colonization of South Africa, our predecessors did not massacre the indigenous population. Instead they exerted hegemonic control, which resulted in a frightening sense of responsibility in all spheres of life. We take the right to decide where people of colour should live, what work they may do, with whom they may socialize – and we regard our actions as in their best interests.
> (The Star *23.6.1988*)

Rape is widespread in South Africa. The official figure is 19 000 rapes a year (this was the number reported to the SAP in 1988). The unofficial estimate (based on the National Institute for Crime Prevention and Rehabilitation of Offenders (NICRO) estimate that only about one in twenty rapes is reported) is 360 000, or about 1 000 a day (quoted in *The Weekly Mail* 17.2.1989). Much of this rape has been institutionalized. There is the phenomenon of 'jackrolling' in Soweto, where young men go out in groups and rape for entertainment. Neither the official courts nor 'people's courts' are always sympathetic to rape victims. Recently (1990) youngsters in Alexandra township put a woman on trial in a 'people's court' and flogged her when they found her guilty of stabbing a man. Mrs Elizabeth Hlatshwayo, a mother of two, was sentenced to a R200 fine or 100 lashes. When she did not pay the fine, the youths took turns in flogging her on the buttocks. Mrs Hlatshwayo said a man broke into her home and tried to rape her:

> In self-defence I grabbed a table knife and stabbed him in the arm. He ran away and returned with a crowd of 'comrades'. I was taken to the people's court, where I was found guilty. I was not allowed to give my side of the story. I was stripped half-naked in front of the crowd and flogged on the buttocks by 12 of the comrades. I did not report the matter to the police because of threats that my shack would be burnt down if I did.
> (The Star *7.5.1990*)

Women's collective resistance to rape is taking various forms. The organizations Rape Crisis and People Opposed to Women Abuse (POWA) do important work making connections between violence against women and their abuse as sex objects, and counselling and assisting rape victims. There is also some evidence of a violent organized resistance to rape. A recent newspaper report announced:

> The women avengers have struck again. The group of Pistol-Pack in Soweto (women who raid shebeens in search of suspected rapists) attacked two more drinking establishments, killing two patrons .... The heavily armed women were described by one shebeen owner as professionals who knew what they were doing. They attacked shebeens at Orlando East and Diepkloof, killing two men while terrified customers watched in horror. It is believed the female vigilante group was formed five weeks ago after a group of men ... abducted nine women and sexually assaulted them .... The seven gun-toting women, some clad in bizarre and colourful robes, others disguised as men, were said to be hunting down the group of men.
> *(*Sunday Times *19.2.1989)*

> The female 'hit squad' is believed to include one of the rape victims.
> *(*The Weekly Mail *17.2.1989)*

The household

Much gender inequality is evident within the household and the family.

> The family is still a major sphere in which the domination of men is secured at the expense of women. Each family is a site for individual men to oppress women in their own particular way.
> *(Ramphele, 1982: 2)*

The most general way is a sexual division of labour which defines cooking, shopping, cleaning, and child care very rigidly as 'women's work'. There are very few reports of men sharing such domestic work in urban African households. Sometimes this is resented:

> I cook for my husband. He's tired from work, lifting up heavy boxes and iron. Sometimes we come in at the same time. He wants his tea. He'll sit down with the paper. You'll be a 'girl' again in the house. He is the boss reading the paper. And that makes you fed up.
> *(Lawson, 1985: 37)*

This resentment is not restricted to African women. A working-class white informant aged 30 and living in Pretoria described her domestic arrangements:

> My husband doesn't even make himself a cup of tea. I don't think he knows how to. Yes, I do mind. We both work, in different government departments. In the evening we catch the same bus home. Then he reads the newspaper while I do the cooking. However, sometimes he lays the table. No, I do all the shopping as well as the cooking, but my husband buys his own clothes.
> *(Informant 16)*

This kind of resentment can lead to a critical stance towards men and marriage (Cock, 1987). The outcome is increasing numbers of single women (whether never married, separated or divorced) and a large proportion of female-headed households. These households play an important part in African townships. Township family ideology still asserts that

> men should take the lead in family affairs on two fronts: firstly they should play the major role in the economic support of their families, and secondly they should take the lead in family decision-making.
> *(Campbell, 1990: 4)*

However, there is a widening gap between social reality and this ideology. Unemployment and low wages are among the factors that make it very difficult for fathers to live up to support functions. The outcome is that

> it is mothers who are the pivot of family life .... It is mothers who often take the major responsibility for managing the scarce resources available to most working-class families.
> *(Ibid.: 6)*

In this process women are subjected to considerable strain:

> Although there is much evidence for the fact that many women are single-handedly bearing the burden of family support and family leadership, there is also evidence that they are not necessarily accorded the respect and authority that has historically been accorded to fathers who played these roles. Thus they have all the stresses that accompany such responsibilities but little of the support and respect needed to carry out this role.
> *(Ibid.: 10)*

It is important to appreciate the extent to which the African family has suffered under the strains imposed by apartheid. In fact the family in South Africa has one of the highest rates of disintegration anywhere in the world. According to Sandra Burman (1990), over 50 per cent of African civil law marriages now end in divorce. The figure is the same for customary unions. Burman has also established that 67 per cent of all African babies born in the Western Cape are born out of wedlock. This, and the fact that over 85 per cent of African men in the region default on child maintenance payments, means that women are subject to considerable strain and hardship.

Law

Much of African customary law is oppressive to women, and much has changed over time to women's disadvantage. Ruth Mompati maintains that in some ways women are more discriminated against now than in the past:

> Certain traditions and customs are being distorted, resulting in even more effective oppression. For instance, the question of 'lobola': this custom was originally used to create good relationships between the families of the couple about to get married. It was not seen as 'payment' for the wife, but rather as an exchange of goodwill. Today, particularly in the cities, we have 'bridepricing' and parents can be sued in court for the non-payment of lobola. The process has been totally commercialized and has lost most of its original meaning. (Daily Mail *3.7.1990*)

It has also lost most of it's original function, which was to protect women – to be an insurance for the woman and her children. It was paid in cattle, which represented a real material form of security. This has changed over time, and now payments are made in cash. These may be substantial, with R7 000 to R10 000 being paid for a well-educated girl (Burman, 1990). People are still very attached to the practice of lobola and it still operates to bind families together (ibid.). But it does not provide the protection to women that it used to do. And this is especially serious given the high percentage of African marriages which end in divorce.

Pre-colonial African society was strongly patriarchal. Much of women's traditional disadvantage was amplified by colonial interpretations. The reconstruction of customary law – as in the Natal Code of 1893 – subordinated African women to male authority, at a time when earlier patriarchal controls were being dislodged by socio-economic change.

The marriage laws in South Africa also illustrate the incorporation of the indigenous legal system into the dominant one, to black women's disadvantage. Until 1988 there were three marital proprietary regimes in South Africa: community of property, exclusion of community of property by antenuptial contract, and customary union in terms of 'Bantu law'. All involved a legal dependence for women. Until recently, more than half of white South African marriages were under community of property, which relegated the wife to the legal status of a minor. She could enter no contracts without her husband's consent. As in the case of a child, he must represent her if she sued or was sued. Antenuptial contract enabled the wife to retain her status as a legal major, but it had deficiencies. Under both marriage systems the father was legal guardian of any children. This created particular problems in divorce, when in most cases the wife got custody but the husband retained his power as legal guardian. Before the 1984 Matrimonial Property Bill, a married woman, whether married in community of property or with an antenuptial contract, was not recognized as a full partner in the marriage.

The 1984 bill significantly corrected this situation. It provided for the abolition of the marital power and provided for the joint administration of joint property in marriages in community of property. It also provided for the accrual regime in marriages with an antenuptial contract (meaning that all property accumulated during a marriage would be divided on dissolution). However, the bill excluded from the reforms all present community of property marriages and all black marriages. During the parliamentary debate on the bill, Helen Suzman said that 'black women get the worst of both worlds'. Unlike white, coloured or Indian marriages, black marriages were automatically out of community of property, with the marital power retained. The Marriage and Matrimonial Property Law Amendment Act of 1988 made it possible to choose how marital property is to be apportioned, and was an attempt to make the consequences of marriage the same for all 'population groups'. However these acts were not retrospective, so many women married before these dates are still subject to their husband's marital power.

Until 1983, labour legislation contained protective provisions for women. The Factories, Machinery and Building Work Act of 1941 regulated working hours for women by prohibiting night work, between

6 p.m. and 6 a.m., limiting overtime to a maximum of two hours per day on not more than three consecutive days and not more than 60 days a year, prohibiting women from employment a month before giving birth and for two months after confinement. However these provisions did not apply to domestic and agricultural workers. The Basic Conditions of Employment Act of 1983 makes no distinction between men and women, and so enables women to work in industry at night.

While it is important to be aware of how gender relations operate to subordinate women, it is also important to be aware of how women are increasingly organizing against this subordination. Afrikaner women are notoriously conservative on gender issues, but the Conservative Party constitution contains a requirement that all decision-making bodies should contain a significant proportion of women. The organization of Afrikaner women into women's associations and mothers' unions has been paralleled recently by the formidable organization of the Inkatha Women's Brigade, rural women being among Buthelezi's warmest supporters. At the same time the resistance of women to the apartheid state has also grown, with their organization in trade unions as well as in the national liberation struggle. That struggle has focused on racism, but it is the intersection of class, racial, and gender domination that creates the particular oppression of black, working-class women.

It is significant how ideologies of gender are fractured by ideologies of race. Many informants interviewed for this study expressed extremely racist attitudes:

> I believe in equal rights for blacks, but you couldn't bring that in overnight. Blacks are told all their lives that they are inferior. This must affect them or make them aggressive. They are inferior to whites if that is defined in terms of civilization or intelligence. I don't like what I know of the ANC. Their leaders can't be quoted. Therefore they must be saying really dreadful things .... No, I've never been in an African township and I don't have any black friends.
> *(Informant 10)*
>
> Blacks are different. They're a very jealous lot because there are so many of them.[5]
> *(Informant 14)*

There are important similarities between racism and sexism. Both define either blacks or women as inferior, secondary, and dependent. The conception of blacks in racism defines them as irresponsible, child-like and incompetent. This conception commonly includes qualities such as passivity, stupidity, or at least a poor ability for abstract thought and logical argument. Sexist definitions of femininity commonly include all these qualities. In addition, females are assumed to have a special emotional capacity for sympathy and compassion. Both sexism and racism are inscribed in South African society and have generated extremely violent and vicious practices.

In 1987 a white 18-year-old Pretoria youth was sentenced to an effective two-and-a-half year prison sentence for running over and killing a black woman domestic worker. The court heard that Breyten-bach drove towards Mrs Maria Ramtsi in Monument Park, Pretoria 'to scare her' (*The Star* 17.3.1987). Nine black men and women have died in or near Pretoria since November 1988 in racial killings characterized by their apparently random choice of victim. The recent trend began with the killing of seven blacks and the wounding of 17 others in central Pretoria in November, 1988. In the subsequent trial of Strydom, a former policeman, a hatred of blacks was a dominant theme. This had been nurtured at home, at church, and at school. Strydom's father, also a former policeman, said in court that blacks were nothing but animals. The accused nodded approvingly at this testimony. The state, in its summing up of evidence, said that the attitude generally was that 'blacks were not people and could be shot like animals' (*The Star* 25.5.1989).

This kind of crude racism has also surfaced in other less publicized cases. For example in the same year two white youths were found guilty of the murder of an eight-year-old black schoolboy by stoning him from a moving vehicle. One white schoolboy told the court he had thrown a stone at a passing black child riding a bicycle as a 'harmless prank' (*The Star* 9.5.1989).

Black South Africans have not only been subjected to cruel racism. Two simple indicators point to the extent of material inequality in South Africa in the eighties: income distribution and infant mortality rates. South Africa has the most unequal distribution of income in the world. This inequality runs mainly along racial lines. Whites, who constitute less than a sixth of the population, earned nearly two-thirds of the income; blacks, who account for nearly two-thirds of the population, earned a quarter of the same (Wilson and Ramphele, 1989). In 1985 nearly two-thirds of black people were living below the minimum living level, fixed in that year at R350 a month. Infant mortality rates are another important indicator of inequality. While these have improved considerably in the last decade, Simkins (1986) calculated that in 1980, per 1 000 births, the rate was 20 deaths of white male babies within their first year, and 15 for white females. African statistics, nation-wide, were then 96 for males and 76 for females. Urban areas in South Africa were predictably better than rural areas, with Soweto having 25.5 deaths per 1 000 births, compared with 130 per 1000 in rural Transkei (Zille, 1986). The outcome of this pattern of racial and sexual inequality is that the key question for many South African women, especially in the rural areas, is survival. As Ruth Mompati has said,

> Emancipation from the kitchen sink is hardly a priority when the chances are you don't even have a proper kitchen and your children are dying from the lack of adequate nutrition.
> (Daily Mail *3.7.1990)*

In this daily struggle for survival, many black working-class women have had to develop extraordinary strengths and competencies. As Angela Davis has written of black women in America,

> Black women could hardly strive for weakness; they had to become strong, for their families and their communities needed their strength to survive.
> *(Davis, 1982: 231).*

Many women were active in the eighties in challenging the structures of oppression through trade unions, popular movements such as consumer and rent boycotts, and the mass democratic movement. There is a narrow sense in which urban African women are 'liberated women': they are women whose economic independence of men provides a material base for a form of social independence expressed in their women-dominated worlds. There are strong traditions of mutual support and loyalty among urban African women. Their energy and resilience, their sharing of resources and mutual support represent a practical expression of sisterhood (Cock, 1987).

The fulcrum around which these networks turn are older women. These are Adrienne Rich's 'raging, stoic grandmothers', the uncelebrated heroines who have endured and who attempt to repair the wounds inflicted by the violence of apartheid (Rich, 1978: 66). Of course the independence of their daughters should not be exaggerated: their economic independence is extremely precarious in view of low wages, job insecurity, and rising levels of unemployment among the African working class. There is a sense in which their subjection to tight controls and restrictions makes it grotesque to describe these women as fully 'liberated'. Yet they exhibit little of the dependence, passivity, and subservience associated with traditional constructs of feminity.

Few of these women would describe themselves as feminists. The words of many of the informants quoted in this book confirm the widespread suspicion and rejection of feminism as anti-men, as bourgeois and divisive, or as essentially reformist and concerned with entrenching and extending privilege. These criticisms of feminism are common in a Third World context, where matters of survival are paramount. Issues such as sexual preference and lesbian rights are often viewed as irrelevant. Furthermore, there is resistance to the Western feminist critique of the family as a source of women's oppression. In the South African context, the migrant labour system and a mass of laws – from the Group Areas Act to influx control – have destroyed African family life. The African family is widely viewed as an arena to be defended against the encroachments of the apartheid state.

There are many examples of women who have fuelled the perception of feminism as exclusively about the promotion of middle-class women's interests. The focus on the achievements of 'successful' women has often ignored the figure, in the shadows who made it all possible – their black women domestic workers. There are also women's organizations which have preached a rhetoric of shared womanhood that has involved a gross insensitivity to the struggles of black working-class women. This insensitivity has fuelled the belief held by many women in South Africa that the priority is national liberation.

The attempts of the most popular organization for national liberation, the ANC, to incorporate women's emancipation are significant.[6] Women have always participated in the campaigns and activities of the ANC. However, the founders of the ANC understood it to be an organization of men. The draft constitution at the founding congress in 1912 classified women as 'auxiliary' members who paid no fee and had no vote. It said,

> It shall be the duty of all auxiliary members to provide suitable shelter and entertainment for delegates to the Congress.

In 1941 women were allowed to become full members of the ANC, and in 1945 the Women's League was formed. In 1954, at the inaugural conference of the Federation of South African Women the Women's Charter was drawn up. This greatly influenced the ANC's most famous document – the Freedom Charter. This begins by saying:

> Every man and woman shall have the right to vote and stand as a candidate for all bodies which make the laws.

Thus, men and women were seen to be equal. The Charter noted that many women are workers and it demanded equal pay for equal work, the building of crèches and the provision of maternity leave. However, the Charter had two fundamental flaws: it clearly implied that women's liberation would follow naturally from national liberation; and it did not have any clause specific to women in which laws would be provided to protect women against discrimination. Many issues such as rape, violence, and the forms of affirmative action required, were not addressed.

In 1988 the ANC published it's Constitutional Guidelines, which took the spirit of the Freedom Charter further. The guidelines began to address the question of women in a more concrete manner. As is stated in the preamble,

... the constitution must be such to promote the habits of non-racial and non-sexist thinking ....

The Guidelines commit the ANC to actively addressing the inequalities-between men and women, both in the home and in society at large, through affirmative action. However, the clause is vague; what is meant by 'affirmative action' and what constitutes 'discrimination' are not defined clearly.[7]

The 2 May 1990 statement from the National Executive Committee (NEC) of the ANC provided a window on ANC thinking on these issues. Six themes are especially significant:

1. The reiteration of the ANC's commitment to the liberation of women.
2. An acknowledgement of women's contribution to the liberation struggle.
3. An acknowledgement that, 'We have not yet fully integrated women's concerns and the emancipation of women into the practice of our liberation struggle.'
4. The recognition that African women have been the most oppressed by apartheid: 'The manipulation of gender relations has been an important feature of state control over especially the African people, and the effects have impinged most harshly upon women.'
5. There is, however, also a recognition that the oppression of women cannot be reduced to apartheid. There is the problem of 'traditionalist' attitudes on the part of both men and women – taking the forms of surrender and submission among the latter. 'The prevalence of patriarchal attitudes in South African society permeates our own organizations. The absence of sufficient numbers of women in our

organizations, especially at decision-making levels, and the lack of a strong mass women's organization has been to the detriment of our struggle.'

6. Therefore the oppression of women has to be separately and specifically addressed: 'The experience of other societies has shown that emancipation of women is not a by-product of a struggle for democracy, national liberation or socialism. It has to be addressed in its own right within our organization, the mass democratic movement and in the society as a whole. There are two aspects to addressing the oppression of women 'separately and specifically'. The first concerns form – the representation of women in decision-making bodies, in leadership and policy formulation. The other concerns content – issues related to women's particular oppression. Problems which must be addressed include domestic violence and wifebeating, rape, male control of household money and resources, the right to control contraception, sexual harassment, pornography, abortion, the sexual division of labour within the household and men's absence from domestic tasks, and the definitions of what behaviour is appropriately 'masculine' and 'feminine'.

To some extent these problems are being addressed within the ANC Women's League. At present 'femininity' is often equated with 'motherhood'. Many ANC statements imply a fusion of woman and mother. Gaitskell and Unterhalter (1989) have analysed the similarities in the way both the ANC and Afrikaner nationalists have constructed an ideology of 'the mother of the nation'. The ANC has always stressed the image of the mother, and their general appeal to all women has been in terms of their common experience of motherhood. During the 1950s, the major anti-apartheid women's organization, the Federation of South African Women (Fedsaw) campaigned vigorously against the introduction of passes for African women which would control where African women could live and work. In their campaign Fedsaw members emphasized the identity of African women as mothers:

> As wives and mothers we condemn the pass laws and all they imply.
> *(Quoted in Kimble and Unterhalter, 1982: 26)*

The appeal to women as mothers, as a source of both strength and suffering, continues today. On occasion this notion was invoked in South Africa during the 1980s to try and unite women against war. It was said that apartheid violence involved a considerable disruption of both white and black family life. As migrant labour fragmented and splintered African family life, so the system of conscription had come to disrupt white family life. At a number of meetings the theme was articulated that all South Africa's children were being damaged and brutalized, as white children learned to use guns, and black children learned to use stones against one another. For example at a Soweto meeting in April 1986, which included black and white women, a Sowetan woman stated:

> Your children are murderers; your ancestors were thieves.

Another woman said,

> We are the mothers of those who burn and throw stones. You are the mothers of whose who shoot and oppress.

In an address in 1986 Albertina Sisulu said,

> No self-respecting woman can stand aside and say she is not involved while police are hunting other mothers' children like wild dogs in the townships .... A mother is a mother, black or white. Stand up and be counted with other women.
> *(Cited by Gaitskell and Unterhalter, 1989: 71)*

Along the same lines, the NEC of the ANC issued the following call in January 1987:

> Black mothers have to live with the agony of having to bury their children every day. Too often they have to search for their sons and daughters who have perhaps been arrested or perhaps disappeared forever without trace. Across the barricades the white mothers see their children transformed and perverted into mindless killers who will not stop at murdering the unarmed and will surely turn their guns on the very mothers who today surrender their sons willingly or unwillingly to the South African death force. These black and white mothers must reach across the divide created by the common enemy of our people and form a human chain to stop, now and for ever, the murderous rampage of the apartheid system.
> *(Ibid.)*

These appeals failed. Black and white mothers did not 'reach across the divide'. Many 'self-respecting women' did stand aside. As Koonz has written of Nazi women, most white women 'resolutely turned their heads away from assaults' against blacks and dissenters. 'They gazed instead at their own cradles, children, and "Aryan families".' As mothers and wives they made a vital contribution to the power of the apartheid state 'by preserving the illusion of love in an environment of hatred ... ' (Koonz, 1987: 17).

Black women have been extremely militant in their opposition to apartheid. This militancy is evident in their opposition to the pass laws, in the defiance campaigns, the food and beer hall riots, and in rent and consumer boycotts. But in all these campaigns black women have had very little support from white women. Historically the appeal to motherhood has not proved to be a powerful and unifying call.[8] This is partly due to the splintered nature of South African society. The situation of black and white women in South Africa presents a challenge to any over-simplified notion of 'sisterhood'. That challenge is sharpest in the institution of domestic service, where the wages paid and the hours of work exacted by white 'madams' from their black 'maids' suggests a measure of oppression of women by women (Cock, 1980; 1989). There is a sense in which the institution of domestic service is a microcosm of the class, racial, and gender inequalities on which the entire social order is based.

The SADF is also a key institution which both reflects and maintains this inequality. The SADF is predominantly, though not exclusively, white, and its commanding heights are occupied exclusively by white men. The exclusion of Africans and women from conscription, and their subordinate position within the SADF reflect relations of exclusion and subordination operating in the wider society. Armies and wars are gendering activities. In times of war the discourse of militarism permeates the entire society. It touches men and women differently, drawing on existing definitions of gender, but also reworking them. War implodes the distinction between the public and the private spheres. There is a real sense in which war is a transformative force: it initiates social change; it restructures relations betwen the sexes; and it provides a kind of springboard from which many women have moved beyond circumscribed domestic roles into new arenas. Perhaps many women feel as Eleanor Roosevelt did: 'The war was my emancipation and education.'[9] This was not only true of middle-class women in World War Two. According to Elshtain:

perhaps the most poignant testimony to the Second World War change is a single sentence from a black domestic who was sprung from domestic work to a high-paying factory job: 'Hitler was the one that got us out of the white folks' kitchen'.
(Cited by Elshtain, 1987: 190)

Undoubtedly the war in South Africa produced some powerful new identities for a number of women. But on the whole the process of militarization mobilized the traditional gender conception of men as 'the protectors' and women as 'the protected'.

Notes

1. Gender is a relational concept. This approach 'avoids the pitfalls of isolationism, which stresses the uniqueness of women's experience and, because it examines that experience virtually in a vacuum, cannot always explain changes in women's lives' (Higonnet and Higonnet, 1987: 4).
2. This woman's career is an interesting illustration of how the removal of institutional barriers does not automatically grant women access to power. In 1923 legislation was passed which, for the first time, permitted women in South Africa to practise at the bar. In 1952 Leo van den Heever was admitted to that bar and in 1969 she became the first woman in South Africa to be appointed a judge of the Supreme Court. Twenty years later she is still the only woman judge among 130 colleagues on the bench.
3. However this is not always as restrictive as that described by George Eliot: 'A loving woman's world lies within the four walls of her home; and it is only through her husband that she is in any electric communication with the world beyond' (Eliot, 1932: 54).
4. The situation has improved somewhat since the government banned sex discrimination in Wage board determinations in 1981. The Wage Act existing until then gave the Wage Board the power to lay down different wages for men and women, although it excluded discrimination based on race. The Women's Legal Status Committee submitted to the Wiehahn Commission more than 240 examples of Wage Board and Industrial Council wage determinations where women were paid on average 25 per cent less than men.
5. For evidence of very crude racist attitudes see Cock, 1980.
6. Kimble and Unterhalter (1982) have given an extremely insightful account of ANC women's struggles.
7. The Guidelines have been subject to harsher criticism. For example Driver argues that the silences on women in the Constitutional Guidelines 'suggest that any statements about women's "equal rights" are nothing but a smokescreen over the patriarchal desire to preserve gender relations as they are at both the private and public level' (Driver, 1989: 11).
8. Gaitskell and Unterhalter suggest that there were two strategic reasons for this emphasis: firstly motherhood was seen as a unifying experience for all black

women, in towns and rural areas, in wage employment or working in the informal sector; secondly, it was understood as a unifying experience for both black and white women. As an experience black and white women shared, it could win the support of white women for African women's opposition to passes. This appeal to women as mothers is not only ineffective but it is also problematic because it inscribes women in a reproductive role. Feminism asserts that women have other roles as well. But there are complex issues involved here. Gaitskell and Unterhalter point out that this connection 'must be read in the context of the vernacular African languages where the word for adult woman and the word for mother are the same' (Gaitskell and Unterhalter, 1989: 72). Furthermore, when challenged on this point at the 'Women in the Struggle for Peace' conference in Harare in 1989, Ruth Mompati insisted that the term 'mother' was simply a term of respect for women.

9. Elshtain asserts that the war liberated her: 'She emerged from the war years a transformed person, her own woman: an identity she owed to the war's corrosion of the brittle and imprisoning "social self" she had once been' (Elshtain, 1987: 188).

3

The protectors:
White men and the SADF

'Bruce' feels threatened by black people and believes that he has to protect his wife and two children against them. He believes that black people are 'animals' and that 'we're different – even under the skin'.[1]

> I once saw the body of someone who had been 'necklaced' in the 'location'. The necklacing was done by placing a petrol-filled tyre round the man's neck, forcing his mouth open and pouring it down, and then lighting a match. There've been lots of necklacings here. But this man – all this skin had been burned off – the flesh underneath was pink just like ours. No ... I don't think that means natives are like us underneath, really they're like animals.

'Bruce' had this experience while he was in the SADF. A blond, ruddy-complexioned young businessman, he felt threatened, but was also resentful of the demands the SADF made on his time.

> We were only paid R10 for a weekend and we had to get ourselves to town. We weren't given any petrol money. We were called up about one weekend a month during the 1984-6 period to keep up a show. We rode around the township in a buffel [military vehicle]. We were ordered to shoot dead anyone seen picking up a bottle because it could be a petrol bomb. And a petrol bomb thrown into a buffel would be bad – everyone would be burned.
> Sometimes it was fun ... the food was very good. But mostly it was boring. The worst thing I saw was a man being stabbed – cut up in pieces really. It happened just in front of us. It happened very quickly. The culprits ran away before they could be caught. We [SADF soldiers] were not allowed to get out of the buffel because we would be blamed, and quite a crowd had gathered. But you know, they're not like us. I feel sorry for the women, but the men just drink. This necklaced body I saw – he was supposed to have raped someone. But there's no such thing as rape among blacks. Blacks are only

interested in violence and drink. They should bring back the curfew [there used to be a siren at 9 p.m. every night in his village, after which time all Africans had to remain in the township]. There was no housebreaking when there was the curfew. However, it wasn't always fair. If my boys [adult African workers] went fishing at night, they sometimes had to swim across the river to avoid the police, and there's sharks in the river.

There are other white men who share Bruce's racism:

If we saw a well-built kaffir, we'd know he was a terr. If he had soft feet that would prove it beyond doubt, at least if we were out in the bush, because who else wears shoes? Sometimes you could also see marks on his shoulders or his waist from the webbing. We'd interrogate him, and if he was stubborn he could have trouble. Maybe we'd tie him to the front of the Buffel and do a little bundu-bashing. Feel it? Why should I feel it? I wasn't on the front of the Buffel. If he's still okay when we get tired of driving around maybe we'd give him a ratpack (a seven-day food supply) and tell him to shut up. Sometimes they shout and complain, and then we have no choice, we have to finish him off. Sometimes he's finished off when we stop driving. Then we just untie him and say farewell.
(SADF soldier, quoted in Frontline, *August 1985)*

One time we captured a terrorist and tied him onto the front of a Ratel [military vehicle]. Then we went 'bundu-bashing'. We had captured him for interrogation – that was the interrogation. He didn't say anything. He died in the first day. We used to pull into villages for everyone to see, as a warning sign. After a few days we took him off. He just fell apart. It wasn't a pretty sight.
(Informant 64)

It would be comforting to think that the people who commit these acts of violence and cruelty are 'different'; that they are vicious, sick, mentally ill, psychopaths – pathological in some way. But there is powerful evidence to the contrary – evidence that acts of group killing, torture, and cruelty are often performed by 'normal' people. Hannah Arendt wrote of this 'banality of evil' in her coverage of the trial of Nazi war criminal Adolf Eichmann:

The trouble with Eichmann was precisely that so many were like him, and that the man was neither perverted nor sadistic ... [but] terribly and terrifyingly normal.
(Arendt, 1970)

Many South Africans who engage in acts of cruelty are 'terrifyingly normal'. They are people who have been socialized into conformity; into unthinking obedience to authority, and into the belief that some human beings (Jews, 'moffies', 'kaffirs' or communists) are non-human and outside the boundaries which define humane treatment. This chapter demonstrates that SADF soldiers such as Bruce are the products of a conditioning process. This process is designed to overcome the individual impulse for self-preservation and make people capable of killing or dying on command. The key theme in this process is socialization into a rigidly masculine and militarized construction of self.

Military training as socialization into brutality

Military training involves stripping young men of their individuality and moulding them into soldiers. During 'basics' soldiers are taught two major requirements: to be submissive to authority and to be aggressive to the enemy. One of the most powerful processes is a dehumanization of this 'enemy'. Military training in South Africa and elsewhere involves inculcating what Gray calls the 'totalitarian image', which sanctions seeing the enemy as the representative of a principle of evil one must destroy. In the South African case this is linked to 'the sub-human image' that sees the enemy as a creature not human at all, a noxious species of 'animal'.

> In South Africa this dehumanization process takes place within the 'kaffir syndrome', where black South Africans are stripped of their human status. Our SADF instructors often used words like 'kaffir' during training, suggesting that the word was synonymous with the terrorist enemy on the border. This process of dehumanization has special relevance and affect in the South African experience, for it draws on an already deeply entrenched psychological basis of racial bias within the wider society. The average white South African male, on entrance into the SADF, has, if not racial hatred, at least some degree of racial insensitivity and insecurity, and thus is in most cases fairly open to the particular process of dehumanization used in the SADF. The racism is simply entrenched in the SADF. It's expressed in statements one heard often, like, 'What are we doing here? I didn't come to run around, I came to kill kaffirs on the border'.
> *(Informant 100)*

'Know your enemy' courses in the SADF emphasize the difference and 'otherness' of black people. The equation of blacks with 'the enemy' is usually made implicitly, but not always. Giving evidence in mitigation in the trial of Saul Batzofin, who was convicted for refusing to serve in the SADF, independent MP Jan van Eck said national servicemen were shown a film in 1988 of a black church leader and others attending a carol service in Mamelodi (the African township near Pretoria). They were told, 'They are the enemy' (*The Weekly Mail* 17.3.1989). Within the SADF the linkages between the ANC, communists, and 'terrorists' easily slip into a racial enmity:

> It's a short slide from the red scare to the black scare.
> *(Informant 104)*

> ... the really dangerous part is that ... the evil images of the terrorist enemy that they project automatically generalize to one's view of blacks. Like when you are taught to salute, you are told that you must hold your hand flat and firm, the same way as you would when you slap a kaffir. So it all combines to confirm the stereotypes about blacks.
> *(Richard Steele, quoted in Frederikse, 1986: 82)*

In the experience of some conscripts there was an explicit identification of blacks as the enemy in a war:

> I remember this officer giving us a speech during training. He held up his rifle and said, 'See this in my hand? This is the only thing that talks to a kaffir'. And the other thing he said was, 'Gentlemen have a look at your hands. You'll notice they are white. That is your privilege and that is what this war is all about.'
> *(Quoted by Frederikse, 1986: 84)*

Within the SADF many conscripts were given an extremely racist and distorted picture of political confict in South Africa. For example a Bureau for Information pamphlet issued and widely distributed in 1988 describes the 'unrest' since 1984 as a confrontation

> between two groups in Black communities: those who favoured evolutionary reform and revolutionaries committed to violence.

The theme of the pamphlet was to justify the detention of children on the grounds of the shocking role

> played by children as intimidators, inciters, enforcers and executioners.

This was supposedly the fault of the ANC:

> As in the case of other revolutionary organizations around the world, the abuse of children as revolutionaries is an established strategy of the ANC.

However, not all conscripts absorbed this picture uncritically:

> The pressures are subtle. The political education was absurd ... too crude really. The world was divided into red and blue – the war in Angola [where this informant fought] was backed by reds .... But we were explicitly told we were fighting the kaffirs as well as the communists. My commanding officer said, 'You're here to kill kaffirs.' Blacks were definitely viewed as sub-human .... I didn't do cadets or go to veld school, but I went to an all-male school and it was very macho. The whole emphasis was on competition. Sexual competition was very important. I think we saw war as a way of affirming one's masculinity and competing successfully with other men.

Notions of 'masculinity' are a powerful tool in this process of making men into soldiers. There is a connection between masculinity and militarism; the traditional notion of masculinity resonates with militarist ideas. The army is an institutional sphere for the cultivation of masculinity; war provides the social space for its validation.[2] The military encourages a form of ultra-masculinity which requires aggressiveness, competitiveness and the censure of emotional expression:

> A soldier must learn to dehumanize other people and make them into targets, and to cut himself off from his own feelings of caring and connectedness to the community. His survival and competence as a soldier depend on this process. Military training is socialization into masculinity carried to extremes.
> *(Roberts, 1984: 197)*

Most military environments are excessively masculine to emphasize the break from the feminine influences of civilian life. Lack of feminine companionship encourages vulgarity, almost completely eliminates courtesy, and channels emotions into rigid male bonding. An American soldier of the Vietnam era was frank. He said:

> I wanted to go to war. It was a test I wanted to pass. It was a manhood test, no question about it.
> *(Keegan and Holmes, 1985: 261)*

His words were echoed by a platoon commander in the Falklands:

> The only real test of a man is when the firing starts.
> *(Ibid.)*

This process of fusing masculinity and militarism is used extensively in the SADF to turn young boys into soldiers:

> One guy in the SADF had not yet started shaving when he was called up for his national service. He was continually ridiculed, his masculinity insulted and his sexual identity threatened. On one occasion he was forced to shave with a brick in front of his entire regiment until his face bled.
> *(Informant 61)*

> The main motive forces in the SADF were the *swartgevaar* [the black danger], the *rooigevaar* [the red danger], and manliness. Fortunately I was classified G4K3 for medical purposes, allowing me to do duty only of an administrative nature. For the remainder of my two years I was branded by superiors and at times fellow national servicemen as a 'moffie' or 'pansie' [derogatory terms for homosexuals]. As a group of G4's we were often called 'sissies' or 'girls'. As a result, many of those classified G4K3 attempted to be reclassified. I think it was largely because they felt their manhood was threatened. Anything associated with weakness was considered effeminate.
> *(Informant 65)*

> Any inability to keep up was associated with a lack of masculinity. There were frequent references to being a 'moffie'. Anyone who couldn't compete effectively [that is, who didn't have the required levels of physical stamina, or cleanliness, or ability in drills and so on] was often ostracized by the platoon due to him having caused us more exercise than we would have done if the weaker one kept up .... These people who could not make the grade were pushed further and further behind. I saw this happening to a chap who was in my training platoon. He eventually shot himself in the bungalow .... He was continually abused and victimized by the corporals, who didn't see what they were doing to the poor guy.
> *(Informant 66)*

> My instructor's favourite expression on the failure of our section to accomplish a task was, 'Julle is net soos 'n klomp vroumense met nat broeke'. ['You are just like a bunch of women with wet pants'.] He made this comment often, and we all found it very humiliating.
> *(Informant 67)*

An aggressive sexuality is encouraged in sexual slang and bawdy verses. Also,

> The instructors make a lot of jokes about sex. They'd say things like 'Don't bend over in the shower'. They encouraged this heavy masculine image of 'so horny he'll fuck anything'.
> *(Informant 82)*

> There was a lot of emphasis on military training as affirming one's masculinity. The norm was always of the virile, heterosexual male. It was quite a homophobic culture ... with a lot of banter about homosexuals.

As in other armies, in the SADF male genitals were frequently objectified in this process of fusing masculinity and militarism:

> Soldiers in a world of ritualized masculinity both consciously and subconsciously came to regard their weapons as extensions of their virility.
> *(Costello, 1985: 120)*

The famous chant that was used to teach marines how to name their instruments correctly (how, in other words, to distinguish between the rifle in one hand and the penis in the other) was also reported in the SADF:

> This is my rifle,
> This is my gun,
> This is for fighting,
> This is for fun.

Conscripts who failed to perform were often called by derogatory terms for female genitals. Soldiers who admitted to fear were 'old women'.

It seems that in basic training it is insensitivity, dominance, competitiveness, and aggression that are encouraged and praised. Many informants emphasized that the core of military training was to equate aggression with masculinity.

> This happens from day one of training in the SADF. My most recent example is of a friend of mine who was doing his national service in the SADF. On his very first day he was pulled from a long line of men awaiting the regulatory hair cut. He was selected due to the length of his hair and was told, 'Let's cut your hair first so that you can stand up when you piss – you no longer have to sit like a woman.'
> *(Informant 78)*

It is important to note how many of these accounts make contemptuous references to women; femininity is clearly associated with weakness, vulnerability, and feebleness.This hatred and contempt for women was built into training for the American marines, according to Eisenhart (1975). One informant was familiar with his description:

> In my own experience in the SADF, the tactics described by Eisenhart were used fairly regularly. The platoon was often called 'a bunch of old women' or told that the SADF was not for 'girls' or 'queers'. Such labelling came always when the group was not performing efficiently, quickly or aggressively enough.
> *(Informant 72)*

The image of 'woman' mobilized in this process of equating aggression with masculinity is generally negative. This is true whether women are viewed as symbols of weakness, sex objects who may be abused, or even as dependent loved ones who must be protected.

The process of dehumanization in military training applies both to the enemy and to the soldiers themselves. The process is best illustrated by Eisenhart, who described an incident from his training in the marines:

> On the last day of training before leaving for Vietnam we were ushered into a clearing where a staff sergeant stood holding a rabbit. He stroked and petted it. As soon as we were all seated and with no word of explanation, he crushed its head with a rock and proceeded to actually skin and disembowel the animal with his bare hands and teeth while showering the entrails on us. As we left the clearing he stood there with fur all around his mouth and blood running down his throat.
> *(Eisenhart, 1975: 18)*

There is some evidence that this kind of brutalization process involving cruelty to animals is also practised in the SADF. I have heard that some SADF special élite training involves soldiers having to carry a puppy around with them for four days – feeding and caring for it. They are then required to kill it with their bare hands. However, I have not been able to locate anyone who actually has had this experience. There have been newspaper reports of gruesome acts of animal cruelty, slaughter, decapitation, and mutilation committed for pleasure by members of the SADF.

> Some national servicemen have claimed that animal cruelty was rife in bases in Namibia and South Africa. Midnight satanic rituals are said to have been held in which drunk soldiers skinned and beheaded cats, drank their blood and chopped off their tails to sell to tribesmen.
> *(Sunday Star 8.5.1988)*

The Star newspaper had in its possession a picture of two smiling conscripts holding a decapitated kitten's head in their teeth.
(The Star *9.5.1988)*

One soldier spoke of having a pet kitten while he was on a chef's course at a military base in Pretoria. One afternoon he walked into the camp kitchen to find that someone had poured boiling water over his kitten and then set a dog on it:

He was still alive but in terrible pain …. I called a private to help me. He chopped the kitten's head off with a spade.
(Ibid.)

During 1987 this informant witnessed another case of cruelty:

A regimental sergeant-major walked into the kitchen. Three kittens were playing on the floor. He shouted that he wanted them killed. A corporal and private then started kicking them around. I was not the only one who saw what they were doing. There was also a woman sergeant. After they had played their game there were two dead kittens on the floor. The other was alive. They left them there and went to call up one of the black workers to clean up the mess.
(Ibid.)

A number of servicemen said shooting monkeys 'for fun' was quite common on the border.

One female monkey with her baby clutched to her chest was shot by a private …. In the black townships where the guys go out on patrol at night, it's a game to shoot the scrawny dogs wandering in the streets.
(Sunday Star *8. 5.1988)*

The equation of masculinity with extreme aggression and violence also involves an emphasis on exceptional levels of stamina and physical fitness. This often involves physical exhaustion, which presumably makes soldiers more amenable to the conditioning process.The emphasis on physical fitness is carried to extreme lengths in training for the 'Recces':

They are the silent warriors, the men of the night, with an army that can reach into any part of Africa and strike at any foe. They are acknowledged by friend and enemy alike as without equal – anywhere – when it comes to bush warfare.
(Special report in Scope *magazine, 10.3.1989)*

Recce training is tough and specific. These guys are the élite and their training shows why. It's tough and at the end only the best make it.
(Special report in Scope *magazine, 24.3.1989)*

Interviewed Recce members offered a diverse range of motives for joining, from patriotism to adventure:

... your ego dictates that you be apart from the herd, one of the élite. Then there is just the basic desire for adventure and the enjoyment of a good war.
(Ibid.)

Another said,

Some of us just enjoy fighting ... as a professional soldier that is what you train for.
(Ibid.)

The emphasis on physical fitness is also extreme among the 'Parabats', 1 Parachute Battalion:

It's no child's play being a parabat. You have to have the kind of physical and mental toughness that characterizes the men who make the Royal and US Marines the crack outfits they are.
*(*Saturday Star *8.7.1989)*

In order for 'the standard of combat to remain high and efficient', the three-month basic course in the Parabats includes:

PT twice a day, no walking in camp, and a 5-10 km run to end each day; a further 6 weeks' advanced individual training with the PT level increased to seven-and-a-half hours a day and a 16 km run with poles or 'dogs'. Later the runs include running with 'marbles', hessian-covered concrete.
(Ibid.)

Several informants mentioned the physical strain involved in SADF training. This was sometimes a source of satisfaction:

What I remember most about my national service was the feeling of exhaustion, but also a pride in coping and becoming really fit. They really do try to break you down. You're put through a gruelling programme of physical fitness. PT is also used as a very harsh and arbitrary form of punishment. You get little sleep. Also it's very depersonalizing. You have the same uniforms, and haircuts and just become another number.
(Informant 75)

This depersonalization was a common theme in conscripts' accounts:

> Basic training was very depersonalizing, humiliating and aliena-
> ting .... There's the monotonous tasks, the petty regulations, inspec-
> tions in the middle of the night. All the petty regulations are enforced
> very harshly. There's a lack of privacy .... Altogether it's a very harsh
> environment. And there's enormous sleep deprivation in basics. This
> is to make you more receptive to the political education.
> *(Informant 68)*

This conditioning process often involves an intense male-bonding.
According to Studs Terkel,

> For the typical American soldier, despite the perverted film sermons,
> it wasn't 'getting another Jap' or 'getting another Nazi' that impelled
> him up front. 'The reason you storm the beaches is not patriotism or
> bravery,' reflects the tall rifleman, 'it's that sense of not wanting to
> fail your buddies. There's a special sense of kinship.'
> *(Terkel, 1984: 5)*

This male bonding in the experience and training for war means a
sharing of sacrifice and danger. It seems to have a particular intensity.[3]
However, according to one informant this notion of 'male bonding' was
a myth:

> No, people say there's this intense bonding, but my main feeling was
> of aggression against other guys. There was a lot of distrust. I once
> saw someone shot by accident. For me it was a very lonely time. I
> found it hard to relate to the other guys.
> *(Informant 68)*

What is significant is that when it occurs, this male bonding and social
cohesion are achieved through emphasizing the 'otherness' of both
'women' and 'the enemy'; women represent home and hearth, to be
protected and defended against a conception of the enemy, who represent evil and disorder.

However, the connection of masculinity to militarism involves deception. John Keegan (1976) breaks with the tendency of previous
military historians to treat soldiers in the aggregate and investigates the
experience of individual men in specific battles. At the Somme in 1916,
Keegan discovered the 'will to fight' was, for many men, an uncertain
phenomenon at best. Men often have deeply ambivalent feelings about

aggression. War experiences also reveal deep fear, disorientation, and doubts about masculinity. Keegan argues that the modern battlefield has an inhuman face; that military technology reduces the warrior's role 'to that of mere victim'. Military technology has made warfare impersonal. In this process

> combat was invalidated as a test of individual heroism that could serve as a masculine initiation ritual.
> *(Gubar, in Higonnet and Higonnet, 1987: 251)*

The stressful effects of combat have been well documented since the Vietnam war (Lifton, 1973).[4] The Namibian conflict bears many similarities to the Vietnam war, hence its psychological effects may be similar:

> 'Like the American GI's, the South African conscripts are fighting in a war with no clear or immediate objectives, such as the gaining of terrain; there is [mostly] no clearly defined or identifiable enemy; they are part of an unwanted foreign army of occupation which is technologically superior to the enemy's; drafted often against their will; often in their teens [the average age of those Americans who fought in Vietnam was 19]; and may return to situations or places [e.g. universities] where their participation in the Namibian conflict may be seen as inhumane, immoral and unjustified.
> *(Davey, 1988)*

Davey's study involved subjects who were all involved in the Namibian conflict. In 1985 there were 90 000 SADF troops in Namibia. This suggests that there may be a great number of very damaged young men in South Africa at present; a 'scarred generation' as Bruce Moore-King describes those whites who served in the Zimbabwe war (Moore-King, 1988: 132).

> There's no doubt in my mind that my experience of military service and action [I was involved in two contacts] has damaged me emotionally. My ability to feel as a human being towards others has been damaged. At the time there's a numbing, an insensitivity, you feel nothing. I remember feeling a great distance from everything .... No, I don't think you ever really get over it. I'm still unable to feel very deeply or strongly about anything.
> *(Informant 68)*

This informant was a conscript into the SADF. The structure of the SADF shows an extensive reliance on conscripted manpower. This manpower is obtained through various forms of coercion – legal, ideological and social. Gender is an important dynamic in all three forms of coercion. Despite this coercion there are different responses to conscription in the white community, which may be categorized as compliance, retreat, and challenge. Those young men who challenge the system of compulsory service in the SADF do so at considerable personal cost.

A conscript army

> It is a peculiar contradiction of this country that every white man is obliged to undergo military training, while black youths who go and do military training end up in court.
> *(D. Kuny SC, quoted in* The Star *11.4.1986)*

This 'peculiar contradiction' is anchored in the fact that the key function of the South African Defence Force (SADF) has come to be the protection of white minority rule. Therefore the system of conscription in South Africa is race-specific. Furthermore, in the 1980s it was distinctive in two additional ways. Firstly, the length of military service demanded from conscripts was among the longest of the 76 countries in the world which have conscription. Secondly, the penalties for objection were among the harshest in the world. During the decade of the 1980s South Africa had the largest army in sub-Saharan Africa, with a total mobilization strength of about 500 000. It drew on two types of manpower – about 18 000 professional soldiers who constitute the Permanent Force, and part-time manpower in the form of five categories:

1. National service conscripts who had to serve a two-year continuous period of duty.
2. Members of the Citizen Force – national servicemen who have completed their initial military training but were obliged to render periodic service to the SADF in the form of 720 days spread over 12 years.
3. Active Citizen Force Reserve members who served 12 days annually for a further five-year period.

4. Commando members who served 12 days a year until the age of 55.
5. White males between the ages of 55 and 65 who are included in the ranks of the National Reserve.

This part-time manpower amounted to almost 58 000 national servicemen, and nearly 300 000 members of the Citizen Force and commandos. This meant that more than 70 per cent of the SADF was part-time and that the army was totally dependent on the white conscripts for its functioning. Recently the racial composition of the SADF has changed somewhat, as there are now a number of 'coloured', Indian, and African volunteers, but 76 per cent of full-time SADF personnel are white, and its high-ranking officers entirely so.[5]

Overall South Africa's draft policy in the eighties had the following characteristics:

1. It was race-specific, applying only to the country's white population of 5 million.
2. It was gender-specific, applying only to white males.
3. It was obliquely class-specific in the sense that if a young white man has the resources to be admitted to a university, he may apply for deferment to delay his military obligations at least until he has earned his bachelor's degree.
4. It involved extremely heavy demands on all white men, who could be required to serve over 1 600 days in the SADF.
5. It involved various levels of coercion. There was direct compulsion in the sense that those who refused to serve were punished.

There was also indirect conscription into an ideology that defines such service as necessary. Conscripts were liable for service in Angola, Namibia, and in the townships. Many conscripts fought in the operational area of Northern Namibia, where South Africa's occupation was held to be illegal by the International Court of Justice in 1971. Conscripts have been involved in Angola's civil war since 1973. They were active in 'destabilization' activities in neighbouring countries such as Mozambique. They have risked death and injury there, as well as the hatred of many of their black compatriots in the townships, where they were widely viewed as 'an army of occupation'. They did so largely because they were subject to legal, ideological, and social coercion.

Forms of coercion

Legal coercion

This form of coercion applied only to a race- and gender- specific category of South Africans. The liability of a white male citizen to render service in the SADF is contained in Section 3(1)(b) of the Defence Act, no. 44 of 1957, which states,

> Every citizen between his 17th and 65th year, both included, shall be liable to render service in the South African Defence Force ....

Section 63 of the Act requires every male citizen to register during his 16th year. Persons liable to serve may apply to an Exemption Board for deferment or for exemption from service.[6] During 1983 and 1984 a series of amendments to the Defence Act were promulgated to allow a narrowly-defined category of religious objectors the option of serving in non-military roles or doing community service.[7]

Conscripts were often not aware of these options, due to the ideological context within which the SADF operated. Section 121(c) of the Defence Act made it an offence, punishable by a fine of R6 000 or six years' imprisonment, to encourage or assist any person to refuse or to fail to render military service. This was amplified by State of Emergency regulations which defined as a 'subversive statement' anything which undermined the present system of conscription. 'Subversive statements' were punishable by large fines or long periods of imprisonment. Any person who was liable to render service in the SADF and who refused to render such service or failed to report for service was guilty of an offence in terms of Section 126(a) of the Act. A refusal to render service carried the penalty of imprisonment for a period of one-and-a-half times as long as the aggregate of the maximum of all periods of service the offender would otherwise still have been compelled to render, or for a period of 18 months, whichever was the longer. This meant a six-year prison sentence for those who had not done their initial two years. Such refusals were rare, largely because white youths have already been socialized into an ideology of militarism.

Ideological coercion

The increasing militarization of the white educational system was an important aspect of this ideological coercion. This has

involved the conscious creation of a social atmosphere that makes
military service seem attractive, military responses to policy issues
sensible, and greater military strength and expenditure seem acceptable – one which in general prepares the population for conditions of
siege and war.
(Grundy, 1983: 109)

The practice of compulsory SADF registration for white males through
schools at the age of sixteen has been described as using schools as
'recruiting bases'. A parent complained that

> this method of recruitment is yet another example of the increasing
> militarization of our society. Do other parents feel concern about their
> sixteen- and seventeen-year-old sons signing away two years of their
> lives without even a family discussion?
> *(Letter to* The Star *7.4.1987)*

Refusals to register appeared to be uncommon. All the informants
interviewed for this study reported that they had registered along with
their entire class. Perhaps this is because pupils have already been
exposed to paramilitary training through the school cadet system. This
was officially launched in 1976 and is co-ordinated by the SADF and
the various provincial educational departments. According to the SADF
it was introduced for three reasons:

1. for the youth to develop a sense of responsibility and love for their
   country and national flag;
2. to instil civil defence in the youth;
3. to train them in good citizenship as a forerunner to their national
   service.
   *(*Paratus *September 1980)*

It has been described as 'not a case of brainwashing, but an attempt to
cultivate the military spirit' and 'a positive attitude to the SADF.'
(Captain Willem Steenkamp, quoted by Evans, 1983: 184). As Frankel
has noted,

> cadet training serves a number of distinctively useful purposes when
> viewed from the perspective of the military. It periodically exposes
> young men to martial routines, it serves as a nursery to national
> service, it stimulates patriotism, and ... creates a favourable climate
> in respect of national defence.
> *(Frankel, 1984: 99)*

The Cape Education Department's 1986 Cadet Training Manual gives some insight into how this climate is achieved. In the first lesson, Standard Six pupils are warned of the 'threat to peaceful co-existence and prosperity in South Africa'. Cadet training is necessary to 'prepare themselves against this threat, because young people have been selected as the target group for revolutionary attack'. It is absolutely necessary that information about 'actual and potential enemies' be gathered by them and reported to the cadet officer 'as soon as possible'. This is necessary because the enemy is desperate and 'aims to overthrow the present government and create a black majority government'. In Standard Eight the focus shifts towards the SADF itself. Sections covered by the syllabus include 'the necessity of compulsory military service', 'the meaning of National Service', map reading and navigation, and 'the protection of hearth and home'.

Pupils are told that 'some governments look with envious eyes at the resources of other countries', and that they therefore aim to create a 'revolutionary climate through getting people to create violence' and 'inciting people not to do military training'. There is a heavy emphasis on physical fitness, and the manual praises Nazi Germany in this respect:

> ... in the case of National Socialist Germany, the physical prepared-ness of the whole nation was very good, because they used every opportunity by way of physical exercises, sport etc., to improve the whole nation physically.

Among the gains of military service mentioned in the section on the 'meaning of National Service' are self-knowledge, responsiblity, leadership, insight, selflessness, endurance, self-discipline and self-confidence. There is also an emphasis on building masculinity.

> National Service may virtually be regarded as a modern initiation school. It is generally considered that the Defence Force makes a man of boys *(sic)*. In between tears and reproaches of loved ones, every national serviceman is nevertheless admired, and those who have already completed national service enjoy a particular status in their family circle and in society. As they are denied this opportunity, women especially admire national servicemen.

The 'safety of hearth and home' section includes practical advice such as ensuring that the telephone is working 'before you go to sleep', working out alternative routes to school and allocating each family member his/her duties in case of attacks. Standard Eight pupils are told that the enemy's propaganda is

> not restricted to verbal statements, radio and TV, but can be used in magazines, articles, music, books, posters, art and the media. It aims to cause demoralisation amongst us ... we must be cautious not to fall into the enemy's trap.

The cadets were closely integrated with the Youth Preparedness Programme, a compulsory subject in all white schools. This also emphasized military preparedness, discipline, and patriotism. It was first launched in the Transvaal in 1972 and was intended to make white pupils accept the new SADF extended two-year period of compulsory military service. A simple, conspiratorial world view was elaborated and no debate, questioning or discussion encouraged. Central to this world view was the belief that South Africa faced a 'total' or 'revolutionary onslaught' from the USSR and its allies.

The 'veld school' is an outdoor extension of this pedagogic programme. Veld schools were run on military lines and activities included inspection and flag raising, survival training, tracking and camouflage, marching, and practical field training, as well as group discussions, lectures and films. There was a strong emphasis on the 'communist onslaught', and the need for a military response:

> There wasn't outright anti-black racism, but a lot of talk about how we must defend our country against communism.
> *(Informant 103)*

> We had a lot of lectures on politics. They said that any kind of opposition to the government is just opting for communism. They told us things like, 'Do you like the kind of things you have in your house, your luxuries? Then how would you feel if half your stuff was given to some black man?'
> *(Quoted by Frederikse, 1986: 10)*

According to another pupil,

> In veld school we did communism, we did the South African flag, we did terrorism, and one whole lecture was about how sex, communism and drugs all goes into the music we listen to.
> *(Ibid.: 9)*

There is some doubt as to how efficacious this attempted indoctrination really is. One pupil, asked whether she agreed with everything she was told in the lectures, replied,

I think it was too old-fashioned. I mean listening to music doesn't automatically make you take drugs or have sex every night or become a communist.
(Ibid.)

The propaganda was too crude and obvious.
(Informant 108)

Possibly the ideological lessons learned from participating in games such as *Nats versus Terrorists* are more deep-seated. But the essence of the process is that

our education teaches us to conform to authority. You don't make decisions. People make decisions for you, and you learn to obey them.
(Informant 103)

The military nature of the white educational environment has become more marked over time. During 1987 it became known that the Transvaal Education Department had instructed certain teachers to carry guns; and fences, barbed wire, and high walls have been built around many white schools. The outcome is that many young white South Africans

... are pretty staunch racists by the time they reach eighteen. Their education is indoctrination. They're locked out of the truth ... they've had no exposure to alternatives. Their parents are role models of racists. They've never been in the townships and don't understand the situation there.
(Informant 106)

The school system was not the only agency which indoctrinated. Some media promoted a glamorized image of the SADF. For example an article in a popular magazine gives a particularly glowing account of the 'Parabats'. 'Operation Reindeer' in May 1978 is described as 'the Parabats' finest moment' (*Scope* magazine 23.9.1988). 'Operation Reindeer' was the code name for what has come to be called the Cassinga Massacre in which 600 Namibian refugees – mostly women and children – were killed by SADF paratroopers.

Many young white South Africans were ignorant of these important events in their history. The SADF operated in a sealed environment, shielded from public knowledge and scrutiny. A mass of laws and emergency regulations hid its powers and activities behind a veil of secrecy. This secrecy applied particularly to the SADF's activities in Angola. Many conscripts were unclear as to why the SADF invaded

Angola in the first place. There has been a great disparity between SADF casualty figures and those provided by the Angolans and independent sources. Most South Africans rely on the state-owned and state-operated radio and communications networks for information. These popularized the belief in an onslaught against the country. The patriotic response was an ideology of militarism which romanticized the SADF – the 'boys on the border' – and 'criminalized' and dehumanized political opponents.

> The SABC has excelled in its stereotyping of the ANC as a demonic force. The ANC is almost invariably reported on in terms of violence and terrorism …. They have been portrayed as folk devils – incarnations of evil and inhumanity who are without conscience in their single-minded determination to overthrow the norms of civilized society … in a revolutionary take-over of power.
> *(Tomaselli, 1988: 22)*

Not only were the ANC depicted as indiscriminate and ruthless killers, 'demon-terrorists', but they were portrayed as having close links with the USSR and operating largely as Moscow's tool.[8]

Generally, the SADF's war with the ANC was often glorified and its encounters mythologized.[9] This glorification is part of what Raymond Williams has termed 'consumerist militarism'.[10] In South Africa this takes a number of different forms. For example, war games are advertised as 'the family game of the future'. A demonstration by two of South Africa's top war games teams advertised for July 1987 promised 'an ideal opportunity to experience a war-type situation and to have fun at the same time'. Advertised experiences include a 'leopard crawl through the bush' and 'hunt a terrorist' (*Northern Review* 3.7.1987). War games and war toys became increasingly popular during the 1980s. A local toy manufacturer reported sales of over 250 000 toy models of a Casspir in 1987. The effect was either to glorify war or to trivialize it, and promote the notion that violence is a legitimate solution to conflict. This violence was frequently linked in the media to notions of masculinity.

The 'Let the army make a man of you' theme was often stated by public figures. The Minister of Defence, General Magnus Malan, has referred contemptuously to male members of the End Conscription Campaign (ECC) as 'mommy's little boys' (*Eastern Province Herald* 6.4.1987). This, together with the demonizing of the ANC as 'communist-inspired terrorists' who threatened all 'civilized' values, resulted in considerable social pressure on young white men to conform to the requirements of compulsory military service.

Social coercion

Social expectations were enforced in a range of social relationships. It was argued in the previous chapter that in South Africa gender identities are rigidly dichotomous, with men being taught to be dominant, competitive, and aggressive, while women are encouraged to be passive and supportive. Girlfriends are an important source of the connection between masculinity and militarism. One woman stated:

> All these long-haired fairies should be forced to do their military training. Maybe they will become men.
> *(Saturday Star 23.7.1988)*

Peer group pressure reinforces the notion that military training is essential to building manliness. Objector Richard Steele has stated,

> Defending your country is supposed to be a good thing, it's the manly thing to do. This is quite an important factor in young men's lives, that you somehow become a man through military training. It's like playing in the first rugby team, in terms of manliness and also the way girls respond to you.
> *(Quoted by Frederikse, 1986: 82)*

Overall these pressures may be extremely coercive. One informant stated:

> If I had to refuse to go on camps I'd lose my girlfriend, I'd be dropped from the first rugby team and I'd be chucked out of res.
> *(Informant 119)*

Parents are also a source of social pressure. This is particularly true of fathers who have records of military service which they equate with 'manliness' and serving their country. Many informants reported sadly that their decision not to serve in the SADF was a source of considerable family tension, particularly in their relationships with their fathers.

> My father fought in Suez and Malaya. He wants me to serve. He worries about my career. My decision not to go into the SADF has made us more distanced. We try not to talk about politics, so as to avoid conflict. My brother was on the border for 18 months. He was a hero to everyone in my family. My father is very disappointed that I'm not prepared to be a soldier. He sees it as a man's duty to protect the white way of life.
> *(Informant 106)*

Given all these forms of coercion – legal, ideological and social – it is not surprising that the response of the majority of white South African males to the conscription issue can be categorized as 'compliance'.

Different responses to conscription

Compliance

'Compliance' is the response of the majority of the thousands of white South African men called up to do their initial military service each year. However it must be stressed that 'compliance' is an extremely broad, and even crude, categorization. It includes both acquiescence and allegiance. A more nuanced approach would include an analysis of various forms of informal resistance within the SADF, such as drug abuse, malingering, petty theft, sabotage, and so on.[11] Informants were not questioned on such forms of resistance. Thus 'compliance' refers to a formal response – obeying one's 'call-up'.

A number of informants who had completed their military service felt positively about their experiences within the SADF. They felt that they had developed in personal terms – were more mature and self-reliant – and had acquired new skills.[12] A number also felt that the role of the SADF was generally a positive one, not only in terms of protecting the country's borders, but also as regards protecting black people's rights and freedoms within the townships. These informants regarded the SADF as making a positive contribution to peace. Two informants stressed that their experience of military service had been 'fun':

> The SADF was a big jorl [party]. We had a lot of fun in the townships in 1986. We drove around and looked at the sights. We used to play with the kids and share our canned food with them. We did a lot of trading. Altogether there was a very friendly atmosphere. We were meant to be a peace-keeping force, but there was no trouble. We really had a ball.
> *(Informant 109)*

> I grew up during my national service. I became a man, physically fit and independent. I'd heard it was tough, but I never imagined how tough it would be. I handled it, but it was a battle. I'm proud of the way I handled it. I was fighting for the safety of the people in South Africa.
> *(Informant 107)*

The SADF had to go into the townships. The police couldn't cope with all the violence. The violence was terrible. I once saw some black youths pour petrol over a dog and set it alight. It was terrible. But there would have been even more violence if we hadn't been there.
(Informant 111)

The first time I went into a township was when I did my national service. I was shocked at the conditions. But several black middle-aged women came up to me and thanked me for what the SADF were doing in the townships.
(Informant 112)

The army does 'make a man of you'. It brings out the best in people. I learned to relate to people better. My own personal belief in myself and my capabilities deepened. My self-confidence increased. I learned to push myself forward, to be more aggressive, and get my own way.
(Informant 113)

Other informants were resentful of the interruption to their studies and careers, and described their time in the SADF as:

a complete waste of time. They didn't know what do with us. It didn't benefit anyone. I only did it because I had to.
(Informant 108)

Some were defensive:

People point fingers at the SADF, but they won't say a bloody thing about the Cubans in Angola, which is despicable and two-faced.
(Informant 112)

Some conscripts' views were dramatically changed by their experiences in the SADF. For example Steven Louw went into the army in 1983 feeling 'positive' about the SADF, which he believed to be 'protecting the people of South Africa'. His experiences with the SADF as a driver in three African townships from 1984 to early 1986 so disturbed him that he joined the ECC after leaving the army. In a court case he said that the turning point came when he intervened as a soldier flailed a young African boy with a stick. He had stood between them and asked 'Why?' to which the reply was, 'Prevention is better than cure'. Louw found it difficult to intervene:

The South African army cultivates this macho, tough boy image. I was wary of breaking with this.

Louw reported that many conscripts had been bored, and tried to provoke township residents to take action against them.

Most people were keen to get involved in the action and to fight against the people in the townships.

In Port Elizabeth he had been ordered to drive up a street and the troops had been ordered to disembark and hide. Louw was told to drive 'up and down' the street 'hoping to provoke stone-throwing or retaliatory action'. He said, 'I remember thinking that this was not the way to keep peace.' In Adelaide nothing had happened until a township resident gave them a power salute.

He was placed in the back of the Buffel and beaten several times. He was very scared and very quiet. He never tried to defend himself. He started to cry when we sjambokked him. Some of the troops said he was not a man because he was crying, and it seemed to justify them beating him.

Another conscript whose experiences in the SADF changed his views is Etienne Marais. When he was conscripted aged 17, he believed that the SADF was in Namibia to defend the people against an external aggressor. While serving as a rifleman in the SADF in Namibia and Angola from 1980 to 1982, Marais came to 'believe that the SADF's presence is a brutal and unpopular one'. He said incidents of 'intimidation and degradation' included

soldiers stealing beer, exposing themselves to Ovambo women, tearing down village fences and shooting rifle grenades into villages without checking to see if people had been evacuated.
(Interview, 1989)

Marais also said he witnessed the 'shooting of a 13-year-old Namibian girl in cold blood' and the eight-hour torture of a 16-year-old Angolan girl. He said:

Collecting ears and fingers as souvenirs happens quite often on the border.
(Ibid.)

He had also seen an SADF member 'use the corpse of a SWAPO guerrilla as a pillow'. He describes the war in Namibia as 'an atrocious war' where

atrocities go largely unrecorded .... Atrocities do occur on a wide scale – and they occur primarily because of the total disregard for blacks that apartheid teaches many young South Africans. People reacted very differently to these atrocities. There was a lot of pressure on us to turn a blind eye. It wasn't done to question.
(Interview, 1989)

Another informant reported,

I became a Christian while serving in Angola. I was terrified ... sitting in a fox hole being strafed by an aeroplane. I was scared most of the time, but there was some fun. I made close friends there. I still see them. We share a nostalgia.
(Informant 113)

I was in charge of a 'mortar pipe'. I was said to be responsible for killing some of the enemy in a contact. I felt very confused ... half proud and half ashamed.
(Informant 68)

Compliance was frequently embedded in a set of extremely racist attitudes. Sometimes the experience of military service reinforced this racism:

When I was on township duty it was clear that the kaffirs hated us. They used to come and urinate against my Buffel. It used to make me very angry, but then the blacks here are scum – they're worse than animals.
(Informant 60)

This reinforcement of racism spread wider than the conscripts themselves:

I have a lot of contact with people in the security forces and the stories that they bring out of the townships are hair-raising .... Our troops are treated with contempt. These young hooligans walk around spitting at them, and pulling their trousers down and baring their arses at them, and that sort of thing. I don't know how these boys keep their control, and I certainly don't think they should be subjected to that sort of business .... I think that the reason that we have this degree of violence in the townships is because these criminals detect softness and then they excel themselves in cruelty. I think that a few of them should actually experience the burning murder treatment themselves, that would stop it very quickly.

(Interview conducted in 1986 by Lesley Lawson with Clive Derby-Lewis – a former Nationalist MPC for Edenvale. Clive Derby-Lewis left to join the Conservative Party in 1982. After the May 1987 election he became a CP (nominated) MP, and their spokesman on Economic Affairs and Technology.)

While little research has been done on conscripts' experiences, there is some evidence that many find their time in the SADF extremely stressful. This stress has become intolerable for some conscripts, even resulting in suicide.

Retreat

The response of retreat manifests itself in four forms: suicide, deferment, evasion, and emigration. There has been a sharp increase in attempted suicides within the SADF. According to figures announced by the Minister of Defence there were 429 attempted suicides in the SADF in 1986, and a total of 24 'uniformed personnel' killed themselves (*The Star*, 21.2.1987). A total of 260 conscripts attempted suicide in 1985, and 16 succeeded (*The Weekly Mail* 31.4.1986). According to figures supplied by General Magnus Malan in parliament, 21 members of the SADF committed suicide in 1988, and 344 members attempted suicide. While white South Africans have one of the highest suicide rates in the world, experts find these figures alarming. It has been suggested that one contributing factor was

> that many service men were involved in inner turmoil because they did not support the government and felt they had become part of the government system.
> *(Brian Goodall, quoted in* The Star *22.2.1987)*

This is an addition to the stress of army life and training.

> Basics [the initial three months' training] is tough; you're in a situation you don't want to be in. Someone else is thinking for you. It's very physical, you've to fight for yourself and there's a lot of group pressure too. If one guy lets the group down he feels like dirt 'cos they all get punished. This gruelling 'Rambo Syndrome' takes its toll. Your only possible support network – your buddies – get

pitted against you the minute you fall behind. The victims are usually 'weaklings', or those who refuse to become 'Rambos'.
(Ex-serviceman, quoted in Wits Student, *vol. 39, no. 2, March 1987)*

I knew a guy who committed suicide in the army. He hanged himself while we were at supper. I think he was a 'moffie'. Everybody picked on him and made him their scapegoat.
(Informant 104)

Dirk Coetzee was a SADF conscript who had completed six months of his military service and committed suicide at his parents' home when he was due to return to camp. His father said that when his son first started his military service he was a very happy person but his attitude later changed and he appeared depressed (*The Star* 29.5.1986).

During the eighties quite a number of white South African men postponed their response to the conscription issue by obtaining deferment from their military service for university study. Their motives in applying for deferment were very mixed:

I've done my two years' national service. Now I've got deferment to study. I object to camps beause they're a waste of time. I feel I've given my two years. Camps would be OK if they were beneficial, but I've been on two and they are a waste of time. They didn't benefit anyone. There was no planning for us – nothing.
(Informant 62)

Some conscripts responded to their call-up papers with evasion, attempting to evade military service by simply not reporting. It was announced in parliament that 7 589 conscripts failed to report for their initial two years of military service in the SADF in January 1985, as opposed to only 1 596 in the whole of 1984 (*At Ease*, ECC newsletter, May 1986). The SADF challenged the former figure as incorrect on the grounds that it included some students and scholars. In January 1986 General Magnus Malan refused to reveal in parliament the number of people who had failed to report to the SADF because the statistics were 'misused' by the ECC. 'It is suspected that the number of those failing to report for camps was much higher .... An ECC organizer has estimated that more than 2 000 men evaded military service every month of 1987 in this way' (*Saturday Star* 30.7.1988).

In 1988 a significant number of Citizen Force and Commando members failed to report for service at camps – almost 15 per cent of those who were called up according to Defense Minister, General Magnus Malan (*The Weekly Mail* 21.4.1989).

A common response to the conscription issue within this category of 'retreat' was emigration. Emigration of white South Africans increased during the eighties, and 'the brain drain' reached headline proportions. According to statistics released in parliament in 1987, a total of 2 164 professional people emigrated in 1986. Over 47 per cent more professional and technical people left the country in 1986 than had left during 1985 (*The Star*, 4.3.1987). Overall from 1984 to 1987 more than 45 000 people left the country (*The Weekly Mail* 27.4.1987). This was often because of conscription.

> While the motivations underlying emigration vary from the political to the most intensely personal, it is significant that many of the younger English speakers are moved to action by the prospect of extended military service.
> *(Frankel, 1984: 139)*

After Frankel wrote these words, the prospect of military service within South Africa's black townships accelerated this process:

> I left the country because the use of the SADF in the townships made it clear to me that the army is defending an untenable political system. The troops going into the townships was the turning point for me and I left South Africa.
> *(Informant 105)*

A 1987 survey conducted of all male students at Rhodes University found that 55 per cent were contemplating emigrating. Of these, 28 per cent were contemplating emigration solely to avoid conscription, while a further 28 per cent gave conscription as one reason (Adams and Bernstein, 1988).

The anguish this response may involve should not be underestimated. The fracturing of family relationships is not only geographical. In 1988 for example, 33-year-old computer expert Tammas Alexander went into exile rather than serve in the SADF. He received a hostile and public rebuke from his father:

> I totally disassociate myself from his action; it was uncalled for and not the slightest bit patriotic. I'm very disappointed in him and ashamed of his action. What is wrong is wrong .... Military service may not be pleasant, but it is a duty, and the law of the land. What would happen if everybody did what he did? We'd be in a real mess.
> *(Quoted in the* Sunday Star, *30.10.1988)*

Alexander chose to go to Zimbabwe so as 'to keep my roots in Africa'. It is this sense of being rooted here that informs some young men's decision to remain in South Africa and simply not report for military service.

The numbers of people who retreat from military service are difficult to quantify. For example conscientious objectors leave the country under a variety of guises. The London-based Committee on South African War Resistance estimates that about 10 000 people have emigrated to avoid conscription since 1978. The lengths to which people will go to to avoid military service are illustrated by the case of a 21-year-old South African man 'trying to dodge military service' who 'assumed a new identity, took out an insurance policy of almost R200 000, and then allegedly set a drugged hobo alight in a car to fake his own death (*Saturday Star* 4.2.1989). Other young men have chosen to remain in South Africa and actively challenge the system of compulsory military service.

Challenge

In the course of the 1980s an increasing number of young white South Africans came to believe that to perform military service in the SADF was to contribute to a political system that the majority of South Africans defined as illegitimate and immoral. Since the late seventies, twenty-one politically motivated objectors have been charged with refusing to serve in the SADF.

Many objectors came to their position after serving in the military. For example Saul Batzofin, who was imprisoned for refusing to serve in the SADF, said that the process began while he was on border duty in 1981, when he witnessed Owambo civilians being assaulted. He told the court that he started his military service in 1980 'without any moral problems with the army'. However, having completed two years' service and six camps, he was no longer prepared to serve in the SADF in any capacity. The seed for his convictions was laid when he volunteered for a vehicle patrol in northern Namibia:

> We stopped at a kraal, and when our corporal was told by an old woman that there were no Swapo members in the area, he assaulted everyone in the kraal, including all the women and children. The officer in charge just looked on and did nothing. I was shocked to find we were using violence against innocent local people.
> (The Weekly Mail *17.3.89*)

When Swapo members were killed, their corpses were left in the camp for the soldiers to see and kick

> if they felt the urge. They were then buried in a few inches of sand outside the camp and I watched them being eaten by wild dogs.
> *(Ibid.)*

> In the morning there would be bits of people strewn all over the place. The manly thing to do was to gloat over the corpses and enjoy killing.
> *(Wits campus speech, 1989)*

For many young men the deployment of the SADF in the townships was a turning point.[13] Harold Winkler has stated for example,

> The deployment of the SADF in South Africa's townships and reports of troops beating township residents, raping women, looting houses, conducting house-to-house searches and sjambokking [whipping], shooting and tear-gassing people makes it impossible for me to participate in the SADF.
> *(ECC Focus, vol. 1, no. 3, 5.9.1985)*

The challenge of people like Harold Winkler took a variety of forms. An increasing number applied to the Board for Religious Objection for alternative service as 'religious objectors'. By December 1987, 1 500 conscripts had applied for religious objector status. A total of 959 had been granted category 3 status (refusal to serve in any capacity). The great majority of these (787 out of the 959, or 70 per cent) were Jehovah's Witnesses. Their refusal to participate in wars extends to not doing military duty or wearing military uniforms. At least 15 people are known to have been refused Category 3 status because their stands were politically related, or not of a 'universal, religious pacifist nature'.

One of these was Peter Moll, who refused to participate in what he believed to be 'an unjust war'.[14] Another was Dave Hartman, who applied to the Orange Free State Supreme Court in April 1986 to have a court order set aside the Board for Religious Objections refusal to classify him as an objector. He was refused in November 1984 because his religion – Buddhism – was not based on the premise that there is a supreme or divine being.

In 1988 a total of 222 national servicemen were granted the status of religious objectors and placed in alternative service. Alan Goddard was one these successful applicants. He was employed as a teacher in the Transvaal Education Department (TED) when he applied to the Board, and was classified as a religious objector in category 72D(1)(a)(iii). He was ordered to do 2 175 days' (6 years') community service. He wished to perform his community service as a teacher, but was told that the Department of Manpower policy was to place religious objectors in non-teaching positions. He was sent as a clerk to the accounts department of a TED office and was given a job filling in forms. A Supreme Court application failed to reverse this decision, but made it clear that the TED does not wish religious objectors to have any contact with school pupils.

> I miss teaching. The only thing I enjoy about my work is the odd truancy investigation. Mostly I do paper work ... pen pushing. The work environment is pretty hostile, especially at the beginning. I was hauled over the coals at every opportunity. My superior even queried why I had an 'I love Soweto' sticker on my car.
> *(Interview)*

The challenge to the system of compulsory military service was even sharper in the case of the 20 white South African men who have been charged over the past ten years for failing to report for military service. Among them was Richard Steele, who was court-martialled in 1980 for refusing to serve in the SADF, and sentenced to 12 months in a military prison. During that period he experienced long stretches of solitary confinement and spare diet. Over the past two years, six people have been charged and four convicted. Philip Wilkinson, aged 23, a SADF corporal, was fined R600 for failing to report for military service in 1986. Dr Ivan Toms, aged 36, a SADF lieutenant, was sentenced to eighteen months imprisonment for refusing to report for an army camp in 1987. David Bruce, aged 23, and Charles Bester, aged 18, were each sentenced to six years' imprisonment for refusing to report for national service in 1988. Bruce was the first South African to face six years imprisonment for refusing to report for his initial two years' service. Leaving the country was not an answer for him because

> by leaving I would be runnning away from something I am strongly committed to – working to end apartheid.

When David Bruce was sentenced on 25 July 1988 he gave evidence in court to explain why he was not prepared to serve in the SADF.

> ... From quite an early age I was aware of being opposed to racism. From when I was in primary school I became aware of the kind of

thing that happened in Germany during the period of the holocaust, and became aware that my own family ... had suffered as a result of those things .... The basic function which the SADF plays in this country is one of upholding and defending a racist political system.

Bruce did not argue that he was a pacifist. He said he would be prepared to serve in an army

that is involved in fighting for the people of the country as a whole, that was not involved in fighting what I understand to be essentially a civil war.

The perception that South Africa is a society at war was expressed by all the young men interviewed for this book. Their identification of the main protagonists in this war variously included the state, Swapo, the people, the ANC, the revolutionary onslaught, the powers of evil, Afrikaans nationalism, African nationalism, ANC terrorists, and the communists. All the young men interviewed believed that they had 'to take sides'.

South Africa is in a state of civil war and we have to take sides. I believe that the side of justice and truth is the side of the poor and oppressed in our country. I stand on that side. I am committed to South Africa and I believe that the truly patriotic action for me is to go to prison rather than to deny faith and my beliefs.
(Toms, quoted in Combat, *no. 2)*

Toms said that his decision to become an objector was based on religious grounds and his experience of security force actions in the townships of Cape Town, where he had worked as a doctor and where few white people go.

... since October 1984 troops have been used to control the black townships of South Africa and to suppress resistance to apartheid. The border is no longer thousands of miles away in Namibia, but right on our doorstep .... Friends who might have gone to the same church school are now facing each other across the barrel of a gun in the townships. For most conscripts this is the first time they have entered a black township, and they drive in high up in a Buffel with teargas, grenades, rifles and with fear welling up within them.
(ECC pamphlet)

Toms said that he was unable to

> reconcile the Christian injunction to love my enemy and the demand
> of the SADF to shoot him.
> *(ECC Focus, vol. 1, no. 3, September 1985)*

The stands of Toms and the majority of objectors are rooted in deeply-felt religious views. Philip Wilkinson, for instance, describes himself as

> a Christian, brought up in the beliefs of the Catholic Church. I am
> committed to peace. I believe that all armies legitimize the use of
> violence.
> *(Quoted in* The Times *5.11.1986)*

Christianity provided several informants with alternative standards and criteria which strengthened their capacity to resist conscription. For example, when asked to comment on the slogan, 'Let the army make a man of you', one replied,

> The more manly thing to do is not to be a soldier. To acknowledge
> weakness is the greatest strength. Christ was the greatest and most
> manly man who ever lived. He wasn't afraid to admit weakness.
> *(Informant 106)*

Christians have three grounds for conscientious objection: the rejection of violence as an ideal; the public calling to witness to Christ's mercy and compassion; and lastly the judgement that a particular conflict is unjust (South African Catholic Bishops Conference (SACBC), 1985: 164-5). These grounds have been extensively debated within the English-speaking churches since 1974, and many churches have come to constitute a source of support for conscientious objectors (Law, *et al.*, 1987).

> My church does support me. It must. Christians failed to demonstrate
> a non-violent way against the Nazis. The church must teach non-
> violence. We're in the passing summer of that opportunity in South
> Africa now.
> *(Informant 103)*

However, this support is not total:

> Charles Bester is too idealistic. And he's not biblically based. Christ
> called for obedience to the government.
> *(Informant 13)*

Many objectors stressed the connection between their political and religious views. Charles Bester, for example, described the SADF in court as 'an evil institution'. He told the court that his Christian conscience would not allow him to serve in it. He cited army raids into neighbouring countries, and the role of the SADF in crushing resistance to apartheid in the townships. He affirmed,

> I am a Christian, and as a Christian must follow the path of love in every situation. I cannot put my life into compartments, so that my religious life has no bearing on my political, sporting and other areas of my life.

Asked why he had not approached the Board for Religious Objections, Bester said,

> I may be exempted by the Board on religious grounds, but they would not recognize my political or moral objections to serving in the SADF. My political and moral objections are intrinsically tied up with my religious beliefs.
> *(Interview)*

This connection was also emphasized by an earlier objector, Richard Steele, who believed that serving in the SADF would lessen his humanity:

> The only way a soldier can be effective is to deny the humanity of his opponent; he is a terrorist, a communist, a racist – whatever word in a given context that makes him better dead than alive .... In dehumanizing the other, you lessen your own humanity as well.
> *(Cited in CIIR, 1988: 83)*

Most of these objectors supported the End Conscription Campaign. This organization, formed in 1983, presented the sharpest and most direct challenge to the present system of conscription (Nathan, 1987). It opposed conscription on the grounds that it intensifies the violent conflict in our society, a conflict engendered by a political system which denies most South Africans basic human rights. In the five years before it was banned, the ECC campaigned for constructive alternative national service. It achieved considerable public support, with over 50 affiliated organizations and thousands of active members and supporters. However, it drew largely (but not exclusively) from a somewhat narrow class base: middle-class, English-speaking people.

Not all the informants interviewed were sympathetic to the ECC:

> It's not a bad idea, but ECC publications are full of propaganda and
> lies. It puts its own views across and neglects objectivity and balance.
> *(Informant 113)*

Many ECC members were subject to persecution. During 1986, 98
members were detained, and others subjected to systematic harassment
and intimidation. Meetings, publications and activities of the organization were banned. Disinformation, death threats, fire-bombings, assaults, break-ins, and anonymous counter-propaganda against the
organization were commonplace. Evidence in a Cape Town court in
1988 revealed that the SADF itself had been running a disinformation
campaign against the organization. Its banning in August 1988 reflected
the extent to which the state felt threatened by its very existence.

> The ECC was one of the best organisations ever to appear in the white
> community. They may have destroyed it, but ECC was only one part
> of the war resistance movement. The war resistance movement is far
> bigger than ECC ever was.
> *(Informant 104)*

In 1988 Mark Rudd, the American leader of the student rebellion of
1968, concluded his review of the youth revolt against the war in
Vietnam with the words:

> What other war in history has been stopped by those who were meant
> to fight it?

This was the challenge that faced white South African men in 1989.

Conclusion

Historically conscription has been linked to both coercion and citizenship.[15] In the South African context the state relies on coercion at a
number of levels to deny the majority of people the rights and responsibilities of citizenship. In this sense conscription for white men into the
SADF throws into sharp relief the system of denial which apartheid
involves. The personal cost to those who challenge this system is high.
Toms has said,

> The thing about South Africa is either you live a comfortable, cushy life like most whites, or you become involved. And if you become involved there is a cost. But in the end I think it is a small price to pay.
> (Christian Science Monitor *23.2.1988)*

The price of imprisonment may well be considered too high by most young white South African males. South Africa in the period under review treated its conscientious objectors more harshly than any other country in the world. The six-year jail sentences handed down to David Bruce and Charles Bester were longer than those handed down to objectors in any other country in the world during the last 15 years. It was unlikely that their trials would trigger large-scale war resistance in South Africa in any way analogous to the anti-war sentiment which helped force the US withdrawal from Vietnam in 1973. But certainly the models of refusal and resistance, albeit on a small scale, are increasing. Toms (released on bail) said,

> We're seeing the start of a peace movement. It's no longer just one individual, but a group of people deciding to make a stand against the system.

In August 1988, 143 young white men throughout the country pledged themselves never to serve in the SADF.[16] This first public, collective stand involved a good deal of courage. Many men interviewed for this book expressed a horror and fear of prison. Not only the informants who had been active in the ECC reported a fear of right-wing violence and of the state. Everyone interviewed acknowledged deep-seated fears such as 'being detained and spending a long period in solitary confinement', 'having my place wrecked', 'being killed', 'being injured on the border, or even blinded by a township kid shooting me in the eye with a bit of wire from a catapult', 'being forced into exile and living in a cramped, shabby little flat in London, knowing only other exiles'. Overall fear was an important thread in many of the informants' tangled web of motives.

In 1989 a total of 771 men publicly declared that they would not serve in the SADF. This event was especially remarkable in that it came a year after the banning of the ECC, and after three years of emergency regulations which made it illegal to undermine the system of military conscription. The register of conscientious objectors at the time of writing stands at 1 289. The number of South Africans refusing conscription into the SADF has increased as more whites are coming to believe that the SADF is directly involved in maintaining and defending minority rule and the apartheid system. They are demanding some form of alternative service.[17] Their resistance is clearly informed by political considerations, linked in some cases to a religious commitment.

The obligation of white males to participate in the SADF is enforced by law and reinforced by social pressures of various kinds. The manipulation of gender identity is an important source of such pressure. As Elshtain writes,

> The pacifist stance, in the modern West, has not been an easy one for men to attain and to sustain.
> *(Elshtain, 1987: 203)*

The construction of the male sense of self has conventionally required a militancy; militancy is the culturally-endorsed way to be manly.

The equation of masculinity with violence and aggression rests upon a cruel myth: many men seem to go to war partly in the hope of becoming heroes, but in reality war emasculates men. It does so by depriving them of their personal autonomy, responsibility, and choice. Military training involves a kind of social programming that teaches unquestioning obedience. In war men become sheep, not wolves. They follow and obey. In this sense war is servility. In another sense war strips men of their humanity and reveals their capacity for violence and evil.[18]

Another irony in this manipulation of male gender identity is that the image of 'hearth and home' is used to motivate soldiers.[19] Women are at the centre of this image of social order to be 'protected' and 'defended'. But advances in military technology and strategy have blurred the boundaries between the 'battlefield' and the 'home front'. This blurring is especially clear in a civil war such as that fought in South Africa during the 1980s. The idea that war compels men to go and fight in order to protect their women, who remain passive and secure at home with the children, is a myth. It is a doubly cruel myth because in reality women are increasingly incorporated into war and contributing to the militarization of South African society.

Notes

1. This is the opposite of Caute's (1983) title *Under the Skin*, which refers to the hidden racism of many white Rhodesians.
2. This has a much wider relevance than South Africa. According to William James, the main function of war is 'preserving manliness of type'. He points to

a pervasive anxiety about the construction of masculinity, the fear that martial experience alone can make a man. Peace is sometimes denigrated because 'the greatest danger that a long period of profound peace offers to a nation is that of creating effeminate tendencies in young men' (Maurice Thompson, cited in Kimmel, 1987: 147). According to Roosevelt, 'The nation that has trained itself to a cancer of unwarlike and isolated ease is bound, in the end, to go down before other nations which have not lost the manly and adventurous virtues .... There is no place in the world for nations who have become enervated by the soft and easy life, or who have lost their fibre of vigorous hardiness and masculinity.' (Cited in Kimmel, 1987: 148.) Woodrow Wilson's reluctance for America to join the Great War was characterized by Roosevelt as 'a lack of manhood' (Macdonald, 1987: 21).

3. The intensity of war has sometimes been compared to the power of childbirth: 'It is, for men, at some terrible level, the closest thing to what childbirth is for women: the initiation into the power of life and death' (Broyle, quoted by Elshtain, 1987: 200). It has also been argued that soldiering and mothering are similar. They are both powerful 'boundary events, a particular structure of experience discontinuous with the expectations of everyday life ... the soldier is expected to sacrifice for his country, mothers are expected to sacrifice for their children ... uniting the two experiences is duty and guilt. The soldier and the mother do their duty and both are racked by guilt at not having done it right or at having done wrong as they did what they thought was right.' (Ibid.: 222). 'Both are boundary experiences that forever alter the identities of those to whom they happen or through whom they take place .... Soldiers like mothers are involved with food, shit and dirt .... Women are excluded from war talk; men from baby talk. Men conceive of war as a freedom "from" and find themselves pinned down, constrained; women see mothering as the ticket to adulthood and find themselves enmeshed in a dense fabric of responsibility that con strains even as it enables. Perhaps we are not strangers to one another after all.' (Ibid.: 225).

4. Much has been written of the 'post-traumatic stress disorder' experienced by Vietnam veterans. By 1971 almost 50 000 Vietnam veterans in the US had died since their discharge and return to civilian life. There were three main causes: suicide, drug overdose and vehicle accidents. Approximately one third of the Vietnam veterans who have turned to the Veteran Center in Fort Wayne for help of one type or another have been involved in violence directed at women or children since they left the military (Ritter, 1989).

5. The periods of compulsory military service have been extended over the last 20 years in a chronology that parallels increasing black resistance. The year 1961 marked the introduction of a ballot system of conscription. In 1967 the ballot system was abolished and universal conscription of nine months' service for white males between the ages of 17 and 65 was introduced. In 1972 the period of compulsory military service was extended to an initial period of 12 months followed by 19 days' service annually for five years. In 1977 the period of compulsory military service was extended to an initial period of 24 months

followed by 30 days' service annually for a number of years. In 1978 tough new penalties were introduced for failure to render compulsory military service (The Defence Amendment Act no. 49 of 1978). Legislation was adopted to pressurize immigrants between the ages of 15 and 25 years into service in the SADF. This was done by denying citizenship or permanent resident rights to those who refused to accept citizenship (and therefore liability to render military service) within two years of taking up residence within the country.

In 1984 the South African Citizenship Amendment Act was introduced. Under these changes all immigrants between the ages of 15 and 25 years who have lived in South Africa for more than 5 years automatically become South African citizens and are forced to do military service. If they refuse, their residence permits are withdrawn and they face deportation. This link between citizenship and national military service is an important one. Not all of the excluded communities are denied the political and property rights of full citizens, but there is a clear implication that blacks and women stand in a different relation to the state. Exclusion from military service is often thought to signal inferior status.

6. Exemption is granted where in the opinion of the Board it is justified: (a) in order to prevent the interruption of the course of education studies of the person concerned;   (b) by reason of the nature and extent of a person's domestic obligations or any circumstances connected with any trade, profession or business in which he is engaged; (c) on the grounds of physical defect, ill-health or mental incapacity on the part of the person concerned; (d) on the grounds that a person is being compulsorily detained in an institution; or (e) on any other ground it may deem sufficient.

7. Religious objectors have to be universal religious pacifists. No provision is made for those who object to service in the SADF on moral, ethical, humanitarian or political grounds. The Board for Religious Objection may classify the applicant:

(i) as a religious objector with whose religious convictions it is in conflict to render service in a combatant capacity in any armed force; (ii) as a religious objector with whose religious convictions it is in conflict to render service in a combatant capacity in any armed force, to perform any maintenance tasks of a combatant nature therein and to be clothed in a military uniform; or (iii) as a religious objector with whose religious convictions it is in conflict to render any military service or to undergo any military training or to perform any tasks in or in connection with any armed force.

A person classified as a religious objector in terms of Section 72D(1)(a)(i) shall render service or undergo training in a non-combatant capacity in the SADF for the same period as military service. A person classified in terms of Section 72D(1)(a)(ii) shall render service which shall be one-and-a-half times as long as the periods to which he would otherwise have been liable, wearing clothing other than a military uniform, and the service shall be rendered by performing prescribed tasks of a non-combatant nature. A person who is classified as a religious objector in terms of Section 72D(1)(a)(iii) shall render 'community service' which shall be completed in a single continuous period equal to one-and-a-half times as long as the aggregate of all periods of service which would otherwise have been applicable, in a government structure.

8. The use of the media to promote conscription and 'demonize' the End Conscription Campaign (ECC) is well described in Graaf.

9. The creation of war 'heroes' is illustrated by the case of Wynand du Toit. He was an SADF officer captured in Angola who was subsequently exchanged for Klaas de Jonge and others. His return to South Africa involved a blaze of positive publicity.

10. He writes, 'We have become accustomed to the integral militarism of the modern nation state, at its most formal and official levels. It is not surprising that this has spread to stain the whole society. But we may also now be facing something worse than this: a vigorous, spectacular and consumerist militarism, extending from the toy-missile flashes of the children's shops and games arcades, to the military tournaments and air displays of general public entertainment and finally to the televised images of safely distant wars' (Williams, 1985: 239).

11. According to some accounts, 'fragging' (the killing of American officers by their own troops) happened frequently in Vietnam (Saywell, 1985: 255).

12. Some comments echo the pride and satisfaction reported by Parker in his interviews with soldiers in the British army. For example, 'When I think of all the things I've learnt since I started the army, it's fantastic .... Sometimes it seems as though you can go on learning for ever. Another thing it does for you is it builds up your character and makes you a stronger-willed person' (Parker, 1985: 31-2).

13. In a similar way to the widespread use of troops in the South African townships between 1984 and 1986, the 1982 war in Lebanon seems to have triggered resistance among Israeli conscripts. Both situations raised painful moral dilemmas for conscripts.

14. Some of the problems with the Board for Religious Objection are identifed by Moll, 1986: 113-15.

15. Many western countries have compulsory military service, and many of these are ambivalent about the rights of war resisters (Young, 1986). The coercion involved in conscription used to be more direct. Medieval armies were made up of peasants who were the virtual slaves of their landlords, and when these were an insufficient source of defence manpower, press gangs captured men into service using a form of body snatching.

16. Of these, 39 had completed their military service (17 as officers or non-commissioned officers), 14 had completed or were completing community service as religious objectors, six had served or were serving prison sentences, and 84 were liable for their full four years of military service. Of the 143, 60 were professionals, 68 students (including 13 medical students) and there were 15 others. Ironically, the same number of Israeli conscripts – 143 – refused to fight in the Lebanon war (Linn, 1986).

17. Twenty-three countries which practise conscription have alternative service in

some form. The period of alternative service is the longest in South Africa, at six years.

18. A British ex-soldier cited by Parker said, '... the army doesn't help you to know yourself: it teaches you to subjugate yourself and your own personality to something much bigger, which is why it can't cope with non-conformists. In a way it brainwashes you: you not only *wear* uniform, but you are, and you have to be, mentally in uniform yourself' (Parker, 1985: 230). Soldiers everywhere are socialized into a notion of 'the enemy' and a respect for authority which legitimizes instant, unquestioning obedience. 'I would certainly carry out any order as long as it was legal, and I would take it it was legal if my superiors gave the order that peace protestors were to be shot at. (Lieutenant in the British army, cited by Parker, 1985: 189.)

19. Elshtain emphasizes the importance of images of femininity, nurturance, and the family, which can be invoked to restore the balance and protect our faith in the social order '... the image of woman as other, as the "Goddess of Peace", retains its power in spite of women's active involvement because it symbolizes qualities that fend off the barbarianism implicit in war. The otherness of femininity ... establishes the social limits of war and guarantees the possibility of post-war normalization' (Higonnet and higonnet, 1987: 2).

4

The 'protected':
White women and the SADF

Colonel 'Kotze' is one of only ten women colonels in the Permanent Force of the SADF. Now in her forties, she is a tall and forceful woman who moves with energy and purpose. Her home language is Afrikaans. She has spent 'eighteen years in uniform', having joined the Permanent Force in 1971 for the 'career opportunities' it offered.

> I was young at the time, with no responsibilities. I could get on an aeroplane at an hour's notice.

She left the teaching profession because of the discrimination she experienced there:

> I had zero chance of becoming a school principal. I was promoted to colonel at the age of 38. I'm not scared to make a decision. I was brought up to take responsibility. I was the middle child. I grew up in a below-average household – in the economic sense. We weren't poor but, we didn't have money to throw around. My parents wanted us to have a good education. My mother raised poultry and my father grew vegetables for the market. All four of us children were involved in this. At the age of five I had to help deliver the eggs. This all inculcated a sense of responsibility. I had to work in the school holidays. Even during term time I worked in a dairy every Saturday. I had to be there at 5 a.m. I had to order stocks.
>
> There was a time when it seemed that the Lord didn't mean me to be married. But I bought a new car every year, I had my own flat in Pretoria and my own holiday house. I enjoyed my independence. I married late – to a SADF Permanent Force officer. Some people in the SADF think that once a woman is married, her career is no longer important to her. If I had to choose, I'd put my marriage and being a wife first, but why should I have to choose? Men don't have to.

Colonel Kotze emphasized that the number of women in the Permanent Force of the SADF has increased dramatically since 1975, when there was an investigation into its use of women. Almost 14 per cent of the Permanent Force in January 1989 were women. This increase has come about partly through necessity – 'manpower shortages forced us' – and partly because of 'women's satisfactory performance in the SADF'.

> In the beginning I concentrated on recruiting girls aged 18-22. Since then I've changed my attitude completely. I now prefer us to concentrate on the 35-40 age group. These women are more mature. Most, in fact 99 per cent of them, have children who are in high school or out of the house. These women are now coming to the SADF as a career. They are the most dedicated and committed to the job. They say they've got 15 years to catch up.
>
> Lots of our women are married to Permanent Force soldiers. In the early days there was a very strict division. In the 1970s we said women were never to be employed in the face of the enemy. Then we found that many of our women were married to fighting soldiers. So we often have to transfer both of them to the operational area. At bases, such as Omega, in South West Africa, the wives are all employed in the SADF, and the SADF provides a crèche. The SADF wants to make it possible for women to straddle both roles – that of wife and career officer. On the whole it works well. Though wives sometimes ask if their promotion can be held back because their husbands would object to having to salute them, I can count the number of military couples divorcing on one hand. In every single case the woman was the stronger and was promoted over her husband …. Like in the civil service, the husband gets the housing subsidy. We get no maternity benefits, but we do have maternity rights; you can take 12 months' unpaid leave and your post is reserved for you. I think that's right. Women have a social responsibility to have children. Therefore the country has a responsibility to the child-bearers of the nation.

Colonel Kotze emphasized the value of the SADF as a means of social mobility and a career for white women like herself.

> In 1971 women were only in five or six job fields: administration, logistics, telecommunications, radar operators, nurses and social workers. In those days Hilda Botha was a commandant and the

highest-ranking woman in the army. Today we have one woman brigadier, who is Director of Welfare, ten colonels, and 103 commandants. But there are no women generals. Today men and women can only get officer's rank after matric plus three years' service. The salaries at all levels are exactly the same for all races and both sexes, depending on equal qualifications .... By the year 2020 there should be more women in positions of authority.

Today the Permanent Force of the SADF offers women great career prospects. We have opened up 65 different fields to women. The typical fields not open to women are those where people are trained for deliberate contact with the enemy. Women are employed in the infantry – for example they give gun instruction – but not for direct contact. Overall women are very involved in training, which is a recent development. This isn't unique to us. In Israel women dominate training .... There are problems because there are still prejudices against women. In the next five to ten years the situation will change. Men will overcome their prejudice. A lot of the officer training is shared. We train women at the combat school. They do everything with the men in training for conventional war.

Of course we constitute a small proportion. In my day there were only three women out of 60 men. We had to work hard to get the men to accept us without losing our femininity. For the first time men realized that women have the ability to think logically. I had to do combat team courses and the combat group course to become a colonel. I was among the first group of six women to do the course. We had to work through the night often. We wanted to prove ourselves. On the whole we women did better than the men. Women in general are more disciplined.

I was one of three women who applied to go on the staff course in 1981. This is a residential leadership course for future generals; 53 people applied and 21 were accepted. We were warned beforehand about sexual misconduct. I experienced this warning as an insult. Actually we had more problems with jealous wives than we had problems with the men making overtures.

While women in many armies – the US army for example – complain of sexual harassment from men, Colonel Kotze maintained that

Our sexual problems in the SADF are not with men, but with two types of women – lesbians, and *losmeisies* ('loose girls') who have no morals. Lesbians are easy to identify though, and this is an important factor in recruiting.

Colonel Kotze believes that men and women are very different:

> The general nature of women is to be life-giving rather than life-taking. But women could make better combat soldiers than men. Women can be more aggressive and hate-filled killers than men. For the first five or six years I was the only woman officer in the Signals Corps. I got to know men. Women are not more emotional than men. Men can become just as emotional and be just as bitchy as women. Men gossip even more than women. Men aren't as honest as women. Men have mastered the technique of hiding their feelings. It's said that women can't cope with authority. But I've had many men come to me and say they prefer working under the command of a woman. Men are less sympathetic to their own gender and vice versa. Women are better listeners, more gentle, sympathetic and more person-oriented. We can be more logical about things. Women can also be more tactful.

In her experience there is sometimes ambiguity within the SADF on the behaviour required by gender roles and military hierarchies.

> Social conduct in the army should not be different to that we were brought up with. I expect to pour the tea and have men stand aside for me. If we have a military parade, the general walks in front. But walking down the corridor the general must stand aside for me. The general will stand aside for a woman messenger with Standard 4 if she's not in uniform, but – and this happened this morning waiting for the lift – he won't stand aside for me …. Sometimes the system confuses me. It confused women a lot when the men wouldn't help them. The lesbians enjoyed it because they could act in a masculine way. The more feminine women were confused. But slowly we brought the situation back to normal.

Colonel Kotze was part of a delegation sent to Israel in 1988 to investigate the question of conscription for white women. (She is opposed to it, for reasons given in Chapter five.)

> I would rather extend the voluntary system. President Botha is very committed to promoting women. In fact at one time President Botha was keen on conscripting women. The issue of conscription was

considered when there was a crisis in defence force manpower in South Africa at the end of the 1970s.

Colonel Kotze complains of discrimination against women within the SADF:

> Yes, there is discrimination within the SADF as there is in the world outside. It's a man's world – men make 99 per cent of the decisions. There's the most prejudice against women at the middle management level. It's clear to me that they have no intention of promoting more women to brigadier rank. They use excuses like age. For me to become a brigadier I need to do one more course. Formally that should be done before the age of 45, but many men do it later. The other excuse they use is combat experience .... Anyway, ten years from now there'll be women brigadiers in the SADF. Manpower needs require this .... The other way in which there's discrimination within the SADF used to be in clothing allowances. Our clothing allowance is the same, but I have pointed out the extra costs of court shoes and stockings. A man can wear one pair of shoes for two years. I have to buy five pairs of court shoes a year. We are now (thanks to me pointing this out) given an allowance of 40 pairs of stockings a year.

However, in white South African terms the SADF is a progressive employer. Its policies, regarding maternity benefits for example, are cited as reasons why 'it has reaped the benefits of a stable and valuable female labour force' (Prekel, 1980: 65). In the final analysis the treatment of women is a secondary consideration for Colonel Kotze:

> The ultimate aim of the SADF is to win the land battle. Organizational aims come first for me. Equal rights and responsibilities for women come second.

The first woman to have reached the rank of brigadier in the SADF is now 59 years old, and divorced with three children. An extremely likeable, articulate, and honest woman, she describes her divorce as the main incentive to establishing a successful career:

> I married at the age of 25, and when my marriage failed I felt I had to make a success of something. As a social worker I started off working for the church and the Johannesburg City Council, before I joined the Prison Service. I was the first woman commissioned

officer in the Prison Service. I was in charge of the rehabilitation of all prisoners and in charge of the training of all female staff. I was the first woman lieutenant, and the first woman ever to work in the maximum security prison with 700 prisoners.

Her voice softened with affection as she spoke of the prisoners she had known:

You needed a magnifying glass to see the good in some of those prisoners. But I think a woman let the softer, more positive things surface in them. I was in charge of all 700 prisoners. I knew them all by name. I knew their offences. We were a kind of family. I was a link with the outside world, and they became very dependent on me. I became attached to them. But there were also lots of sodomists and homosexuals, and of course they're a different species. I was the first officer to attend church with the prisoners, and that gave me access to their inner lives. They got upset when I didn't come. I told them I had three kids at home. They said I had 700 kids there. One Christmas service they all clapped me .... I was promoted to major, the highest rank ever for a woman in the Prison Service. I resigned in 1973.

She moved to the SADF from the Prison Service, and encountered some hostility when she was promoted:

I was invited by the SADF to supervise the social workers in the SADF. They made me a colonel. The men social workers were all professional soldiers ... they didn't have a professional aproach to their clients. They were very authoritarian. When I was made a colonel there was a lot of hostility from the men. It was difficult for them to work under a woman. There was also hostility because I hadn't done any military courses. Those staff courses are very tough – they try to break you. So I was Director of Social Work Services in the SADF. This was a challenge. I was trained to put the client first, but in the SADF the client can't always come first; you also have to take account of the organization's interests. Lots of the problems I dealt with were to do with young marriages. Many men said, 'If at the age of 18 I'm capable of defending my country, then I'm capable of marriage'. There were only about 28 women social workers in the SADF. The men social workers were very feminine, not the masculine type that a soldier expects. A soldier won't accept a homosexual. It was difficult to utilise national servicemen as social workers.

In total this informant spent 15 years in the SADF. She often experienced tension between military and gender roles.

I think they made me a brigadier because I was the right person in the right place when we had the war in Angola. I became friends with Mrs Malan. I had to escort her to the border. I got to know the Minister of Defence through her. Often I was the only woman. We had to travel a lot. I went to the border about every three months. They needed a lot of support. They said you can't be a soldier if you don't drink. I spent a lot of time in bars, but I don't drink alcohol. At times I had to abuse my femininity to get things done. At times I was a woman first and a soldier second. But in these bar situations I often felt that I blocked their spontaneity. They didn't tell the same jokes or use the same language when I was around, and I was often the only woman in a group of 40 men. So I often left them and went to bed early. Then they could get on with it. Rank was the other problem. The highest rank always walks in front. Only two generals ever walked in front of me. The others would stand back for me. Rank would be broken because officers are meant to be gentlemen.

She left the social work division to become Director of Women's Affairs in the SADF.

Today a significant proportion of the Permanent Force are women. Women are used to set men free to do more operational tasks. Also women want to play a part in the defence of South Africa. Women are utilized in about 68 different tasks in the SADF. But women in the SADF have to prove themselves all the time. In the beginning the men soldiers were amused by women, but women are now accepted as an integral part of the SADF.

Then I went on a senior staff training course. It was nine months long and I only got two hours sleep a night. But the next highest post after brigadier is a general, and there are no general's posts for women. With no possibility of promotion, I asked for an early retirement. It was unfair that I had no chance of further promotion, but there were equal conditions in the SADF in terms of pay, leave, perks such as a car, housing and so on.

The Brigadier believes that she achieved high rank because of three personal qualities:

I'm very disciplined, I worked hard and am skilled at relating to people. I was an identification model for women. I could relate to anybody – from the lowest IQ national serviceman to the Minister of Defence or the State President. I can even relate to non-Europeans. I believe everybody should have a say in the matters of this country.

I've got a soft spot for the blacks. We needn't have a guilty conscience. Change won't come overnight. But we must change. Being a Christian, I feel there must be a place for everyone under the sun … I haven't much respect for the ANC. The ANC is the enemy. But they've got reasons to feel wronged. The trouble is that they've got tunnel vision. They don't acknowledge the changes that have occurred. Swapo is also the enemy.

She enjoys her time in retirement:

My parents and children are very proud of me. I've lost faith in men as far as an intimate relationship is concerned, but I prefer men's company to women's. I can't sit for a whole morning talking about servants. Women have no respect for time. I have many old women friends from Potchefstroom University days. I was nominated by *The Star* as Woman of the Year. That year Steve Biko's wife got it. I felt amused.

The Brigadier looks back with a sense of accomplishment and satisfaction:

Looking back now, my 15 years in the SADF weren't easy. I'm outspoken, and sometimes I had trouble when I spoke my mind …. Also it was difficult juggling work and home. I'd be in my office just before 7 a.m. and I'd only get home about 5 p.m. I was always the first in and the last to leave. The people I was working with found it irritating. I had to spend time with my three children, but I also had to travel a lot. The accomplishment I'm most proud of was getting the Southern Cross Medal for excellence and dedication. It is the biggest decoration ever awarded to a woman. I'm proud of that, and the fact that I could hold my own as a brigadier with all those men.

These two women – a brigadier and a colonel – point to the fallacy of the idea that women are excluded from war. Women's part in modern war has been obscured, but in fact they have faced danger in a variety of military roles. These have tended to be supporting roles:

On the battlefield, quite like on the Elizabethan stage, only men have been permitted to be fully-fledged actors. Any war narrative will teach us, however, that there are a considerable number of supporting roles which get handed out to members of the female sex and which are essential to the unfolding of the plot.
(Huston, 1982: 274)

The ways in which women have historically been incorporated into war are sketched by Huston (1982: 275, 279) as follows:

1. As pretexts for war – the Helen of Troy syndrome. As Huston points out, women can be 'a valuable that needs to be defended, but they can also represent value itself, an ideal incarnating peace and virtue by Huston. It is in this sense that women have been termed 'the ultimate cause of war'.
2. As wives and prostitutes – women can fulfil Nietzsche's injunction to provide for the warrior's rest and recreation.
3. As entertainers they provide diversion.
4. As victims – in Huston's words, 'they are more and more numerous among those bit parts known as casualties'.
5. As sympathetic nurses – the 'Florence Nightingale syndrome'.
6. As seductive spies – the 'Mata Hari syndrome'.
7. As cheerleaders, running along the side of trains and waving goodbye to the uniformed departing men.
8. As 'castrating bitches who belittle and berate men for refusing to become macho murderers'. (Huston's words)
9. As mothers of soldiers.
10. As co-operative citizens, according to Huston, 'suddenly developing quasi-masculine stamina for field and factory work, which will just as suddenly evaporate when the war is over'.

White women are incorporated into the militarization of South African society in all these roles. These points of incorporation will be discussed in two main sections – direct and indirect incorporation. The direct incorporation is clear in the increasing use of white women within the SADF in a variety of roles, from nursing through to radar, intelligence work, and cartography. Indirect incorporation is also extensive as white women provide a considerable degree of support – both ideological and material, to members of the SADF. The distinction between these direct and indirect linkages cannot be drawn in clear terms. One of the defining features of South Africa as a militarized society engaged in a 'war' (as viewed by the black majority), or in defending itself against the 'total onslaught' (the view of the state and many whites), is that the battlefield is the entire society. A clear demarcation of the battlefield is the fulcrum of the connection between militarization and gender. If the military is viewed as a bastion of male identity, then

It must categorize women as peripheral, as serving safely at the 'rear',
on the 'home front'. Women ... must be denied access to 'the front',
to 'combat' .... The military has to constantly define 'the front' and
'combat' as wherever 'women' are not.
(Enloe, 1983: 15)

In a civil war or struggle such as that waged in the eighties in South
Africa, the limits of combat are redrawn as the experience of war spreads
among the general population. In this process, an important breach in
the ideological constructions of gender is threatened. As Ruddick has
written,

Dividing the protector from the protected, defender from defended,
is the lynchpin of masculinist as well as military ideology.
(Cited by Schweik, 1987: 552)

Considerable efforts are made to avoid this breach and to elaborate a
traditional but expanded notion of femininity for women within the
SADF

Indirect linkages between women and militarization

The most remote connection between women and militarization lies in
the importance given to women's procreative role. Writing of Nazi
Germany, Mason has pointed out that

all racialist movements which take the biological pseudo-scientific
elements in their ideologies seriously, are bound to attach particular
importance to women's procreative role.
(Mason, 1976: 88)

In South Africa, as in Nazi Germany, the state attached a particular
importance to family, domesticity, and child-rearing in the white community. Although not official policy, the raising of the white birth rate
had an important place in the strategy to maintain white racial supremacy. There have been a number of appeals to whites to double their
reproductive efforts:

A Johannesburg doctor recently published a book arguing that family
planning is a plot by South Africa's enemies to reduce white strength.
Mrs Bessie Scholtz, a Nationalist MP and mother of eleven, called
for more white children. Newspapers like *The Citizen* regularly run
plaintive wails from readers about the decline of the white birth rate.
(Beckett, 1982: 11)

What this implies is a celebration of white women's domestic roles as mothers and wives; an equation of femininity with domesticity. Women's role is 'to keep the home fires burning', to stay at home, produce babies, and 'support our boys on the border'.[1] At the indirect material level, there are three linkages between women and war, or three ways in which white women contribute materially to the militarization of South African society. Firstly, many white women are active in support organizations such as the Southern Cross Fund, which provides food parcels and recreational services for 'the boys on the border'. Secondly, they are active in Civil Defence and Commando units. Thirdly, they are engaged in armaments production for Armscor.

Women and support organizations

The Southern Cross Fund is an important agency through which white South African women provide material support for the SADF. It was founded by Elizabeth Albrecht, who was its national president for 20 years, until 1989. Her

> overriding ideal in starting the Southern Cross Fund was to build morale .... I believe that no fighting forces in the world can be successful until they are quite sure they have the sympathy and reinforcement of the people at home. The folks at home must stand full square behind their men in uniform.
> *(Albrecht, quoted in* The Citizen *7.3.1989)*

> I think we in the Southern Cross are more realistic and down-to-earth than a lot of other people in South Africa because we've been dealing with the problem of war, and the man – especially the young man – who goes to war. I've been up to the border eight times and we've gone up with the idea of helping to keep their morale up and bringing a bit of cheer. And there we've seen the men living and working and sometimes fighting in very difficult circumstances, which is the most inspiring thing I've ever seen. And we come away with our morale built up.
> *(Interview with Albrecht by Lesley Lawson, 1987)*

The work of the Southern Cross Fund was described by Mr Pik Botha (then the Minister of Foreign Affairs), as 'memorable, inspiring and dignified (*Paratus*, vol. 37, no. 71, July 1986). The Fund's motto is 'They are our security'. It has 300 branches throughout South Africa, and raises money for the security forces generally, in other words both the SADF and the SAP. Since its inception in 1968 it has raised over R14 million (*The Citizen* 31.5.1986). The money is used to provide medical aid and comfort, particularly to soldiers in the operational area. For example, the Fund has donated recreational facilities such as snooker tables, swimming pools, cold water and ice machines, video and television sets, as well as sending parcels to conscripts. Members of the Southern Cross Fund also regularly visit hospitalized soldiers at the military hospital near Pretoria. In 1985 they decided to change their *modus operandi*:

> ... the whole thing had become clear to me as it has now become clear to everybody – the real borders of our country are no longer only the faraway borders. The borders of our country are right here on our doorsteps; you know, in the Western Province and the Eastern Province. I've been to all those places to look at the situation there; and in the Northern Transvaal and here in Soweto. So the war is no longer that faraway war to the north of South West Africa, it's here. For example a mother says to you, 'You give parcels for the man in Ondangwa, my son is in Soweto and he is in as much danger as they are, if not more. And what are you going to do about it?' ... So we decided to give to all the boys ... we handed out a parcel at each of the intakes. I had the honour of doing the first two ... I was deeply moved. It was at the gymnasium at Heidelburg and there were thousands and thousands of people, which was terrific. The whole pavilion was full and the bands were playing and the choir was singing and the flags were waving. It was simply fantastic.
> *(Interview, 1987)*

So for the conscript,

> basics can't be all that bad, not with the useful packages handed out by the Southern Cross Fund .... The parcels consist of an elegant brief folder in which one can find writing paper, envelopes, a pen knife, a tin opener, nail clippers, pens, cleaning utensils and many other useful artifacts that the troopie would find a need for during his army service.
> *(Paratus, vol. 38, no. 5, May 1987)*

Asked whether the black community supported the SADF, Elizabeth Albrecht cited the occasion when she was presented with a cheque by the black community in Potchefstroom:

Then this black man got up and he gave a first class speech. He said, among other things, 'We hear a lot about freedom fighters to the north of us, and we get messages that say they're coming to set us free. Why do they want to set us free? We are not in jail. We know why they are coming. They want to take what we have away from us. The things we have worked for, they want to come and take that.'

In Mrs Albrecht's view, Russia was behind the 'total onslaught:

The truth is that Russia needs what we have got. Russia's ideal is to rule the world, and to do that you need an awful lot of power and an awful lot of money, and we really have got so much in this country. We're literally sitting on the world's riches. If Russia could get hold of South Africa's gold and diamonds, within 24 hours they could rule all the stock exchanges of the world .... If you study the communists' methods, you'll find that they have certain fantastically well-thought-out rules. One of these is that if you go into a country, study that country. Look at its history and the whole way it's put together. Pick out the grievances, because there's no country in the world where people don't have grievances. Then you find groups of people with grievances, and very often they are legitimate. They touch on very fundamental things – housing, education, jobs. And then of course we don't have it to the same extent, but a lot of these black countries have hunger .... I think grievances play a great role, but they are used in this particular instance as levers, to get the whole thing off its feet and make it wobbly so that it will fall down.
(Interview, 1987)

Elizabeth Albrecht says:

In the whole operation my husband was a wonderful help and support.
*(*The Citizen *7.3.1990)*

She has received various awards, and was the first woman to be given the honorary rank of colonel in the police, in 1979. Presumably this is because

the actual effect of Southern Cross activity is to market militarization in a way which encourages public identification.
(Frankel, 1984: 98)

A similar function was fulfilled by the 'Bel-en-Ry' (Phone and Ride) organization, which organized lifts for national servicemen and involved women in 52 towns across the country (*Paratus*, vol. 38, no. 15, May 1987).

These organizations have other functions as well. 'Marie' is 48 years old, and one of the very few women Nationalist Party MPs:

> The Southern Cross Fund provided my political apprenticeship. I was the National Organizing Secretary for a time. I gave my first public speech on behalf of the Southern Cross Fund when Elizabeth Albrecht got her dates confused and didn't pitch up. I had no notes and had to speak at a large and distinguished Rotary dinner. I'm a good speaker; I won the speech competition at school. I can take an audience with me. I started about half of all the branches of the Southern Cross Fund in South Africa. I used to drive around a lot and sometimes I would address three or four meetings a day. I've got a lot of energy and drive.
>
> The SCF was started in 1968/9 and at first we mainly raised funds – first for Portuguese soldiers in Angola and Mozambique. We understood the conflict to be East versus West, not a black-white confrontation. The East-West thing was creeping down on us. There were terrible atrocities suffered by those Portuguese soldiers. The SCF built the wing of a hospital in LM. I got very upset about the amputees. Many were hospitalized and treated here in South Africa secretly. Conditions on the border were very bad. There were lots of mental breakdowns among those kids. Then when our own boys went up it became easier and more open. We gave swimming pools, ice machines, and started a coffee bar in Walvis Bay.

She organized functions attended by prominent Nationalist politicians:

> As National Secretary I organized functions attended by PW Botha as Minister of Defence, and Hendrik Schoeman, the Minister of Agriculture. He once asked me, 'What would your husband do if you went into politics?' He invited me to discuss the issue with him in Cape Town at parliament. That was the beginning. I went on to become the first woman in the Nationalist Party in the whole of South Africa to become chairman *[sic]* of a constituency. Of course my husband felt very threatened, and this eventually led to our divorce.

Women in civil defence and commando units

White women are increasingly active in commando units and civil defence organizations. The Civil Defence Programme was consolidated by the Civil Defence Act of 1977. The aim of the programme is to

... provide, by means of planning and provision of emergency measures, with a view to an emergency situation, the RSA and its inhabitants with the greatest measure of protection and assistance, and to curtail civilian disruption in the most effective manner.
(White paper on defence 1977)

Local authorities bear the primary responsibility for the implementation of the programme. They have the responsibility of establishing an effective organization that can

... go over to organized action with a view to saving lives, protecting property and maintaining the essential services necessary for the survival of a civilized community.
(Ibid.)

Industries, commercial undertakings, schools and universities are also expected to create their own civil defence organizations that can co-operate with the local authority. At a local level, in urban areas the programme is co-ordinated by a block co-ordinator who can mobilize the volunteers in the area. Volunteers are expected to serve at least 96 hours a year. They can be called upon at any time and are expected to be ready for duty. Regular drills take place and the SADF has a rating system for the various civil defence organizations, depending on their emergency plans, their speed of mobilization and their level of pre-paredness.

Civil Defence involves people in various aspects of work such as traffic control, fire fighting, first aid, drill, fieldcraft, crowd control, explosive identification, weapon training, roadblock routines, anti-riot procedures, and lectures on internal security. One such course in Bloem-fontein in 1987, aimed specifically at women, included warnings from a SADF lecturer on 'the revolutionary onslaught', and the comment:

Men get involved in the defence of the country through national service, but womenfolk do not get even half of this exposure.
(Paratus, vol. 38, no. 4, April 1987)

The Civil Defence Programme provides such 'exposure' and attempts to mobilize the general civilian population for the military defence of the apartheid state. It fits neatly into the overall programme of 'total strategy'. The Johannesburg municipality Civil Defence Programme involved approximately 800 volunteers, about half of whom were women:

The women are mainly involved in first aid, whereas the men are
more involved in fire fighting.
(Interview with Civil Defence Corps official, June 1989)

For one informant this programme was a very positive experience:

I was employed as a nurse by the Sandton Municipality and was
involved in the Sandton Civil Defence Programme. I enjoyed it ... it
was organized along very military lines. There were very strict
rankings and firm discipline. Overall it was a very good working
atmosphere.
(Informant 10)

The literature advertising the Civil Defence Programme's Open Day in
June 1989 stated that 'a typical disaster/emergency situation will be
staged'. This turned out to be a car bomb, with various white bleeding
and mutilated bodies strewn around. A Council official explained:

We hope people will look at this and think, 'It could be my wife or
my child lying there'.

Another said,

We expect an escalation of terrorist attacks by the ANC around the
time of the election, as there was around the time of last year's
municipal elections. Our biggest publicity agent is the ANC.

The Open Day included prominent displays of 'terrorist weapons',
including AK47s, limpet mines, and various types of explosives. The
training manual covered bomb-threat management, hostage-taking,
fire-fighting, evacuation, first aid, and how to recognize bombs and
other terrorist weapons. In the training manual, the 1983 Pretoria bomb
which killed 19 people and injured 217, and the 1985 Amanzimtoto
bomb which killed five people and injured 43, are cited as

examples of the violent increase in the use of the bomb across the
RSA as weapons *[sic]* of intimidation, destruction and death. Terrorist and criminal bombings have taken the lives of scores of people,
maimed and injured hundreds of others ....

The bomb as a terrorist weapon was the major theme of the Open Day.
While some white women are increasingly active in civil defence

organizations operating in urban areas, their involvement in commando units in rural areas is also increasing. In 1982 provision was made for men who had done their national service to be put on the controlled reserve for five years, and then to be liable for allocation to their local commandos. Men who have had no training at all are allocated into the national reserve. Both reserves can be called upon to do commando duties in certain 'primary areas' which correspond roughly with the country's border areas. These include the whole of northern Natal and a number of northern and western Transvaal areas. A headline in a local newspaper in 1988 read:

> On the danger border, the school lift club is provided by the SADF and the mums are Uzi gunslingers.
> *(Sunday Times 3.4.1988)*

The article described how farmers and their wives are integrated into commando units in border areas. These

> tough white farmers of the Limpopo valley insist they live normal lives, but they are definitely a society under siege ... they drive land-mine proofed vehicles, live behind towering barricades of razor wire, and sleep with high powered automatic rifles close to their beds. Most of them walk about with handguns strapped to their sides.
> *(The Star 22.2.1988)*

The commando units are aimed at counteracting insurgency in these areas, and white women are an increasingly useful part of this process:

> My men cannot be everywhere at once, but by training farmers and their wives in the use of weapons and communication systems we have an answer to terrorism in the area.
> *(Col. Swanepoel in Paratus, vol. 38, no. 2, February 1987)*

In this process of incorporation traditional notions of femininity are restructured and expanded. For example in the Soutpansberg Military Area, commando members gathered recently for an evaluation:

> In the past two years the Soutpansberg Military Area Unit has concentrated on taking counter-insurgency skills to the farming folk in the area, turning *oumas* and housewives into trained auxiliaries of the Defence Force.
> *(Ibid.)*

On this particular occasion,

> Ouma Marina Hogenboezen strode into the evaluation with a rifle
> under her left arm and picknick *[sic]* basket in her right hand and
> said, 'Shooting comes as naturally as baking in the kitchen'.
> *(Ibid.)*

It is important to stress that 'traditional' notions of femininity are not
abandoned in this restructuring. For example on this occasion, the day's
programme included a fashion show:

> Bidding to take the best-dressed category, the women's teams par-
> aded in a variety of colourful outfits. Red bush-hat-cum-stetson,
> safari suit pulled in with red leather belt, and red pumps was about
> the best.
> *(Ibid.)*

Women in armaments production

The final indirect, material linkage between women and militarization
in South Africa is the involvement of women in armaments production
for Armscor. The indirect material contribution of women to the militarization of South African society is probably most significant in the
sexual composition of the defence industry workforce.

Armscor had twelve nationalized subsidiaries in 1983. It distributed
work to over 1 200 private contractors and subcontractors. It claimed
not to trespass on the field of private enterprise, so its subsidiaries were
responsible for those weapons systems regarded as of special strategic
importance and those which were uneconomical for private production.
Armscor subsidiaries produced weapons, ammunition, pyrotechnical
products, aircraft, electro-optical instruments, and missiles. Private
contractors produced armoured vehicles, other vehicles, vessels, radar
and computers, telecommunications equipment, weapons electronics,
marine technology, and warfare electronics (Ratcliffe, 1983: 77). The
defence industry employed 105 000 people, 29 000 in Armscor subsidiaries and 76 000 in private industries (*Financial Mail* 11.9.1981).

Many defence industry workers are women. For example, Pretoria
Metal Pressings is an Armscor affiliate which produces a large variety
of ammunition and employs a high percentage of women (Ratcliffe,
1983: 81). So does Naschem, an Armscor affiliate which fills and
assembles large calibre ammunition and bombs, and produces

explosives and propellants. Lyttleton Engineering works make guns and components for guns, cannons, and mortars:

> Its workforce consists mainly of women, who are increasingly replacing men in production.
> *(Ratcliffe, 1983: 83).*

Webster (1984: 57) quotes an employer who observed that in a munitions factory '80 per cent of the machinery is already run by women'.

It is extremely difficult to gain any more detailed information on the workforce in the armaments sector. However, Ratcliffe identified a clear pattern in which women appeared to be the predominant sector of the Armscor workforce. He suggests this is because

> Women are one of the weakest sections of the workforce. Women are perceived to be less militant than men and are thought to have greater dexterity for intricate assembly line production.
> *(Ratcliffe, 1983: 85)*

The increasing and extensive involvement of women in such 'militarized work' is a global phenomenon.[2] However, much of this work is distanced from the eventual weaponry, so that the military connection between women's daily work and killing is obscured. This was not always the case. Women have, at various periods in the history of the West, been conscripted into armament production to meet serious manpower shortages.[3] At present in South Africa economic forms of coercion propel women into providing an important source of labour power for the defence industry.

Women as a source of ideological support

Another point at which women are indirectly incorporated into the militarization of South African society, is that they provide a crucial source of ideological support:

> Womanpower is winning power.
> *(Paratus, vol. 36, no. 4, April 1987)*

> Our women form a large and powerful part of the indirect fighting force.
> *(Venter, 1983: 11)*

The importance of this ideological support has been articulated by many SADF leaders on numerous occasions. Its function in maintaining soldiers' morale was expressed by General C.L. Viljoen, the chief of the SADF in 1984:

> My congratulations to all those who worked so hard to make this exercise [Exercise Thunder Chariot] the success it was. I would especially like to thank those who stayed at home to keep the fires burning while the men were at the P.W. Botha Training Area. Without the support of their loved ones at home, the men on the ground would not have been as successful as they were. The support from their loved ones is an important factor for the morale of the men who took part.
> *(Paratus, vol. 35, October 1984)*

Colonel Honzhauen gives even greater significance to women as a source of ideological support. He believes women to be

> the mightiest weapon against the current threat. It's not just the man who has to *vasbyt* [stand firm] but also the wife, mother and girl-friend …. A woman can do a lot to influence her husband, son or boy-friend. She must understand the implications of his duties and she must be prepared herself to pay the highest toll. A man whose wife overwhelms him with household problems cannot work effec-tively. The woman whose man is in the operational area must make him feel he's doing something for her and for his country. A border soldier's senses are definitely affected by his wife's attitude to him and his work.
> *(Paratus, vol. 35, no. 2, February 1984)*

However, gender roles must remain intact in this process:

> Remember the woman must remain a woman and keep on allowing her man to feel like a man, because the men are fighting throughout our country not for material things, but for their women, children and loved ones.
> *(Ibid.)*

Women are 'the mightiest weapon', and each is enjoined to develop these manipulative qualities in order that the SADF may reach her man. A good deal of effort is invested in this process of indirect recruitment. For instance a girls' school was asked to supply dance partners for conscripts serving in a parachute battalion in Bloemfontein. Afterwards this group of girls, and their mothers, were invited to visit the unit. The wife of the Officer Commanding explained the rationale:

We want to reach the woman and try through her to work on the man. A mother has influence over her son and a girl-friend over her boy-friend.
(Paratus, vol. 34, no. 9, September 1983)

The importance of 'working on the man' is that it is not always easy for the armed forces to acquire the manpower they claim to need. In South Africa manpower is acquired directly by the conscription of white males into the SADF, and indirectly through an ideological conscription into militarism. It is in this latter respect that white women are crucial. Many of them elaborate an ideology of gender roles which link masculinity to militarism. In this process they are a vital source of emotional support and incentives to men to 'act like men', both in battle and during their national service. Sometimes this female quality is claimed as part of the Afrikaner cultural tradition:

In the early history of South Africa it was the women who were prepared to sacrifice themselves and their loved ones for their beliefs. It was the women who were prepared to make an honour of danger and to help build a future for their descendants in a new and strange land.
(Venter, 1983: 16)

The 'total onslaught' is widely understood to be directed at the family:

The well-being of her family is of the utmost importance to the married woman. Therefore the onslaught against our country affects her very deeply. The psychological war being waged has a direct bearing on the women, because the aim of the psychological war is the disintegration of family togetherness, especially as the family is the cornerstone of spiritual strength ... the woman is the fulcrum of the nation's well-being.
(Ibid.: 17)

The presence of domestic servants in the family is thought to represent a potential danger:

Domestic servants occupy an unusual position in the average South African household. In most cases they are trusted family members ... [but] uninformed she [the domestic servant] is an important target for the enemy. Unprepared, she is not only easily influenced, but can also be used as a valuable source of information. In the sociable atmosphere of the kitchen it is easy to tell her what Johnny has written in

his latest letter, thereby telling her things that may be of importance
to the enemy.
(Ibid.: 19)

This message – that black people are potential enemies – is reinforced
by the author of a recent book, *The Gun and You*, who advises his readers
to view domestic servants with suspicion as a 'potential security risk':

> No matter how trustworthy you may believe them to be, servants
> should be regarded as a potential security risk, because they will talk
> to their friends. Intentionally or otherwise, there is a likelihood that
> such talk may alert a thief to the fact that you own firearms and where
> they can be found.
> *(Hamann, 1990: 7)*

The connection between masculinity and militarism is often mediated
by women. They socialize men into a particular definition of masculinity that is violent. They do so from an early age through the provision
of war toys and the censure of emotional expression. The army then
carries this process to an extreme. Chapter two described how a masculine identity is incorporated into military performance in the SADF
basic training. This training is often legitimated by women in terms of
its value in teaching masculine independence and discipline:

> ... do bear in mind that soldiering is, after all, a task for a man, and
> the army has to train and discipline our sons to this end.
> *(Letter to* The Star *24.4.1987)*

This end includes achieving

> the ability to stand on their own feet and become independent
> individuals able to cope with their own lives.
> *(Ibid.)*

This letter urges

> anxious army mums [to] give your sons all the moral support you can
> and help them to adopt a positive attitude to their training.

When young conscripts arrive at the Voortrekkerhoogte polo grounds
in late January for their first day of national service they are usually
surrounded by

> anxious moms and dads and sorrowful girlfriends ... come to bid their
> final farewells to the new troopies.
> *(Paratus March 1989)*

They clearly fulfil the cheerleader function delineated by Huston (1982):

> Mrs Heather McKain ... was in good spirits when she said goodbye to her son, Ryan (19), 'I'm feeling in an expectant mood. I know my son won't need any encouragement to take up sport in the army, especially football,' she said. His father, Mr Jimmy McKain, a former Royal Navy officer said jokingly, 'I'm pleased to see him go. I hope the army makes a man of him.'
> *(Ibid.)*

Women provide this cheerleader function both as mothers and as girl-friends:

> Jacques Kriek (20) – who did a year of a three-year B.Comm. degree at Pretoria University before he opted to 'do my bit' – was tearfully hugged goodbye by his girl-friend, Nolene Thomas, who declared that she was 'feeling sad' and that she would write 'six times a week'.
> *(Paratus March 1989)*

> Holding on to his girl-friend's washing powder present and Mom's biscuits he [the national serviceman] looks around the place that is going to be his home for the next two years.
> *(Supplement to the popular magazine Fair Lady 8.11.1981)*

Clearly 'mom' and 'girl-friend' are critical sources of support. They also provide an ideological legitimation as 'the defended' and 'the protected':

> I'm proud to be a soldier
> In defence of our homes,
> Our wives and children,
> Our liberty, our lives, our God.
>
> I'm proud to wear a uniform,
> I'm proud to take up arms,
> To guard my home and loved ones,
> To keep them from all harm.
>
> I'm proud to be a soldier,
> A link in our defence,
> To heed the call to battle,
> I'm proud, in every sense.

> I'm proud to meet the challenge,
> Proud to make a stand,
> In defending you: South Africa,
> My dear, beloved land.
> *(A national serviceman,* Paratus, *vol. 35, no. 12, December 1984)*

Several informants mentioned the importance of the support of their mothers when they went into the army. One even went so far as to say,

> It's mothers who keep the war going. My mother thought my going into the SADF was a good thing. My father was much more non-committal.
> *(Informant 68)*

This echoes the tradition where

> ... politics was war; the tradition of Sparta and Rome .... The role women play in this dominant narrative is that of Spartan mothers and civil cheerleaders, urging men to behave like men, praising the heroes and condemning the cowardly.[4]
> *(Elshtain, 1987: 121)*

This role can become very judgemental, coercive, and even punitive, when women demand heroism and hardiness on the battlefield.[5]

This cheerleader role can easily slide into the 'Helen of Troy phenomenon' – woman as the *raison d'être* for fighting. When men fight wars as 'the protectors', women often take on a particular objectified importance as 'the protected'. Women are the custodians of the social values that the men are fighting for; the 'woman left behind' becomes a repository of these values. In South Africa the patriotic white mother must prepare both her sons *and* her daughters for military service, although in different terms:

> As our sons are prepared from a young age for military service, so must our daughters at an early time of life be prepared to take their places, later on, as girl-friends, wives or mothers of soldiers .... From their earliest years girls must be prepared to view military service involvement as a natural and logical part of their future.
> *(Venter, 1983: 21)*

Popular magazines often include articles on the importance of supporting soldiers, for example through sending food parcels. One article, titled 'A treat for your faraway troopie', praises a reader because she instinctively knows the way to her soldier's heart is in the parcels she sends him – his one assurance there is someone out there who really cares.

(You magazine, no. 26, 3 March 1988)

However, it is as wives that women are the most important source of ideological legitimation and emotional support. Wives of serving members of the SADF automatically belong to the Defence Force Ladies Association. This Association strives to promote

sympathetic understanding and active support for the husband's duty as defender of the Republic of South Africa.
(White paper on defence 1982: 51)

The Chief of the SADF, General Geldenhuys, has said that

in many cases the Association's support made all the difference to morale not only of the wives and families left behind, but also to the man who was away from home.
(The Star 22.6.1989)

General Geldenhuys was speaking in defence of the State President's wife after widespread criticism of the expense involved in a farewell tea party arranged for her by the Association. The SADF had admitted spending more than R100 000 on a chartered Boeing 707 to fly SADF wives to Simonstown for the party. General Geldenhuys said that the Defence Force Ladies' Association played a major role in the welfare and support of all members of the Defence Force, and was proud of its relationship with Mrs Botha, a former patron of the Association (*The Star* 22.6.1989). The Defence Force Ladies' Association does not only provide ideological support. In the last ten years they have collected more than R1 million for special Defence Force projects (*The Sunday Star* 16.7.1989). The key attribute of these SADF wives is loyalty – loyalty to the point of incorporation into their soldier-husband's role:

Loyalty is the most important feature that binds us together.
(Mrs Viljoen, quoted in Paratus, vol. 34, no. 9, September 1983)

Loyalty has the following components:

1. A knowledge of communism
… knowledge of communism remains of the utmost importance … because communism leads to disloyalty.
(Mrs Viljoen, National President of the Defence Force Women's Association, quoted in Paratus, vol. 34, no. 4, April 1983)

2. Meticulous grooming

Soldiers do enjoy a status in the community, and their lady friends should be an asset to them even when they are only doing shopping together. Certain standards are expected of him when wearing his uniform, and the same applies to the woman accompanying him.

Therefore the following is recommended:

For a formal dinner ... a light material (chiffon) long dress, little jewellery, court shoes in either gold or satin, and matching hand bag. For visiting town ... a neatly tailored outfit, court shoes and handbag. Sandals can only be worn if feet are well looked after and carefully manicured.
(Mrs Schoeman in an address given to the South African Army Ladies Organization at Buffelspoort in 1980. Supplement to Paratus, *vol. 31, no. 5, May 1980)*

This meticulous grooming implies an elaborate cultivation of 'femininity' so as to mirror the soldier-husband's status in the community. This clearly illustrates Virginia Woolf's insight in *A Room of One's Own*, where she argues that women serve as 'magnifying mirrors' which show men at twice their natural size. Such mirrors, she claims, 'are essential to all violent and heroic action' (Woolf, 1957: 35-6).

3. Self-knowledge and sophistication

Happiness always has a woman in the picture. In the first place happiness is a woman who knows who has made her. She is the crown of creation, and no afterthought or accessory. Happiness also is a woman who knows why she was made. For that reason, it is important to be still and ask yourself, 'Who am I?'
(Woolf, 1957)

Mrs Viljoen's own answer to this question is:

I am a woman and a human being in my own right. However, Happiness is also a woman who knows to whom she belongs. This radiates from her own family, to the community, and then the nation. The easiest way to break a nation is to break bonds. That is why a mother is so important. Happiness is also a woman who is not naïve about an enemy's attack on the Republic of South Africa.
(Mrs Viljoen, wife of the then head of the SADF, quoted in Paratus, *vol. 34, no. 7, July 1983)*

4. Optimism

We must prevent thinking that we could lose. What we are dealing with is total onslaught – it is a total war on all aspects of our lives.
(Speaker at a conference hosted by admirals' and generals' wives, quoted in Paratus, *vol. 34, no. 4 April 1983)*

5. Shared values

… the loyal wife is bound to her husband by a shared love of your fatherland, people and Provider.
(Ibid.)

6. Domestic competence

The wife must know where her husband's salary is paid out, and where accounts must be paid. She must be able to drive a car. She must be able to fix fuses and taps. She must assume responsibility for locking doors and windows and for turning off water and electricity after use.
(SADF booklet, While He is Away, *cited by Human Awareness Programme (HAP), 1986)*

7. Regular correspondence

It's up to you to make sure that your letters and actions while he is away show him beyond any doubt that you love him just as much as always, and you're going to wait for him, no matter how long. One very important way to show your love for your man is through the post. A family that does not write weakens the whole platoon.
(Ibid.)

8. Responsibility

The wife of a man in uniform has to show responsibility to her calling as wife, believer and citizen. The first phase of the psychological war takes place in the home, as the smallest unit of the population. If the enemy succeeds in winning the wife away from her task, then half his battle is won. Therefore the wife has to form her own opinion and has to develop in a dextrous manner, to cope with all the demands that are presented.
(Mrs Naude, wife of the Chaplain-General, quoted in Paratus, *vol. 38, no. 1, January 1987)*

9. Commitment

Being a wife implies being supportive of her husband in all areas. It implies a job and is hard work. The current lifestyle, with its tendency towards questioning of authority, pessimism, and lack of concern are little pricks which work on us daily and lead to disloyalty. We are confronted with a choice between loyalty and disloyalty. This is no longer a simple and logical choice, but a personal one. Disloyalty is the neglect or disobeying of the human calling to be part of a particular situation and to do within that situation what is appropriately adult.
(Speaker at a conference hosted by admirals' and generals' wives, cited in Paratus, *vol. 34, no. 4, April 1983)*

10. Independence

You, as the wife of a soldier, must learn to be as independent as possible – both practically and emotionally. You must maintain the smooth running of the household without your husband's help, and handle the day-to-day routine without his support.
(Venter, 1983: 27)

11. A competence with guns

Women are generally not eager to handle weapons, but it is essential that, before your husband leaves, you know where the weapons and ammunition are kept, and that you become so adept at handling them that you feel completely safe and at home with them.
(Ibid.: 29)

These interpretations of loyalty as the key quality of the soldier's wife all underscore the importance of the home in the official formulation of 'total strategy'. Furthermore, they suggest a notion of an 'incorporated wife' (Callan and Ardener, 1984), who is entirely submerged in her soldier-husband's role, lacking any autonomous identity. While the prescriptions of that role are onerous, at the end of the day the woman is simply a mirror or shadow.

Overall

a woman's behaviour must always be of such nature that it is worth the trouble for a man to defend her.
(Venter, 1983: 34)

The protector or defender role is presented as a natural one:

> At a very deep level of their nature men are protectors. If they then
> have the support of those nearest to them, they will go to the ends of
> the earth to protect their women.
> *(Ibid.: 39)*

> It is especially tough for the wives of commanding officers. The wife
> of a commanding officer does not only have her own duties as wife
> and mother, she is also the cornerstone and confidante of all the wives
> in her husband's unit.
> *(Ibid.: 51)*

The extent to which the wife is incorporated in her soldier-husband's
role is best illustrated by the Johannesburg City Council's decision to
restrict paid maternity leave to women employees whose husbands were
presently doing or had done military service. Those to be excluded were
'specifically the wives of religious objectors', as well as all blacks,
coloureds, Indians, and single women.[6]

The effectiveness of this notion of the incorporated soldier-wife is
illustrated by the case of Louwna du Toit, wife of Wynand Du Toit, an
SADF officer captured in Angola:

> Wynand knew his gutsy wife encapsulated all the qualities he ad-
> mired. A former soldier, she was a product of the Women's Army
> Training College at George, in the south-western Cape. She clearly
> understood the meaning of 'duty' and 'loyalty'. No one could identify
> more strongly with the cause her husband was fighting for than
> herself. She was the wife of an army officer, a highly specialized
> soldier whose duties carried him into the dark realms of top secret
> counter-insurgency operations.
> *(Soule* et al., *1987: 5)*

Du Toit was eventually captured in Angola on one such operation. While
he was held as a prisoner of war, Louwna coped on her own:

> The first three months were not so difficult, as I was used to Wynand
> being away from home, but reality dawned soon after this. I realized
> that the sooner I learned to stand on my own two feet, the better.
> *(Ibid.: 90)*

At the same time she had their small son Kippie to care for:

> The stork delivered him just like any other baby son ... in a white
> basket with a blue ribbon. I fed him with blood-red hyper-energy
> syrup, with purity bottles full of impossibility and with the pink
> candyfloss of love.
> *(Ibid.: 92)*

However, for some women this role of incorporated wife sometimes breeds resentment:

> Yes, I was married to a Permanent Force soldier and we're now divorced. In the beginning he gave me security. I came from a really poor family. My father worked for the South African Railways. There was no money for a second dress to go to church in.
>
> My husband gave me no assistance in the house at all. He wouldn't bathe a child [they have four children], attend a school concert or take a sick child to the doctor. He wanted me to stay at home all the time. I didn't expect him to cook the supper, but to provide some emotional support, especially as I began to get active in NP affairs. He just sat in front of the television and played badminton two or three evenings a week. I've always had a strong self-image, but a low self-esteem as a woman. My mother was very repressed. I'd never heard the word 'sex' when I got married.

The power of the wife's role in maintaining militarism is underlined by the Minister of Defence's response to an article in a woman's magazine in 1988 on the issue of conscription. Replying to a parliamentary question from Mr Clive Derby-Lewis, the Minister warned that he intended to

> take action against publications containing articles which encouraged wives to influence their husbands to resist doing national service.
> *(The Star 7.5.1988)*

However, the wife is only one source, albeit crucial, of the ideological legitimation and emotional suport which connects women to the social process of militarization. Other crucial sources are women in their roles as providers of entertainment and diversion. This 'Vera Lynn phenomenon' was an important theme for many Britons during World War Two:

> There'll be love and laughter and peace ever after,
> Tomorrow, when the world is free.

Vera Lynn ('the forces' sweetheart') believes

> I was reminding the boys what they were really fighting for, the precious personal things rather than ideologies and theories.
> *(Quoted by Costello, 1985: 99)*

Much of the content of this type of entertainment reinforces an ideology of domesticity in which women and 'loved ones' provide a rationale for the soldier's privations. In South Africa the message is conveyed through radio and television programmes, such as *Forces Favourites*, and tours of the operational areas on the part of female entertainers and beauty queens.[7] During the 1980s many top South African beauty queens donned military uniforms and visited soldiers in the operational areas, the beloved 'boys on the border'. For example Miss South Africa, Janine Botha, went on a tour of operational areas in Namibia:

> The smiling, fresh, beautiful Janine moved among Owamboland's desolate, dusty camps, glaring heat and dreary camouflage .... The willowy Miss South Africa moved gracefully among the troopies with a smile for one, an autograph for another and gentle words of encouragement for the homesick and the lonely. Tanned young men gathered around the girl who reminded them of their own sweethearts and sisters back home, eager to talk to her and take her photograph .... Like true royalty the beauty queen never once lost her composure. Not even when the pilot of an Allouette helicopter kidnapped her from the base at Rundu and smuggled her to a wild party on the Kavango river. And she gamely tried her hand at firing AK47s, blasting practice targets with LMG machine guns and launching grenades.
> *(Sunday Times 4.12.1988)*

The previous year,

> Miss South Africa stormed the border ... and conquered all before her. Wilma van der Bijl charmed the Rambos of Owambo, gave the troopies a treat and admitted it was one of the most rewarding jobs she'd done since her crowning.
> *(Sunday Times 16.8.1987)*

Women such as Esme Everard, Patricia Kerr, and Diane Chandler fulfilled this morale function in radio programmes. Their contribution to maintaining soldiers' morale did not go unrecognized. July 1987 marked the twenty-fifth anniversary of the popular radio prograMme for soldiers – *Forces Favourites* – which is described as a 'great morale booster'. For the past twenty years this has been prepared and presented by Patricia Kerr. Her commitment earned her 'The Order of the Star of South Africa for exceptional service of military importance' (*Paratus*, vol. 38, no. 4, April 1987). Her programme sent about 300 weekly messages of love and support to and from soldiers, made pen pal arrangements, and so on. Many of these messages reinforce the ideology of gender roles. Pat Kerr has paid 20 visits to the border since her first in 1972. Another radio personality, Gail Adams, who was producer of the Sunday evening radio pogramme, *Salute*, reported that she 'fell in love about forty times' on her four-hour visit to seventeen base camps. After this experience she planned to

> feature girls regularly, in the form of a 'radio centrefold', which could be a chat-up with a reigning beauty queen.
> *(Paratus, vol. 34, no. 2, February 1983)*

This 'centrefold' type of woman is a further component in the linkage between masculinity and militarism. A sexist abuse of female sexuality is evident in at least two different ways: the indirect visual abuse of women as sex objects in 'pin-up' illustrations, and the direct physical abuse of women in the case of rape. As regards the former, it is interesting that *Paratus* used to have a monthly 'pin-up' page. A photograph of a woman, either fully clothed or in a bathing costume, filled the final page of every issue of *Paratus* until mid-1977. This clearly reinforced a splintered and contradictory image of women – an image split between the extremes of moralism and sexuality, 'Damned whores and God's police'.[8] (Unfortunately it is as 'damned whores' that women frequently suffer at the hands of soldiers, as Chapter seven will show.) 'Sexy' photographs of women are valued by many SADF soldiers, but it is a letter from a soldier in World War Two that best illustrates the importance of this imagery:

> You won't find one barracks overseas that hasn't got an *Esquire* pin-up girl. I, for one, have close to fifteen of them. Those pictures are very much on the clean and healthy side and it gives us a good idea of what we're fighting for.
> *(Costello, 1985: 191)*

In South Africa, as in the Second World War, the pin-ups contributed to boosting soldiers' morale as reassuring symbols of what most soldiers believed was worth fighting for. In most cases, what 'was worth fighting for' had less to do with abstractions of freedom or patriotism than with the need to protect the personal values represented by sweethearts, wives and families.

> Sex therefore played an extensive role in the war experience, whether it was pin-ups of Hollywood stars, or well-thumbed pictures of 'the girl back home' ....
> *(Ibid.: 28)*

This notion of woman as the *raison d'etre* for fighting has been stated by the Defence Minister himself: 'Fight for your wives, children, and future' was the message delivered at a parade to honour the memory of South African soldiers who died in World War One. On this occasion the Minister of Defence, General Magnus Malan, said in a speech,

> In the First World War and the Second, the battlefields were mostly distant ones. Today they are closer. But the enemy remains the same. It is the enemy of freedom, democracy, Christianity, civilization and of human decency.
> *(Rosebank/Killarney Gazette 23.1.1988)*

The direct linkage: The increasing incorporation of women into the SADF

It might be thought that the linkage between militarism and masculinity would be eroded by the increasing incorporation of women directly into the armed forces – a process that is occurring globally as well as in South Africa. However, this incorporation seems to preserve the ideology of gender roles; the definition of femininity is expanded rather than fundamentally reworked.

The global trend to use women increasingly as a military resource is related to a number of factors: changes in military technology; decreasing birth rates in the developed world; increased labour force participation rates among women; changing attitudes to gender roles; and ironically, the rise of equal-rights feminism. The irony stems from the fact that armed forces everywhere have been distinctively patriarchal institutions:

> The military, even more than other patriarchal institutions, is a male preserve, run by men and for men according to masculine ideas and relying solely on manpower.
> *(Enloe, 1983: 7)*

The patriarchal nature of many societies facilitates the connections between the armed forces and other institutions. For example, Enloe writes of the military-industrial complex as a patriarchal set of relations thoroughly imbued with masculine-defined militarist values. The network

> depends on male bonding, male privilege, and militarily-derived notions of masculinity.
> *(Ibid.: 193)*

White women in South Africa have also been subject to this global process of inclusion into military structures. However, the increasing incorporation of women into the SADF has not seriously breached the ideology of gender roles. It is largely maintained by a sexual division of labour, whereby the vast majority of women in the SADF are placed in subordinate positions; there are very few women in the top levels of policy- and decision-making. This sexual division of labour is reinforced by the elaborate cultivation of a superwoman image, whereby these women are encouraged to combine non-traditional jobs with their domestic responsibilities as wives and mothers.

Women now constitute a significant proportion – 13.8 per cent – of the 18 000 members of the Permanent Force, and this proportion has increased steadily in recent years. White women served in the South African armed forces in the Second World War; there were 25 000 women recruited into the Permanent Force and 65 000 women in temporary positions, but they were all demobilized at the end of the war.[9] By 1977 the percentage of women in the SADF had increased to 7 per cent, from 0.6 per cent of the total force in 1973. By 1981, 12.5 per cent of the full-time Permanent Force were women (Human Awareness Programme, 1986: A1; Prekel, 1980: 63). The Deputy Minister of Defence has said that the use of women in this way has reduced the burden on Permanent Force members and has freed national servicemen for other tasks (*Hansard*, no. 11, k1980).

Much of this direct incorporation of women into the SADF was due to President P.W. Botha.[10] It was largely through his initiative as Minister of Defence, that the Civil Defence Army Women's College, a military training college, was opened at George in the Cape (Botha's own constituency), in 1971. The College trains white women for the civil defence structure of the commandos and the citizens' force. At the opening ceremony Botha described this recruitment of white women as

> an act of faith in the women of South Africa and a manifestation of faith that the civilian population was preparing, in an organized way, a national 'wall' against military threats as well as emergencies and national disasters.
> (Sunday Times *12.4.1971*)

In 1976 Botha announced that women would be trained for a range of new jobs in the Permanent Force. Women would also be recruited into the commandos and trained in the use of weapons (*Rand Daily Mail* 17.12.1976). Botha was clearly impelled by SADF 'manpower' requirements and the need to define 'manpower' in race-specific terms. Unterhalter has argued that women's presence in the SADF is used to symbolize a white unity:

> ... in the mid-1980s, as in the early 1970s, political and ideological motives supersede labour requirements in the recruitment of women.
> *(Unterhalter, 1987: 110)*

> ... the use of women in the SADF was born not so much out of the need for women's labour as the need for women's identification with white supremacy ... women's role in the SADF was an advertisement for the modernity of the SADF and an instrument to create white political unity. Women in the military have helped to maintain white identity in South Africa.
> *(Ibid.: 120)*

The fact is that they have helped to maintain both white supremacy and male supremacy. Their exclusion from combat roles is fundamental to the latter.[11] Women's exclusion from combat roles maintains the connection between masculinity and militarism. It is legitimated on a number of different grounds:

1. Women are instinctively unlikely to kill.

> It is the task of women to give life and to preserve it. Women can provide invaluable assistance in the support services. I know there are women who could cope but, generally, the female has no place on the battle front.
> *(Col. Hilda Botha, quoted in the* Rand Daily Mail *18.3.1980)*

2. Women's socialization is inappropriate.

> Women encounter nothing like the extreme physical discomfort and danger of combat in their everyday life, so they're not taught to cope with this sort of thing. The men on the other hand experience something like it with blood sports .... Firstly, without a training programme that could successfully reverse the cultural training women experience from birth, it would be extremely difficult. The normal female role is not an aggressive one, but rather caring and sympathetic. As the instrument of life it would be difficult for her to overcome these feelings, but with the right psychological preparation it could it be done.
> *(Psychologist, Alma Hannon, Ibid.)*

3. Women are incapacitated through physiological function such as menstruation.

> Some women suffer from premenstrual tension and, at this time, they may be less mentally agile and well co-ordinated than at other times. A percentage are also more accident-prone at this time. If this sort of thing were not checked at the outset it could put certain women at a definite disadvantage on the front lines.
> *(Senior Consultant in Gynaecology at the Johannesburg Hospital, Ibid.)*

4. Male chivalry.

> It would be very difficult to use women in an operational task. The physical implications like toilet and sleeping facilities would create endless difficulties. Men would it find it difficult to prevent themselves saying things like 'After you' or 'I'll take that, it's too heavy for you.'
> *(Commander Jurie Bosch, Commanding Officer of the South African Irish Regiment, Ibid.)*

This exclusion from combat roles is essential to maintain the ideological structure of patriarchy.[12] It is essential because the notion of experiencing military 'combat' is central to the social construction of masculinity:

> … To be a soldier of the state means to be subservient, obedient and almost totally dependent. But that mundane reality is hidden behind a potent myth: to be a soldier means possibly to experience 'combat', and only in combat lies the ultimate test of a man's masculinity.
> *(Enloe, 1983: 13)*

However, the distanced and highly technological nature of modern warfare means that the notion of direct, hand-to-hand combat on the ground is a dated conception.[13] As Enloe points out,

> combat is usually left conveniently vague in definition. Are bomber pilots, a thousand feet above their helpless targets, engaged in manhood-testing combat? Is an infantryman, shooting in blind frustration at an enemy he cannot see in the distant foliage, engaged in combat? Are sailors, sitting in front of a computer control panel aboard a ship in a war zone, doing something that qualifies as 'combat'? The myth of combat dies hard. In today's highly technological societies, there is still the widespread presumption that a man is unproven in his manhood until he has engaged in collective, violent, physical struggle

against someone categorized as 'the enemy': i.e. combat. For men to experience combat is supposed to be the chance to assert their control, their capacity for domination, conquest, even to gain immortality.
(Ibid.: 13)

The notion of 'combat' is clearly highly problematic in modern warfare. So are the notions of 'the front' and 'the rear' which appear regularly in military discourse.

The most consistent characteristic of the front surviving into the era of modern warfare is that it remains the place where fighting activities considered to be most important for the success of the military operation are located.
(Yuval-Davis, 1985: 651)

The implication is that women's exclusion from the front zone and combatant roles reflects women's exclusion from roles of power and prestige in the wider society. The sexual division of labour in the military reflects that in society as a whole, and is based on current ideas of the 'proper' areas of labour for men and women. The areas of labour considered 'proper' for women have expanded in recent years. Technological changes in modern warfare have created a requirement for many more auxiliary positions in areas such as communications and administration. Women in the SADF are no longer relegated to the traditional female roles of medical and welfare work, but are involved in telecommunications and signals, logistics and finance, military police and instructional activity.

The women volunteers are trained at the South African Army Women's College in George. Volunteers must be under 22, have matric or its equivalent, be bilingual, never have been married, and be physically fit. Initial basic training lasts one year, which is divided into two phases. For the first six months the women undergo training at the College in physical fitness, with much emphasis on resilience and the use of firearms. They are lectured on a range of topics, and most importantly of all are adjusted to military discipline. They are coached to emphasize their 'feminine' characteristics, to keep up a neat appearance, and they receive instruction in cosmetic application.

After this they are allowed to specialize in different fields according to their interests. Telecommunications, cartography, administration, and stores administration are some of the courses offered by the college. (*Paratus*, vol. 34, no. 2, February 1983). The Swans – women in the

South African Navy – are given eleven weeks of intensive training. The emphasis is on girls who can present the image of women in uniform positively (*Paratus*, vol. 35, no. 9, September 1984). The crucial theme throughout training is that there is no contradiction between femininity and serving in the SADF. Thus the ideology of gender roles is preserved.

Colonel Hilda Botha (now Mrs Burnett) is a confident and articulate woman who for ten years was in charge of training these young women soldiers, often referred to as 'Botha's babies'. Among them was President Botha's daughter, Rozanne. Colonel Botha was appointed Commanding Officer of the George Army Women's College for women by Mr Botha in 1973, when he was Minister of Defence. She accepted the job after her first husband died very suddenly, leaving her with three small sons to support.

> George has an intake of about 220 a year. The Selection Board last year interviewed more than 1 000 girls. We recruit directly from schools and universities, and we always get more applications than we have vacancies.
> *(Interview, 1989)*

Some girls appear to end up at the George army college because of a lack of direction:

> I was at the Afrikaans high school in Kimberley. One day some women from the SADF came to talk to the school. I didn't know what I wanted to study at university. I saw going to George as an opportunity to stabilize myself. I didn't realize that going to George meant joining the SADF. Also I was keen on sports. Quite a lot of the girls at George in my day were in the same position. There were two distinct groups – people like me, and those planning to join the SADF. We lived quite separately.
>
> Basic training lasted ten weeks. We slept four to a room. We had to wake up at 4 a.m. and start cleaning and tidying. You even had to fold your socks in a special way. The instructors would come and inspect almost every day. The food was nice. The girls gained weight … some of them doubled in size. Also the clothes were nice. We wore brown skirts, mustard blouses, brown socks and flat shoes. You were not allowed to have your own clothes at all. The clothes we arrived in were sent back to our parents. We wore browns for training, and crimplene suits for smart – for parades and going to church and so on. For that we had a skirt, top and jacket in turquoise. We were paid about R28 a month in my day.

Actually I hated every minute of it. I hated the instructors, the drilling and the military atmosphere. But I did learn things I couldn't learn anywhere else in the world. I learned there's always something nice about a place or a person – you just have to look for it. You learn your own strengths.

After breakfast we had drilling for two-and-a-half hours, then a tea break. Then we had lectures on military stuff, first aid, the structure of the SADF, military law, etiquette, how to behave at formal dinners, how to behave in front of superiors. We learned that in good company you should not talk about sex, politics or religion. We had lectures on preparedness, which were interesting if you could keep awake. We did weapon training ... learned about pistols and rifles and had lots of tests. The emphasis was on clerical and administrative work. The whole emphasis was on how we should free the men to fight.

After lunch there were more lectures and target practice and camouflage, and then sports and physical training. That was the best part for me. We used to jog in the Outeniqua Mountains. That was lovely. We played hockey, we swam ... it was more relaxed in the afternoons. But we were busy all the time, every minute of the day. On Sundays we went to church in George ... and we worked in the garden. I can't remember ever reading a magazine or a newspaper or a book.

The worst was the instructors. They were rude and shouted. I didn't respect our instructors. They were very unstable and inferior, childish, empty people, not intelligent. The whole emphasis was on looking neat and attractive. But we had no contact with men. There was a lot of emphasis on team spirit. Lots of singing. The whole squad would be punished with an extra hour of drilling if one didn't do well in the inspection. Another punishment was cancelling passes.

I was there at the same time as Rozanne Botha. We thought she got special treatment. She got the merit award for the best student just because her father was Minister of Defence at the time. I thought she was an absolute pain. After supper we watched TV and did our washing. We were not allowed to leave the premises at first. After the first five weeks we were only allowed to go into town on a Saturday morning. Only after twelve weeks could we attend church in town.

Friends were the best part. There were some rough ones, but also some extraordinary girls. We became very close to each other. Most of my close friends now come from that time 11 years ago. Only a

minority joined the SADF. We had six months at George and then were posted to different places. I went to Voortrekkerhoogte and worked at telecommunications. I'd been specially trained for that. We had a ball. There were only a few women among lots of men. The idea was that women should step into the jobs of the men and release them to go to the border. I visited Caprivi and Namibia. I volunteered to carry the mail bag. We flew up there and back the same day. I was more uncomfortable than scared. I had a boyfriend that I met at Voortrekkerhoogte. He wanted to fight Swapo. He was injured and some of his friends were killed in a battle. I had a lot of confidence in the strength and capabilities of the SADF.
(Informant 47)

Another young Pretoria girl, 'Anna', went to George

because I felt I could use a year for myself. It was an opportunity for experience.
(Informant 16)

Prior to this she had had a number of ideologically formative experiences:

I did cadets at school. I went to veld school twice and loved it. I liked the hiking best. Also I enjoyed youth preparedness. It stressed Afrikaner culture and religion and what it meant to be a good Afrikaaner. We talked a lot about communists and communism. Pop music was communism. Communism was really bad – the main source of evil in the world. I was very patriotic. I really believed that what the government said was law, and you shouldn't argue with it. I also joined a youth organization called the Voortrekkers. I joined in Standard 1 because it was the thing to do. We did camouflage, drilling and shooting. My mother was a Voortrekker when she was young. Those girls are my best friends. They were a very positive influence.

I really was very patriotic in those days. I loved my country. I was not exposed to anything to do with revolution or human rights. I was raised in a NP family and we all felt very positive about everything the government did. I wasn't at all critical, very conformist I suppose. Actually it was in the army that I came to question authority. We were asked to do totally illogical things. Like cleaning the classrooms every day. No reasons were ever given. I lost all respect for authority. Going to George was like an adventure. I wanted freedom and to get away from home.

I hated it. From the first day all your identity was ripped away from you. All your clothes were taken away, you looked like everybody else, you're a number, they don't even know your name, no one cares for you. The emphasis was on the group. I felt very depressed and insignificant. Looking back, it was a very positive experience though. It involved hard, psychological work. It made me stronger. You have to think very deeply about your own worth and the things that make you different to other people. Everybody cried and was very unhappy, except for those with a father in the SADF. There were four girls to a room. You had no privacy. We had two uniforms, and the same boots as men, and green berets. We were allowed small signs of femininity. For example we were allowed to wear rings (actually only one) nail varnish (it had to be pale pink) and make-up.

What made me feel very unfeminine was that no one ever helped you to carry anything. The guns were quite heavy. We had to load furniture onto vans. We did a lot of men's work really. We felt very dirty and tired a lot of the time. We also spent a lot of time cleaning – buses and classroom and so on. We did a lot of what we called 'kaffir work'. After basics you had to choose between telecommunications, signals, clerical, or map-reading. I chose clerical work. I was taught how to write a letter, office administration, and to type. After eight weeks training you had a choice. You could stay there or come to Pretoria and work at army headquarters. That's what I did. I carried files all day. I lived in the women's quarters.

Looking back and speaking as a woman, everything in the army was unnatural. There was no contact with men. There was a lot of lesbianism. Many of the instructors were very butch. There were meetings at night, and if the instructors got caught in bed with another girl, they were given 24 hours to leave the unit at George. But they were absorbed in other units. All the lesbians joined the Permanent Force. Headquarters applied pressure to me to join the Permanent Force. They thought I was officer material. They said I'd progress far and gave me lots of praise and encouragement ...

I'm against conscription. Girls are too fragile. But people should have a choice. Women should be allowed into combat roles. Almost all the girls who joined the Permanent Force were insecure people. They needed structure, and the SADF is a very enclosed and protected world. They were weak people who didn't want to face the world.
(Ibid.)

The George college is not the only training centre for girls. In 1989, 84 South African Air Force women recruits started their 'basics' at the Air

Force Gymnasium in Pretoria. Janine Burton-Durham joined because

'I like the air force way of life – the parades and the uniform. I enjoy being smart.' A competitive tennis player, 'the air force offered me a good deal. I represent the SAAF and it pays my tournament travelling expenses and I stay at SADF bases free ... I'm a patriotic person. I like representing my country.' Once basics are over she will be working in personnel administration.
(Sunday Star *12.2.1989*)

'Colonel Kotze' and Colonel Botha both believe that serving in the SADF is good for girls. Inducements to women to serve in the SADF are often posed in terms of appeals to a heady mixture of patriotism and self-improvement:

● Learning self-discipline, independence, and self-reliance. *(Interviews with eleven graduates from the George Army Women's College, reported in* Paratus, *vol. 35, no. 2, February 1984.)*

● Patriotic duty.

The defence of this country cannot be regarded as an exclusive male prerogative. We women have to come forward and stand by our men against the multi-faceted onslaught against this country. We have already made our mark, that's quite clear to see. So much so, that I am convinced that more and more opportunities are going to be created for women in the SADF, and that more women will be attracted to the Permanent Force.
(Captain Fiona Coughlan, Paratus *vol. 30, no. 12, December 1979)*

● Job satisfaction and career opportunities.

I regard my work as dynamic, intelligent and fulfilling. The decision I made to join the SADF is one which I'll never regret. I have total job satisfaction .... Not only that, my job also gives me the constant feeling that I'm doing something significant for our country.
(Ibid.)

There are frequent appeals to women not to allow their role in the SADF to contaminate their femininity. Physical appearance must be carefully cultivated:

With good grooming any woman can look as good in her uniform as out of it.
(Paratus, vol. 30, no. 5, 1979)

It would appear that this injunction is adhered to:

> Wearing medals instead of brooches doesn't make a woman any less feminine .... During the making of this photo feature on the SADF we worked with women who love their job. They enjoy their authority and know that extra effort means recognizable promotion .... Making decisions and getting things done is just part of the job. They also support the armed services and spend their days dashing from one challenge to another. The result, when they sink into a hot tub at the end of the day, is called career satisfaction, and the perks include being saluted by all sorts of interesting men.
> *(Sunday Star 8.10.1989)*

The image of women serving in the Permanent Force tends to be inflated to 'superwoman' proportions. The SADF superwoman usually combines her highly responsible job with domestic responsibilities in the shape of a husband (often a member of SADF personnel) and children. These women tend to be physically active, and to enjoy robust hobbies and sports such as orienteering. They have boundless energy and enthusiasm for their jobs and are often portrayed as extremely attractive. All enjoy cooking, for example the 'master *(sic)* of *bobotie*'. In short, the definition of femininity operating in this image has been expanded rather than fundamentally restructured – the domestic role has not been abandoned, but enlarged to include martial as well as domestic skills. The following may be cited as examples of such SADF superwomen:

1. Attractive Sergeant Major Lauretta Corcher of Signals Unit, Orange Free State Command, has made quite a name for herself in the provincial sport arena, but few realize the superfit 29-year-old is a veritable 'superwoman'. In an apron she is a master of bobotie. In the garden she has the flair that lifts every marigold, head and at work she runs an efficient operation, overseeing two dozen people. All this the slim sergeant major shrugs off as merely 'a busy schedule'. What is important is the enjoyment, she says, 'There's never a dull moment in the Defence Force.'
   (Paratus, vol. 38, no. 5, May 1987)

2. Captain Fiona Coughlan – a translator with Directorate Language Services – also reads a lot, ranging from fiction to international politics. She is at home in five languages, and has a working knowledge of a further three. She is fond of horse riding, swimming,

walking (as a routine she walks over three miles a day) and cooking.
(Paratus, vol. 30, no. 12, December 1979)

3. Captain Lyn Potgieter is a personal Staff Officer to a Commanding
   Officer. The mother of three children, she is also an athletics officer,
   treasurer of the Windhoek SADF Rugby Club, a member of the
   Officers Club Committee and a member of an Afrikaans language
   committee. Her many commitments, 'keep me young – I haven't time
   to get old'.
   (Paratus, vol. 34, no. 5, May 1983)

4. Captain Esterhusen is a nurse at Military 1 Hospital. The mother of
   four school-going children, she wrote exams at the same time as her
   children.
   (Paratus, vol. 33, no. 9, August 1983)

Captain Esterhusen served in the SADF in the traditional female role of
nurse – what has been termed 'the Florence Nightingale phenomenon'.[14]

Another traditional female role in which some women serve is that
of spy – 'the Mata Hari phenomenon.' According to a careers supplement in a local newspaper, 'the Defence Force is relying more and more
on women' in 'posts involving intelligence work' (Careers supplement,
The Star 16.9.1987).[15]

Olivia Forsyth and Joy Harnden are two very different examples of
this role for women. In 1989 they were both exposed as trained intelligence operatives of the Security Branch of the South African Police
who infiltrated anti-apartheid organizations. Both women used their
sexuality – albeit very differently – to get access. This conforms to the
Mata-Hari image; a manipulative sexuality has always been attributed
to the female spy.

Olivia Forsyth eventually infiltrated the ANC and, according to
Major-General Basie Smit, executive chief of the Security Branch,

> during her seven years as an agent she was able to perform her secret
> task and gathered valuable information.
> *(The Star 3.2.1989)*

She was much praised:

> What Olivia Forsyth did for her country is nothing short of heroic,
> even though her detractors label her a traitor for exposing her former
> 'comrades' for the villains that they are. One wonders who the real
> traitors are: Olivia, who sacrificed everything dear to her for what
> she believes in, or the criminals (whites among them) who will stop

at nothing to destroy our free-enterprise society, flawed though it may be. Her actions acutely embarasssed the ANC leadership, causing its image irreparable damage, and made many misguided whites think twice about joining an organization that has only contempt for them. Miss Forsyth has shown the ANC to be a fifth column poised to stab our country in the back and whose object is to create as much social and political mayhem as possible.
(Letter to The Star *27.2.1989)*

In fact the South African media turned Olivia Forsyth into a heroine. This romanticization of a squalid and sordid role is only paralleled by the media treatment of Wynand du Toit. In the *Sunday Times* her story was captioned, 'The Forsyth Saga'. The story began,

> Daring spygirl, Olivia Forsyth, came in from the cold this week. Demure Olivia, the 28-year-old former Rhodes campus agent and ANC plant [revealed that] she had been a trained intelligence operative in the security branch, holding the rank of lieutenant and agent number RS 407. Details of the extent and success of her undercover operation, which took her into the Frontline states and eventual detention in an ANC 'rehabilitation' camp in Angola, are not divulged.

In this interview Olivia stated that

> 'I had very strong radical credentials which I had built up over a period of four or five years in South Africa, and they were unshakeable. By the end of 1985 I was a well-known radical. I had leadership positions in numerous oganizations. That was an iron-clad cover …. Leading a double life as a jeans-clad radical and highly trained intelligence operative was difficult. I joined Foreign Affairs because I wanted to do work for the country. I love this country very much. I also enjoy working with and meeting people and travelling. I had read of Craig Williamson's story (the former security police major who penetrated the ANC in the early 1970s for some years). When I volunteered in 1981 it was specifically for intelligence work …. If I had the choice, I would do it all again.' Olivia, posing as a student activist and committed radical, befriended unsuspecting students on campus …. 'One of the things I had to do was lead a double life. You learn to think in two minds if you want to succeed. I have to admit I am a John Le Carr fan – but I think the truth is really stranger than fiction. And it's not always so glamorous. To a very large extent, I had to sacrifice my personal life.'
> *(*Sunday Times *5.2.1989)*

The ANC seems to have been her main target. Before her exposure,

> I was engaged in an undercover operation involving my infiltration
> of the ANC by posing as a defector. This operation has yielded, *inter
> alia*, a mine of intelligence about the inner workings of the ANC.
> This includes information on conflict within the ANC leadership,
> widespread disillusionment among the rank-and-file membership,
> the dictatorial and intransigent nature of the organization and its total
> disregard for the individual, mutiny, torture and appalling conditions
> at the ANC prison camps, problems relating to inefficiency, alcoholic
> tendencies and AIDS, ethnic and tribal conflict, strategy and tactics,
> underground structures, operations in the Frontline states and the
> ANC's attitude towards the release of Nelson Mandela.
> (*The Star 3.2.1989*)

The two spies apparently used different methods of gaining social and
political access, revolving around sexuality and diligence. Both shared
houses with key political activists for a time. Overt sexuality is alleged
to have been an important weapon in Olivia Forsyth's strategy of
infiltration. According to National Union of South African Students
(Nusas) president, Lindsay Falkov,

> those in Nusas with her knew her to be very promiscuous.
> (*The New Nation 9.2.1989*)

The person in Harare through whom she obtained access to ANC people
describes her as 'very sexy':

> When I first met her at a Nusas July Festival in Cape Town I thought
> she was impressive. She seemed to be very collected both intellec-
> tually and politically. She later contacted me in Harare in February
> 1986. My wife had been away for about a month and the Boers must
> have known that I was feeling lonely and sexually deprived .... Soon
> afterwards she came to visit me at my house wearing very tight canary
> yellow ski pants .... very sexy. That afternoon we slept together ....
> We had an intense affair. I was seeing her almost every day. I came
> to trust her emotionally. I needed her. Afterwards what scared me
> most was realizing how the Boers had manipulated my sexual and
> emotional vulnerability .... There was a pathos about her. She
> pretended a kind of naïvety. This bounced off my arrogance. She was
> also very bright .... We talked a lot. We shared the same contempt
> for Nusas politicians and the bankruptcy of much of the white left. I
> found her comforting. She seemed quite genuinely to understand a

lot. I was shattered when my ANC contact told me she was a lieutenant in the security police ... I was devastated. I was really fond of this woman ... I subsequently found out that she had slept around a lot. In fact there was a joke about a T-shirt in Cape Town which said, 'I didn't sleep with Olivia Forsyth'. Very few men on the left could wear it. She slept with just about everybody. Her nickname in the ANC was 'Kalipinda', which was the name of a bar outside Lusaka that was a cheap whorehouse.
(Interview, 1989)

A very different strategy was used by a second spy unmasked at the same time – Joy Harnden. She spent 'five years as an infiltration agent' (Major-General Basie Smit, executive chief of the Security Branch, quoted in *The Star* 3.2.1989). Miss Harnden (27) was a former journalism student who was recruited by Olivia Forsyth as a security branch operative in 1983. According to her proud mother,

> My girl did invaluable work in the five years she infiltrated anti-apartheid organisations ... I worried about her constantly. It's not easy to be the mother of a spy.
> *(Sunday Times 5.2.1989)*

I knew Joy through our common membership in the organizations of the Black Sash, the End Conscription Campaign and JODAC (the Johannesburg Democratic Action Committee). I believe that Joy's capacity for hard, boring work gained her access, and was (for a while) interpreted as a sign of her deep political commitment. She was extremely diligent and efficient, always volunteering her time and energy. For a time she had a research post in the Johannesburg Advice Office of the Black Sash, which she filled, according to Black Sash regional chairperson Mrs Ethel Walt, 'very efficiently'. She was detained twice for two-week periods. Black Sash ex-President Sheena Duncan described her as

> quiet, quite pretty, she seemed to have had a hard upbringing ... I felt quite motherly towards her.
> *(Saturday Star 4.2.1989)*

Others described her as 'quiet as a mouse'. She seems to have used her sexuality in the opposite way to Olivia Forsyth. Her housemate and main line of access to the ANC says,

Joy had no sexuality .... she was completely non-sexual. Any men that sought her out, she rejected ... She got access through hard work and a kind of girlish vulnerablity. I was used in a very calculated way. She lived with me for about two-and-a-half years .... But we weren't intimate. She was a lodger really. We worked together politically. I was her main access to the ANC, We went to Mozambique together to see my mom. I was never suspicious. Even when Jodac exposed her I thought their reasons were very slender.
(Interview, 1989)

It is important to note that both these women spies were officially members of the SAP. In South Africa in the eighties there was a blurring of the boundaries between the army and the police force, who often acted in concert as 'the security forces'. There are about 4 000 women in the SAP. In February 1989 nearly 200 young girls joined the Pretoria Police College, where they underwent six months' basic training.

The Miss Jean Brodie of the police world, Captain Elene Terblanche has been priming her '*crème de la crème*' for eight years. She likes nothing better than being given a batch of girls and moulding them into shape. Captain Terblanche says that encouraging the girls to retain their femininity – and there is plenty of lipstick in evidence under the jaunty police hats – is an important aspect. 'Some people think to be in the police force means roughing it. That is not true. The girls are encouraged to be very feminine. They clean their own rooms, do their own ironing and tend to the gardens. We arrange fashion shows for them and talks on make-up and deportment. We are putting girls into uniform to do a man's work, but we want them to remain looking like and behaving like ladies,' she says. 'They are all highly motivated. Out of 2 000 to 3 000 applications we can accept only two intakes of 170 a year, so the successful ones know how lucky they are'.
*(*Sunday Star *12.2.1989)*

So why do women volunteer for the SAP or the SADF? The answer revolves around different forms of coercion. Stiehm has posed the question in relation to men:

... why do the men who are called upon to do the actual fighting do so? In large part it is because of coercion. In wartime men are drafted. They are punished if they refuse to serve. Their basic military training is highly compelling and intended to teach an unquestioning obedi-

ence, compliance, and submission. i.e. coercion is used to make coercion unnecessary.
(Stiehm, 1982: 371)

This coercion includes socialization into an ideology of militarism which compels both men and women. It is significant that the increasing incorporation of women as a minority of the armed forces has not seriously breached the ideology of gender roles or the sexual division of labour. The most common functions women fulfil in militaries are clerical, administrative, and servicing. These are jobs very similiar to those held by women in the wider labour market. They do not contaminate the ideology of femininity which reinforces the sexual division of labour. It is therefore difficult to see how this increasing use of women as a military resource can be hailed as advancing equality between the sexes:

> ... women's participation in the military has failed to challenge traditional and very basic sexist ideologies. It reinforces a sexual division of labour sharper and more rigid in the armed forces than in civilian life.
> *(Ibid.)*

This echoes Yuval-Davis' comment on the Israeli case. This

> suggests that the incorporation of women into the military may change the nature of, rather than eliminate, the subordination of women. Women's formal inclusion in the military does not guarantee their equality, either in terms of the actual tasks they fulfil or in terms of the power they exercise. On the contrary, as the Israeli case illustrates, the extremely hierarchical and bureaucratic nature of the modern army can contribute to a gender differentiation and gender inequality even more institutionalized and extreme than in the civilian labour market.
> *(Yuval-Davis, 1985: 648)*

The South African case illustrates the same process. Women's subordination within the SADF is not only evident in the sexual division of labour, which means that most women serve in subordinate and supportive roles, or in women's absence from the higher ranks. It is also evident in the problem of sexual harassment that a number of women reported. It is not possible to establish whether this occurs on the same scale as in the US army, where two out of three women have encountered sexual harassment ranging from cat-calls and dirty looks to pressure for sexual favours, and rape (*The Guardian* 13.9.1990). But it is significant that a high-ranking informant reported that

> our sexual problems in the SADF are not with men but with ... lesbians and '*losmeisies*'.

This underlines the importance that is given to reserving traditional gender roles and the effort invested in policing these roles and ensuring conformity.

The almost universal exclusion of women from combat roles and direct conscription resonates with the much wider question of women's subordination and exclusion from power and prestige. This exclusion is necessary to maintain the existing ideological order. That is why the SADF devotes so much attention to deflecting any potential contradiction between 'femininity' and participation in the SADF. In this process they ignore a much wider set of contradictions upon which the South African state is impaled. One of these is the fact that while the majority of white women contribute to the process of militarization, a small minority of them are a source of resistance to it.

Notes

1. This role is sometimes rewarded in material terms. For example in Israel in the early 1950s Ben-Gurion initiated rewards of IL100 for 'heroine mothers', defined as those who have had ten children or more (Yuval-Davis, in Yuval-Davis and Anthias, 1989: 95).

2. In the 1980s women have become 'the backbone of the militarized micro-electronics industry' (Enloe, 1983: 190).

3. For example, in World War Two there was a mobilization of women for armaments production in Britain. The compulsory registration of women was introduced in 1941, and on the basis of the register women were selectively conscripted into industry, the administration, and the armed forces. By 1943 'it was almost impossible for a woman under forty to avoid war work unless she had heavy family responsibilities or was looking after a war worker billeted on her' (Mason, 1976: 22).

4. The heroic mother role is illustrated by the exemplary mother of Rousseau's Spartan ideal who loses five sons but gives thanks to the gods that Sparta won the battle.

5. An American girl who had been going steady with a soldier posted overseas in 1943 jilted him after receiving a letter from him telling of the emotional strain of life at the front. 'He was sent to Italy where the fighting was very intense for a long time, and he wrote to me whenever he could. Then, in one of those V-mail letters, he told me he cried many nights during the heavy fighting. In my

sheltered life, with my stereotyped notions of what a man constituted, the thought of his crying turned my stomach. I was convinced I had loved a coward. I never wrote to him again' (Costello, 1985: 26).

6. The Council decided that only women employees whose husbands were doing or had done military service would be eligible to receive up to 96 working days' leave on full pay – on condition they pledged to work for the Council for a further year. Controversy resulted, but the Council's Staff Board Chairman defended the proposal, saying it was 'merely a gesture' similar to that made in wartime to women whose men had gone off to fight (*The Star* 28.1.1986).

7. Probably the most famous such personality in South Africa was Perla Gibson, the 'lady in white', who sang to over three million young soldiers who passed through Durban on their way to remote battlefronts during World War Two.

8. As 'God's police' women are a source of moral authority; as 'damned whores', a source of dangerous sexuality (Summer, 1975).

9. According to the Kappie Kommando, they were all prostitutes. The Kappie Kommando was formed in 1982. The name honours the *kappies* (bonnnets) worn by the Voortrekker women who defended Afrikaner nationalism against Britain's imperial policy during the Anglo-Boer War. The women of the Kappie Kommando dress in Voortrekker costumes, often in black, as an indication that they uphold 'traditional' political values.

10. In 1989 the SADF laid on a military extravaganza in Cape Town to say a public farewell to President Botha. He was persuaded to attend because of his 23-year association with the SADF. Welcoming him, the Chief of the SADF, General Jannie Geldenhuys, said President Botha had been responsible for building up the armed forces to their present level. He had created a place for women in the SADF and laid the foundations of the arms industry in the country (*Saturday Star* 2.7.1989).

11. Stiehm points out that women are not the only social category excluded: '... there are certain groups which are generally excused from military service. They include: the young (who later become protectors), the highly valued (superprotectors like the President, his cabinet and his advisers), the despised (homosexuals), the distrusted (communists in the USA), and women (who seem to be simultaneously highly valued, despised and distrusted by male rule-makers' (Stiehm, 1983: 369). A peculiar twist to this is that in South Africa white male ballet dancers are granted deferment from military service so long as they are employed by a state company. It is debatable whether this is because they are despised or highly valued.

12. A similar attempt to preserve the ideology of gender roles, despite the direct incorporation of women into the armed forces, occurs in Israel (Yuval-Davis, 1985). Approximately 65 percent of Israeli girls serve in the army through their two years of compulsory military service (*Jerusalem Post*, 8.11.1986). 'CHEN, the Hebrew acronym for the Women's Corps, as a word means "charm" and indeed CHEN adds to the Israeli Defence Force the grace and charm which make it also a medium for humanitarian and social activities' (Israeli Defence Force spokesman, January 1980).

Israeli women make up about one quarter of the army's regular soldiers, and have served in the armed forces since Israel's 1948 War of Independence. Many women were guerrilla fighters in this war. As such they fought alongside men in combat. However, women came to be excluded from combat roles. Despite the persistence of the image of the tough Israeli woman soldier, women in the military mostly occupied traditional female 'support' roles. In 1980, women were engaged in only 270 of the 850 military positions available, and 65 per cent of women occupied secretarial, administrative, and clerical positions (Macdonald, in Macdonald, 1987: 12). A change has come about in the past few years: hundreds of women are now being trained in combat techniques such as sharpshooting, the use of explosives, chemical warfare, and driving tanks. After being certified as instructors, the women teach these skills to men. Some women also serve in the occupied territories as behind-the-lines operations officers, or help co-ordinate military action and occasionally go on patrol. This concept of moving women to combat training has been accelerated by the Palestinian rebellion, which has put new manpower demands on the army. 'Little by little there has been an increase in the number of women being recruited into the army, and a lack of manpower has led the army to find solutions such as these' Brigadier-General Almog, Commander of the Women's Corps, quoted in *The Star* 14.7.1989). Women are still barred from active combat duty and there are reports that some Israeli feminists are critical of this on the grounds that it prevents true equality. Brigadier-General Almog said that women were kept out of combat for three reasons: the first was to encourage childbearing; the second to keep women from being killed or captured; and the third to avoid conflict with some Orthodox Jews who opposed women adopting the role of men. 'It's a traditional view of women that you have to protect them' (*The Star* 14.7.1989).

It is not only in the Middle East that women's exclusion from combat has been relaxed when societies have been undergoing revolutionary struggles. Frequently however, once a stable state has emerged, its domination by men is reasserted and combat becomes male-exclusive again. This process occurred in the Soviet Union, as well as in Israel.

During World War Two the Soviet Union, prompted by egalitarian ideologies as well as desperate manpower shortages, mobilized women as combatants. 'They were, however, frequently segregated into all-female units or assigned missions that exploited gender characteristics' (Higonnet and Higonnet, 1987: 8). Soviet women served as snipers, machine-gunners, artillery operators, and tank operators. Their peak strength was reached at the end of 1943, when it was estimated at between 800 000 and 1 000 000 or 8 per cent of the total number of military personnel. Despite this experience with women as war-time combatants, the Soviets have returned to the standard model, with women designated as non-combatants and vastly outnumbered by men, at fewer than 10 000 (Elshtain, 1987: 178).

In the USA there is the same exclusion of women from combat. However, since 1972 women have been moved from their traditional confines of health care and clerical jobs into all but 16 of the US Army's 377 military occupations.

More and more jobs have been taken out of the 'direct combat' category so that women can be used. Women make up about 11 percent of US military forces, flying warplanes and performing combat support duties. However, the notion of 'combat' is often ambiguous. Some 600 women were among the troops who invaded Panama on 20 December 1989 to remove General Manuel Noriega from power. Officially, the women were only in 'support' positions, but some of them found themselves under fire and in seconds were shooting back. 'Captain Linda Bray, 29, Commander of the 988th Military Police company from Fort Benning, Georgia, crashed through a gate in a jeep, training a machine-gun on the enemy. Three Panamanians died in the encounter. " I joined the Army for the excitement, the challenge, experience and loyalty to my country," Captain Bray said. "I haven't been let down for a moment. The sounds, the confusion and the excitement – they automatically click in combat" (*Eastern Province Herald* 5.1.1990). Bray is 'reported to be the first woman to lead American men into combat' (*Eastern Province Herald* 11.1.90). However, there have been reports that 'tearful women soldiers ignored orders which they felt would endanger their lives' (*Sunday Star* 21.1.1990).

The Panama campaign has revived the debate on women in combat. The *New York Times* said in an editorial that the issue 'reaches deep into the relations between the sexes and is fraught with politics and prejudice'. At the time of writing, women are among the troops deployed in Saudi Arabia as part of the American build-up in the Gulf.

Several thousand Cuban women served with the 50 000 strong Cuban contingent in Angola, which will have been withdrawn by mid-1991. They served mostly as doctors, nurses, and administrative staff, but there was also an all-women anti-aircraft battery in Angola, the 'Mariana Grajales' battery, who dress in camouflage fatigues but wear earrings and lipstick. Newspapers report they were disappointed that they did not have a chance to prove their mettle in direct combat with the SADF: 'If we had been in direct combat we would have shown the South Africans,' one woman said (*Eastern Province Herald* 9.1.1989). Conversely, one conscript interviewed, who had fought in Angola and claimed to have a 'chivalrous approach' to women, said he would have shot a Cuban woman soldier without any hesitation.

13. '... the output of the armed forces, the business of killing, has become more remote, and the production of armed forces, the organization of men and machines, has become more and more of an industrial undertaking' (Kaldor, 1981: 7). The numbers of military manpower directly involved in combat has consequently declined: 'The direct labour of war, which includes infantrymen, tank crews, artillerymen, fighter and bomber crewmen, fighting ships personnel, who actually do the fighting, has declined dramatically as a proportion of total military manpower' (Ibid.: 9). In the USA fewer than one out of every six persons in uniform 'currently serve in a combat speciality. By way of historical comparison; better than nine out of every ten persons serving in the Union forces during the American Civil War had combat specialities' (Ibid.).

14. The nurse in some ways epitomizes caring, maternal qualities. Yet

institutionalized war nursing by women is a relatively recent phenomenon in Western Europe. The Crimean War brought the first grudging recognition of women's military role, when the single-minded determination of Florence Nightingale broke down male prejudice against female nurses.

15. It has been suggested that women are peculiarly suited to this role. For example in occupied France during the war, women are said to have had certain advantages as secret undercover operatives: 'They did not require the extensive documentation that the German occupation forces issued to every French male who could be challenged about military or labour service, and women could blend more easily into the local population because of a natural (*sic*) lack of suspicion of females' (Costello, 1985: 25).

5
The resisters

The linkages between women and war, the incorporation of women both directly and indirectly, materially and ideologically into the militarization of South African society, are not smooth, uniform processes. The linkages are complex, and straddle contradictions which are embedded deep in the peculiar social conditions of South Africa. While white women contributed to the process of militarization in the decade of the eighties, white women were also more active than white men in the extra-parliamentary struggle against apartheid. Of course the high level of women's participation in such groups has to be set against the high degree of passive acceptance and support for the apartheid regime among white South Africans generally. However, women's and men's participation in resistance was shaped by the politics of gender in contradictory ways. This will be illustrated by focusing on the two very different organizations which constituted important sources of resistance to state militarization in the 1980s: the End Conscription Campaign (ECC) and the armed wing of the African National Congress, Umkhonto we Sizwe (MK).

An MK profile: The knitting needles guerrilla

Thandi Modise has been called 'the knitting needles guerilla'. She was termed this because while she was operating underground as an MK cadre reconnoitring potential military targets, she tried to look as ordinary as possible, and carried a handbag from which a pair of knitting needles protruded. I interviewed her shortly after she was released after eight years' imprisonment for sabotage at two Johannesburg department stores.[1]

Thandi left South Africa during her matric year in frustration at the intransigent and violent response from the police to protests at her Mafeking school:

I was then 17. You know at that age you think you know everything. We were amazed at the Soweto kids. There and in Mafeking peaceful demonstrations were met with violence, with police beatings and shootings. We felt like animals being hunted.

She left in a group of ten school children:

We had one aim – military training.

Two of the five girls in the group later returned home and were state witnesses against her. But Thandi says,

I pity them. I enjoyed better opportunities than them. They are still bowing down to so many forms of oppression. I cannot get angry with them.

At the time, ANC officials in Botswana offered both boys and girls a choice of education or military training, but girls were encouraged to continue their schooling. Thandi was the only girl in the group of 20 that subsequently left Botswana to train as guerrillas. She spent a year training in Tanzania and at two different camps in Angola:

Women were a minority in both camps. At one time there were fewer than 30 women out of a total of 500 trainees. Women guerrillas were a new phenomenon. The male comrades respected us for having the courage to be soldiers. They did everything to make us feel their equals.

Women slept in a separate barracks but wore the same uniforms of camouflage trousers and shirts, with boots of black leather or green canvas. Men and women were given the same training of physical fitness, obstacle courses, engineering, tactics, map-reading, and instruction in the use of weapons and explosives.

Women comrades experienced problems on the obstacle course. We tired more quickly than the men.

However their chores and daily routine were the same:

We dug trenches, did guard duty, shared cooking, washing ... everybody did their own washing. We all did the same things. We ate the same food. We did lots of physical exercises so we all had beautiful bodies.

Everyone woke up at dawn and began the day with physical exercises. After washing and changing into uniforms, breakfast was served in a large dining hall – soup, bread baked at the camp, biscuits and tea, coffee or cocoa. This was followed by an assembly which involved an address by the camp commander and a news bulletin given by the camp's information section. After this cadres were divided into sections and platoons to engage in lessons and day-to-day camp activities. Training was given in the use of an assortment of firearms, cannons and rockets, and machine-guns. The afternoon was spent in lectures or reading.

> Political education focused on events in Africa, and the history of the ANC. There wasn't too much about communism. I never met anyone who hated churches.

Life in the camps was hard. The food was a problem. In both Angolan camps rice was the staple:

> We all craved 'pap' (mealie meal), but it was never on the menu.

There were boiled vegetables, canned food from the Soviet Union and East Germany, sometimes game – buffalo, wild pig or baboon – hunted by the trainees, and sometimes fresh vegetables grown at the camp. One year all 500 trainees at a camp suffered severe food poisoning. Thandi believes the South African Security Police were responsible.

The mosquitoes were also a problem, especially in a camp with only pit latrines. One training camp had running water, but not the other, so water had to be fetched from a river infested with crocodiles:

> Fetching water and doing the laundry were risky without an AK at the ready. Sometimes the trainees saw a crocodile surfacing and would flee in terror. One comrade fled leaving her AK behind.

Weekends were spent in recreational activities such as soccer matches, watching films on warfare and revolution, and cultural activities:

> There were lots of records and we put on plays and sang.

Thandi sang soprano in a choir which ANC President Oliver Tambo joined whenever he visited the camps. There were parties to mark birthdays and other special events. On Thandi's eighteenth birthday she felt very homesick:

I missed my family – I'm the last of six children – and I missed my child, but I felt she was in good hands with my mother. Some boys and girls fell in love and got married. I fell in love with someone in the camp, but we felt we were too young to marry.

On occasions such as Women's Day the women in the camps wore special uniforms. One was an olive green jacket and a skirt with a slit at the back. Another was a grey dress worn above the knee. The latter outfit was nearly discontinued, as it provoked 'wild stares from the male comrades'. But both uniforms

> gave a feminine touch and the women liked to wear them. We drilled in the short dresses on women's occasions and we felt like women. The men whistled but we ignored them .... Looking back it was a good life. We felt very close and we trusted each other. We went through difficult times together.

When I interviewed her in February 1989, Thandi was thirty years old and the mother of two children – the elder of whom is 13. When she was arrested in 1979 she was four months pregnant, and she gave birth to her younger child while she was in detention in Johannesburg. She spent three days in hospital with her baby, and then her mother collected her:

> I was never allowed to breast-feed her.

Both children are now living with her mother in Vryburg, and she has spent her time since she came out of prison getting to know her children. She talks of this time with pain, but says she was reassured by knowing that her mother would care for her children well. She does not see any tension between being a guerrilla and being a mother:

> I'm a guerrilla *because* I'm a mother.

Asked whether children and close relationships are luxuries which guerrillas cannot afford, Thandi answered,

> No, they're necessities. We should be lovers as well as fighters. Having loving relationships doesn't weaken you, but it softens you. Without them you can become rigid and extreme .... Some people have accused me of being an unnatural mother, but I did it for her. It's better to leave your child and fight. I'm very pleased my children will never turn around to me and ask 'Why did you do nothing?' .... We have to have a better South Africa for our children. I do it for the

children – all the children .... People expect guerrillas to be unemotional people, but my last child was planned. She helped me along. You always need someone to love. Guerrillas need to have such things .... Marriage and children are necessities, not luxuries .... They deepen your commitment.

Perhaps this position is not as uncomplicated as Thandi made it sound. Later in the interview she said:

When I returned to South Africa after training and was operating underground there were no fixed rules about whether I could see my mother and children. But I decided it might weaken me, and make me soft .... I returned in January 1978 and was arrested at the end of 1979. I think there was an informer. I have seen her since I came out. The first two years I felt very angry and bitter. Now I just feel sorry for these people ... I used to be a bitter person, but it was making me sick – it was clouding my view. I decided to channel my anger. I'm still a very angry person, but I've learned to channel my anger.

.... In court they said they treated me like a little piece of gold. I think they're right. Gold goes through a refining process – there's a lot of heat ... I was in solitary confinement for six months. Reading the Old Testament fanned my anger, especially the story of David. He tried to rectify the wrongs done to his people. Why should we be judged wrong when we tried to do the same? The psalms are soothing – especially psalm 23. But how can you fear nothing when the people are threatening to kill you?

... They found firearms, and exlosives. I had been making drawings of government buildings in Krugersdorp, Randburg and Roodepoort, and recruiting people. My idea of fighting these people is to hit them where it hurts. I would choose parliament first, then police stations. *As a woman* [my emphasis] I tried to avoid killing people.

Thandi also suffered particular humiliations as a woman during her six-month interrogation. She told the court in her trial that while she was being interrogated, black security policemen had escorted her to the toilet and watched her relieve herself.

In prison I completed my matric and did a B. Comm. through Unisa. My mother visited with the children four times a year for the first six years. She's sickly and works as a domestic servant. I stayed strong in prison through reading and discipline. But it wasn't easy. They made sure that we knew when people were being executed. We had a policy that we wouldn't cry before the enemy. Sometimes they watched to see if we were feeling down and then would say something really nasty. But I found a mother in Dorothy Nyembe ... we got close .... She's the person I admire most in South Africa. She was in her late fifties when I met her. She never married, though she would have loved a houseful of children.

The police wanted me to spy for them ... a fat house in Cape Town, good schools for my children ... that way they win a lot of people.

Thandi defines herself as a soldier who fought in a war:

People must know there's a war on. People think we go and fight because we have nothing better to do.

The achievement of which she is most proud is 'to have become a guerrilla'. She has a strong commitment to equal rights for women, but does not call herself a feminist. She equates feminism with bra-burning and a denial of femininity:

I wouldn't call myself a feminist. I'm proud to be a woman. I can do most things a man can do. I wouldn't go burning my bras. Feminists really want to be men. Feminists are unfeminine. But I do believe in equal rights, and I do think that men oppress women .... My parents were divorced. My mother was awarded the house and the children ... I don't want to change the customs of our people, but women should be recognized as people. The role of women has been underrated. We are responsible and yet we cannot be church ministers. It's unfair that we cannot.

She is a committed Christian,

but I've never prayed twice a day.

Her ideal is

to live in a country where I'm free to say you can't do this to me, to tell the President he's erring, without fear of being thrown into jail. But no such country exists .... Socialism and communism are theoretically the most beautiful systems. But people – we always put ourselves first. So we tend to destroy even the most beautiful systems ... I believe in justice. The 'right-wrong' person is what they called me in jail. I think it's because I'm very definitive in my judgements.

Thandi Modise is a member of the movement that has led opposition to the political subordination of the black population in South Africa, and which today commands mass popular support, the African National

Congress. From its foundation in 1912 the ANC was built on a rejection of violence as a means of attaining political change:

> Throughout its fifty years of existence the ANC has done everything possible to bring its demands to the attention of successive South African governments. It has sought at all times peaceful solutions for the country's ills and problems.
> *(Nelson Mandela's statement to the court at his trial on 22 November 1962)*

It was only after almost 50 years of peaceful protest and a decade of mass-based passive resistance that the ANC took the reluctant decision to continue the struggle as an illegal underground organization. As Oliver Tambo explained:

> We had sought by every non-violent means at our disposal to realize the liberation of our people .... But true to the traditions of colonialist rule and the ideology of race superiority, the rulers of our country paid no heed to the demands of our people. They drowned our efforts in blood and brutality.

The sixteenth of December, 1961, twenty-one months after the organization's banning, marked the start of a new strategy in the ANC's multi-faceted resistance to apartheid: the armed struggle. With it came the formation of the ANC's armed wing – Umkhonto we Sizwe. In the founding manifesto it was declared that MK's resort to armed activity

> would be a blow against the nationalist preparations for civil war and military rule.

Gender and Umkhonto we Sizwe (MK)

The armed struggle has never been the only strategy of the ANC. It became one of its four central pillars of resistance: mass organization and mobilization remained the lynchpin, along with the building of underground structures, and the international struggle to isolate the South African government:

> The resistance of the people took an armed form from 1961 in response to the systematic blocking of all channels of political expression from the time of union, and further to the increasing repression of the 50s, and the mass killing at Sharpeville in 1960. The liberation movement, in choosing armed struggle, was defending the

people and warning the white community. Armed struggle is not a principle of the ANC; it is a tactic, a method of struggle and at all times one among many.
(Informant 49)

In 1976 the Soweto revolt sent many radicalized young men and women into exile to join the ANC. MK in particular received a massive input after the Soweto revolt. According to police estimates, of the many young men and women who left the country to join the ANC in exile in the two years after the initial uprising, 'perhaps as many as 3 000 went into MK' (Barrell, 1990: 33). One of these was 'Edward':

> I left South Africa to join MK after the 1976 revolt. I was in Soweto during the uprising. On 16 June I was there. I saw that white man's murder. They stoned him as he sat in his car. It went on for a long time. It was quite painful. Then a person came with a pickaxe and opened the car door and hit him. I hated what had been done and the fact that no one could stand up and say don't do it. A strong leader would have stopped the crowd …. The main thing that struck me in '76 was how the government felt it could dismiss us. I was shocked at how a peaceful demonstration was turned into something violent …
> *(Informant 51)*

MK now entered a period of armed propaganda. Survival rates for infiltrated MK combatants in an active unit were short – about six months according to one MK officer's estimate (Cited by Barrell, 1990: 60). However, they were often much shorter. According to one MK cadre,

> I came back to South Africa on a military mission in 1978. I was part of an MK unit of four. We were going to be a rural unit. We were caught on the same day. I think we were caught because I was young and impatient and we had an informer with us right from day one. They arrested us within 24 hours of us entering the country. I spent 12 years on Robben Island …. No, I'm not bitter. The informer was on the other side. He was doing his job.
> *(Informant 51)*

Clifford was another MK cadre who was arrested shortly after his return to South Africa. The impetus to his joining the ANC was his frustration when he become a father. He voiced feelings of inadequacy that he could not find a job and support his wife and child properly:

An African man is only a man if he can provide for his family. It was 1978 and my girlfriend gave birth to a baby boy. I was so happy and longing for them a lot. But there were difficulties. There was no education in Leslie ... I felt I had no future. I judged that my difficulties were because of my skin colour .... The Leslie location was a bad place for people to stay. The people lived in zinc houses. There was no electricity. There were few jobs and a lot of unemployment. The streets were not tarred and were in a terrible state, especially when it rained. Apart from two football grounds, there was nowhere that people could enjoy themselves, not even a hall. All this was about 500 metres from the white town of Leslie where we could see conditions were just the opposite – tarred streets, brick houses, schools, free education, better conditions and family life.

Unable to find a job in his community and support his girlfriend and baby, Clifford felt totally blocked and

frustrated at every turn. With two of my friends I decided to leave South Africa and join the ANC in order to try and do something about our position. I wanted to rehabilitate the country. In Swaziland the ANC taught me that it was not white people who were responsible for the suffering of black people, but the government. The ANC people taught me. They gave me a light. They taught me about a democratic and peaceful and non-racial South Africa. I decided to join and stay with them. I thought that way my son could one day have a better life.

(Interview with prisoner awaiting trial, 1988)

This informant underwent military and political training in camps in Angola in 1980. Soon after this the ANC began to place a new emphasis on 'people's war'. This notion was adopted by the Kabwe Conference in 1985, and the ANC committed itself to recruiting and training a greater number of members for military action. This involved the attempt to widen the armed struggle to involve the whole population in a struggle that was both military and political. There was an increasing pattern of armed attacks – an increase of 700 percent between 1984 and 1989. There was also an increase in armed attacks specifically against the South African security forces – especially members of the SAP or municipal policemen.

Basic training of MK cadres lasted about six months and took place mainly in Angola, though there were also significant camps in Tanzania,

Uganda, and Zambia. Numbers in the training camps varied from 700 to 40 cadres. Basic training included instruction in firearms, explosives and engineering, battle tactics, topography, military strategy, and revolutionary politics. Each day had about six periods of instruction of about 50 minutes each. After about six months' basic training, cadres went for more advanced instruction, often in countries like the Soviet Union and East Germany. What impressed someone such as Clifford most about East Germany was that

> you never saw any really poor people. You never saw people scrabbling for bits of food in dustbins.
> *(Interview)*

The numbers of MK within the country also increased, with a new strategy 'to train trainers' who would be able to teach basic weapons handling and guerrilla tactics in the townships without the recruits having to leave the country. So MK was a military organization whose units operated with some autonomy.

> By the end of 1987 MK had trained more than 12 000 guerrillas since the 1976 uprising …. More than half had been deployed in the country.
> *(Barrell, 1990: 64)*

The numbers of whites and foreigners in MK also increased in the eighties:

> With the conflict in South Africa assuming the moral dimensions that the Spanish Civil War did for a previous generation of the international left, it can also be expected that the military involvement of committed whites and foreigners will increase, accompanied by growing international recognition and financial assistance of the ANC. While the ANC has not yet been approached about enlisting foreign brigades, individual white volunteers, such as Marion Sparg and Klaas de Jonge, have been operating in growing numbers.
> *(Adam, 1988: 99)*

In fact Klaas de Jonge referred to the Spanish Civil War as analogous to South Africa in its moral appeal:

> It was so easy to be against Fascism in Spain. You didn't even have to discuss it. South Africa is the same case for me. It is very easy to get angry and to take sides, and if you don't there's something wrong.
> *(Interview, Pretoria, 1986)*

This Dutch volunteer's anger was directed at apartheid as 'a particularly harsh form of racial capitalism' and became focused after Ruth First's assassination:

> I knew her and admired her a lot.

De Jonge was alleged to have brought arms and explosives into South Africa to be used by MK cadres.[2] He had no qualms about the use of violence against military targets:

> I would be very glad to blow up 300 military people. If you choose to wear a uniform, to be a policeman or a soldier, you make yourself into a target …. They have an alternative, even if it's hard and means going to prison, but they have an alternative. People in uniforms are shootable targets. It's a civil war and you have to do these kinds of things.

All those MK cadres interviewed regarded themselves as soldiers in a patriotic army, fighting a people's war.

> It was only when all other forms of resistance were no longer open to us that we turned to armed struggle. It is essential to understand what prompted the ANC to undertake armed struggle in order to appreciate why we stand here in this court as combatants and soldiers of the ANC. We are not criminals, we are not murderers. I myself am a survivor of the Soweto Revolt of 1976, where I suffered the trauma of seeing hundreds of innocent children and young people, including my own relatives and friends, drop dead from police gunfire. That event shocked us all into the realization that the life of the black person has no value under apartheid and will have none until the system is destroyed.
>
> We are soldiers in a patriotic army, struggling to establish democracy and peace. We believe that we are prisoners of war. General Van Loggerenberg stated in Cape Town in the ECC trial that South Africa was in a state of war. Such statements are confirmed by cross-border attacks into countries such as Angola, Botswana, Lesotho, Mozambique, Swaziland, Zambia, and Zimbabwe. These attacks, which have been carried out by SADF personnel, have resulted in the deaths of not only ANC members but also innocent nationals of these countries. The ANC has sought to have the conflict regulated in conformity with the international laws of war, aimed at protecting civilian life and preventing barbarous conditions of combat and captivity. The stated policy of the ANC is that it respects the values underpinning the humane conduct of war. It is for this reason that the

ANC has solemnly undertaken to respect the Geneva Convention and the additional protocols of 1977 in so far as they are applicable to the struggle waged by its combatants. The Convention is one of the cornerstones of international humanitarian law. The South African government has refused to sign these protocols.

...There is a war going on in this country. Massacres have been perpetrated against civilians at Mamelodi, Uitenhage, Queenstown, Winterveld and elsewhere .... In the past we have taken every precaution not to harm civilians. Thus targets such as power stations, strategic installations and military targets have been the subject of attention, and elaborate steps were taken to ensure that no civilians were hurt. We have stated that this remains our policy. However, as in any war situation, there may be instances where individual combatants are responsible for acts that go beyond policy and which cannot be condoned. It is an unfortunate and tragic fact of war that civilians fall victim to the violence. We are more concerned about civilian lives than our adversary, the apartheid government ....

(Court statement by Obed Masina, Frans Ting-ting Masango, Neogriffith Potsane and Joseph Elias Makhura, MK members on trial in 1989 for charges of terrorism)

Men constitute the majority of MK combatants who have been tried and convicted in South African courts. However, women also constitute a significant proportion of MK members. What was the role of women in MK, and how does it compare with the role of women in the SADF? The two armies reflect all the myriad differences between a conventional and a guerrilla army. In fact

... we are speaking of two different things. The SADF is a regular professional army, and a skilled army. The MK started as a guerrilla army, the army of the oppressed and the powerless. We challenged the might of the apartheid state, which was served by a very powerful army. In challenging the state we had to build a guerrilla army to carry out guerrilla tactics.

(Chris Hani, MK Chief of Staff, Lusaka, May 1990)

There are not only different levels of skill, resources and technology, but also of social organization and ideology. The SADF was a force for conservatism; MK was a force for change. However, there are similarities in the two armies regarding the position of women. In both the SADF and MK, women constituted a small minority in the 1970s. According to one MK cadre,

There were very few women in MK in the 1970s. There were only two women out of 700 in my training camp. When I was sent to the GDR for further training, only three out of the 32 in my platoon were women.
(Informant 51)

In both the SADF and MK there were dramatic increases in the numbers of women soldiers between 1976 and 1989. Women now constitute almost 14 percent of the Permanent Force of the SADF and approximately 20 percent of cadres in MK. The two processes were connected in that MK's expansion after 1976 fuelled the SADF perception of 'threat levels' and a 'manpower' crisis, to which the increasing incorporation of white women was part of the solution.

Despite this process of increasing incorporation, in both armies women are under-represented in positions of leadership and authority. There have been only two women to reach the rank of brigadier in the SADF, and there are only ten women colonels at present. In the ANC there are only three women in the National Executive Committee (NEC) and, although there are not the same formal ranks in MK as in the hierarchical and authoritarian structure of the SADF, there is only one woman in a formally acknowledged leadership position within MK – the head of communications, Jacqueline Molefe (47) was appointed in 1983, when Modise became commander of the new MK headquarters. Jacqueline Molefe is extremely modest about her achievements:

Yes, I'm in the commanding structure of MK. There should be more women there; there are many capable women in MK, but most top positions are occupied by men. I think I got this position because I was the longest serving person in the communications department. I left South Africa in 1964 and went straight into MK. I trained in Tanzania and then became a driver at head office. Life was very tough but I had a lot of determination. After that I did a secretarial course in Lusaka and then trained in the Soviet Union in communications. I specialized in radio.
(Interview, 1990)

She believes that the integration of women into the army is a crucial means to achieving gender equality:

In the army people come to respect each other. It's only in the army that I've seen equality practised. In terms of endurance and discipline women have been outstanding in MK. Because of that – because of what we've been doing on the ground – we've been recognized as equals. We are more disciplined than men. We make better drivers. Also women are good sharpshooters – in training we really excelled. This made the men respect us. In mock attacks or ambushes the behaviour of women won respect .... Once I was out on a march in Tanzania when someone said they'd seen a lion. I didn't run away, though I was very afraid.

Molefe emphasized that this respect from male cadres has to be earned:

In MK I feel I'm respected, but you have to prove yourself over and over again .... In the beginning we were not allowed to carry guns in the camps – only pangas. Men did the guard duty at night. But after a time women proved themselves on marches .... We have to prove ourselves all the time. Some men in MK have a negative attitude. Even some of our leaders were against us getting into the army.

Molefe combines the roles of soldier and mother:

I think of myself as a soldier and I'm proud of that. I'm also a mother – I have two litte girls. I didn't used to want children, but they've introduced something new into my life. I'm really responsible for their well-being and their future .... My appearance is not important to me. I'm always shabby.
(Interview, 1990)

The previous chapter demonstrated that in the SADF there is a rigid sexual division of labour, both in basic training and deployment. Unlike the SADF, in MK men and women trained side by side. In MK women receive exactly the same political and military training as the men cadres, and are involved in an extensive range of tasks. A woman who trained in Angola said:

The training was identical. There were only three women out of the whole camp of 500, but we were given the same training in the use of firearms, engineering, the use of explosives and so on .... There was a lot of emphasis on physical fitness. Every morning we ran 5 km, but we women (we were called *mzana*) were given the choice of participating in physical training.
(Informant 90)

The training for women in MK was exactly the same, and on some things they used to beat us. No, that didn't worry me. At school my main competitors were always girls. They could run faster than me.
(Informant 51)

The training was shared equally. On marches, on the shooting range … everything is the same. What we try to get across is that when the SADF comes the cadres will not be able to choose. You must be able to defend yourself.
(Molefe interview).

But there were some problems. According to Jacqueline Molefe:

Some of the women can't cope with the exercises. It takes some time to convince our women; they have the hangovers about how a woman should be treated because of their upbringing. In the beginning they expect help or they say they can't exercise too much because they will come to have legs like men …. In the beginning the boys expected to have their clothes washed, and the girls would do it.

Another informant said,

Yes, there was some sexism in the camps. It mostly came out of a kind of protectionism. The men tried to protect us from long stretches of guard duty for instance … I left South Africa in 1980 … I did one year's military training in the camps in Angola. There was absolutely no difference in the training given to men and women … but there were certain problems. Our anatomical upkeep (*sic*) is not the same. There were certain things in training which can damage a woman. Women had to carry heavy loads like everyone else, but not the very heaviest. I can't try to lift a truck for instance.
(Informant 5)

Another woman disagreed:

The men cadres were very protective. But I used the *dshka*, an anti-aircraft gun which is very heavy, when I was training in the USSR. The men's protective attitude pushed me. MK men expected women to be docile and subservient.
(Informant 90)

The outcome of this integrated training is that the presence of competent and confident women is felt in a wide range of departments. Unlike the SADF, the ANC is committed to the equal participation of women and they are not limited to service roles. However, there is a sexual division of labour:

> Women generally were deployed in clerical and office roles .... In fact women were better snipers then men, so we argued that they should utilize us better.
> *(Informant 90)*

> In all the departments men predominate. Engineering is mainly men, and artillery is only men. The communications department has more women, and there are some women in intelligence .... Overall there are some women in most departments, even in operations, and that means combat.
> *(Molefe interview)*

Molefe's comments raise an important point: women have not generally been used in combat roles, as that is conventionally defined to mean direct hand-to-hand fighting in confrontation with the enemy. As a guerrilla army, MK has not engaged in much of this kind of conventional combat, but the exclusion of women from combat may be significant given that the experience and tradition of actual combat with the enemy is an important ingredient in MK's prestige.

No women combatants are mentioned by name in the NEC's statement delivered by Tambo on the occasion of the 25th anniversary of MK. There are no women's names 'inscribed in the roll-call of honour of our revolution' (Tambo, 1986: 3). The exclusion of women from traditional combat means that no women participated directly in the famous MK actions that are now the subject of myth in the townships – actions such as the 1967 Wankie Campaign, a joint MK-ZAPU infiltration mounted from Zambia across the Zambesi into Rhodesia. Women were also generally excluded from combat roles in Angola, where MK soldiers gained battlefield experience and fought against Unita. Nor were women directly involved in any of the really spectacular MK missions such as the attack on Sasol in June 1980, or the Goch Street shootout led by Solomon Mahlangu. The word 'directly' is important here, because women were extensively deployed as couriers and in surveillance and reconnaissance, so they contributed indirectly to these actions. Furthermore, if 'combat' is redefined to mean direct exposure to danger, then acts of arson and sabotage performed by women MK cadres are part of 'combat'. One woman informant insisted,

For us in MK, sabotage was combat.

When this argument was put to Jacqueline Molefe, she emphasized the significance of women's contribution to guerrilla struggle:

There was no formal ruling excluding women from combat. It was our fault. We didn't put enough pressure, we were not forceful enough. We often protested that we were excluded from selection and it was always women who were chosen for the secretarial courses .... But in Wankie we women were part of logistics; we were part of the support groups. And anyway there were very few women in the bush. There were only about 13 women in MK at the time of Wankie. And there were a small number of women involved in Angola. We were not part of the advance – we didn't go on the offensive. But ambushes of the convoys became battles and there were women among the casualties .... We women have engaged in guerrilla struggle, but not as part of the attacking force. Women did a lot of the work on the ground, like reconnaissance. Women were important on the ground.

Another informant insisted that

Women in MK were not used in combat. But they were used a lot as decoys, couriers and so on .... They were used a lot to smuggle in arms, but not in combat. But then MK hasn't seen much combat.
(Informant 51)

This informant believed

Women should not be used in combat. Women are too special. War is terrible.
(Ibid.)

However, he had no doubts about women's capacity to be soldiers:

Yes, a woman can be a soldier. Many women fight better than men. But I wouldn't deploy women in the front line. They shouldn't be in the trenches ... I'd rather deploy them in support roles, in the medical field particularly .... Men go to war to defend their women and children. The army is like prison – there's no individual attention. Women generally concentrate more on the person. Women have a more caring attitude ... I think that's related to the fact that I was brought up by my grandmother. It was from her caring for me that I learned about caring. My grandfather was dead and I had three sisters. My mother worked in town as a domestic servant. I used to stay with

her in town for two to three weeks a year. In fact it was a society of women, and from them I learned that women are more caring than men .... My grandmother taught me about pride. She taught me that even though we were very poor, I didn't have to feel inferior to anyone.
(Ibid.)

This informant was arrested on his return to South Africa and imprisoned:

In the 12 years I spent on Robben Island I noticed that it was women who did all the visiting and sent the food parcels and wrote letters and did the caring. That's when I came to see women as more sensitive.
(Ibid.)

It is difficult to be definitive about the significance of women's exclusion from traditional combat roles in MK. It was shown in the previous chapter that the notion of combat is problematic. This is true in a conventional war because of changes in military technology, and it is also true of a revolutionary war that does not involve direct confrontation and where the boundaries between 'front' and 'rear' cannot be sharply demarcated. There is no doubt that women have played an important and courageous part in MK activities. Undoubtedly the nature of the struggle and the breakdown of normal male-female roles encouraged many women to discover new capacities within themselves. They formed a complex web of support that sustained combatants in many ways; they provided much of the infrastructure of resistance – they acted as couriers, they provided intelligence and refuge. Through rent and consumer boycotts it was often women who gave resistance its mass character.

At the same time the image of the female fighter – the MK guerrilla – has become a popular mass image of the strong, liberated woman. One of the figures of township mythology is a woman MK guerrilla known by the code name of Zoya. During 1986-7 she is believed to have operated in a two-person unit commanded by Roland Molapo, who killed a number of town councillors and municipal policemen on the East Rand. After a fortnight's action she is believed to have been killed in a shoot-out with the security forces. In June 1988 there were two separate crossings of MK guerrillas, including three women, from Swaziland. A woman was among those shot, allegedly by the notorious hit-squad commander Captain Eugene de Kock.

On the whole, women's reasons for joining either of the two armies are vastly different, though notions of 'patriotism' enter into both sets of ideological motivations. Certainly for many women joining the SADF, the opportunities for 'career' training are important. While the SADF offered social mobility and the opportunity of individual advancement for Afrikaner girls, MK demanded the sacrifice of exile and a life of hardship and danger. In the conventional army of the SADF, where women's subordination and subservience to men was generally unchallenged, the role of women seems to have been extended rather than fundamentally reworked. In the revolutionary army of MK, women were incorporated into new roles. A number of ANC informants stressed that 'Our army is a voluntary army', but this applies to women in the SADF as well. In both armies there is some emphasis on political education, though the content is dramatically different. While the SADF has always operated to defend the *status quo* and thus to maintain both white and male supremacy, MK has always operated as 'freedom fighters', as an army of liberation, with the question of women's liberation explicitly on the agenda (see Chapter six). The issue of women's emancipation figured in political education within MK, though

> most of the guys didn't take it very seriously.
> *(Informant 51)*

While a great deal of emphasis is given within the SADF to maintaining a hierarchical ideology of gender roles and to cultivating a subordinate and decorative notion of femininity, the egalitarian ideology of MK sometimes involved a denial of femininity that at least one informant found irksome:

> My femininity is important to me. The other struggle is keeping my weight down. I enjoy clothes. When I was in the camps wearing a khaki uniform and doing physical exercises I was very strong and fit. But I sometimes used to look at myself in the mirror and wonder.
> *(Informant 5)*

An important difference is that while in the SADF women were segregated during training, in MK the training was shared and identical. I received conflicting accounts as to whether this shared training created sexual problems. One woman said that on arrival at her training camp in Angola in 1981 she was told,

> It's the law here that women have to contracept and we use the loop
> …. There was no sexual harassment, but some people did have sexual

relations. Most women were on the pill or the loop, but there were some pregnancies.
(Informant 5)

There was no sexual harassment in the sense of anything violent or heavy. But there were sexual relations among cadres and sometimes that created tensions.
(Informant 90)

The women in MK in the 1970s created lots of social problems. Sexual overtures used to drive them over the edge. There were lots of problems with jealous boyfriends. Also some of the women had personality transformations. They got conceited from all the attention they got .... But they also varied a lot. One of the women in my platooon in the GDR was very crude ... she talked about sex all the time and made coarse jokes. She was what you call a nymphomaniac I think.
(Informant 51)

Men in MK were resistant to condoms. They think it's the woman's duty to prevent.
(Molefe interview)

Overall both armies draw on gender stereotypes. According to one cadre,

The stereotypes are strong within MK. MK refects the sexism in the wider society.
(Informant 90)

Notions of manliness do seem to be an important theme for male MK soldiers. Furthermore, there is a romanticization of militarization among South Africa's black youth (see Chapter seven) and the theme of resistance militarism and manliness is exemplified for many young South Africans by no less a figure than Nelson Mandela. Mandela visited Algeria in May 1990. He had last visited Algeria in 1961 for military training from Algerian guerrillas fighting France for independence. He is reported to have said that this 'experience of military training made me a man' (*The Star*, 18.5.1990).[3] Ironically this theme is among the grounds on which one of the best known white members of MK, Hein Grasskopf, rejects the role of soldier. The emphasis on a violent definition of masculinity is the basis of his rejection of the army as a career:

I'm prepared to go into the new South African army if necessary. But only on a temporary basis. The army's awful. It's very macho ... I'm not a soldier by nature.

Among the small number of whites convicted in South African courts for furthering the aims of the banned ANC, women form a significant proportion. There have been a number of famous cases, for example Barbara Hogan, Helene Pastoors, Jansie Lourens, Trish Hanekom and Marion Sparg.[4] The latter was a 29-year-old former journalist who was sentenced in 1986 to 25 years imprisonment on charges of high treason and arson. She is the first white South African woman known to have been trained in an MK military camp in Angola and to have served as a member of MK. Pleading guilty to all the charges against her, Sparg admitted planting the limpet mines which exploded in Johannesburg's police headquarters and an East London police station in 1986. She said she knew it was possible policemen or civilians would die in the blasts:

> But my motive was not to injure or kill people. It was one of a soldier in Umkhonto we Sizwe, a military army. I followed orders just like any other soldier.
> (The Weekly Mail, *7.11.1986*)

The politics of gender were used to deny and trivialize the validity of such choice and commitment. Shortly after her arrest in March 1986, several South African newspapers depicted Sparg as a 'failed woman'; as a lonely, overweight, unattractive female who had turned to revolutionary politics not out of commitment, but out of a desire to belong and win acceptance. She was depicted as a failed woman rather than a revolutionary. Paradoxically she was still a woman, and so *ipso facto* could not have acted independently – as a woman she had to be manipulated by a man of special persuasive powers. Sparg was described as acting under the influence of one such man, Arnold Geyer, whom Major Craig Williamson of the South African Security Police described as 'a sort of Charles Manson figure' (*The Observer* 31.3.1987).

A similar theme from the politics of gender has been used in the media to attempt to denigrate the activities of Barbara Hogan, who served a ten-year prison sentence. She was described as

> an academic and trade unionist who was the first person convicted of high treason without committing violent acts. She had run an ANC

cell for ten years after being recruited by her black boy-friend, Pindile Mfeti.
(The Observer *31.3.1987)*

Similarly Jansie Lourens, who served a four-year sentence for sabotage, was said to have been influenced by her boy-friend (now husband), Karl Niehaus. According to the judge, Karl had 'dragged his timid young girl-friend' into his ANC activities and would have to 'bear that responsibility and take the rap'. He said:

> If one has the impression that Lourens is a timid little girl and he is using her for his own ends, isn't he to blame for the embarrassment she finds herself in? That seems to be the truth behind the words. On that basis he is the man responsible for ruining this girl's life.
> (Rand Daily Mail *4.11.1983)*

Lourens' advocate argued that her

> actions were of a peripheral nature. There had been evidence of Niehaus' strong personality. She was in love with Niehaus and was loyal to him.
> (The Star *24.11.1983)*

A newspaper editorial stated:

> The poignancy of the trial of Karl Niehaus and Jansie Lourens on charges of treason has escaped nobody .... This time the tragedy was inescapable, not simply because the young people in the dock were Afrikaners, but because they were so quintessentially Afrikaans. That they were naïve was plain to everybody, and equally plain was the naïvety of their background: the sturdy families, the firm values, the binding loyalties, the unquestioning support for their people's cause. All those qualities so admired when they were employed in the cause of Afrikanerdom, were turned, in Niehaus and Lourens, against that cause. The violence which Niehaus was prepared to contemplate to overthrow the state mirrored exactly the oft-spoken willingness of our military caste to fight to the death to preserve the state. Like so many young Afrikaners, Niehaus does not balk at civil war; like them he will fight – on the other side. And Lourens at his side, gentle and loyal, is the very prototype of an Afrikaner wife.
> (Sunday Express *27.11.1983)*

However Jansie Lourens is very different to the other 'prototype of an Afrikaner wife', Lowena du Toit, described in the previous chapter.

Giving evidence in mitigation my father said I was a very loyal person
who was misled by Karl. This upset me a lot. I was depicted in the
trial and by the press and the judge as this timid little thing who was
dragged along by Karl ... 'timid', 'loyal', 'gentle' were the words
most used. I found it insulting. It made me seem like a fool. I don't
have a domineering personality, but I'm my own person.
(Interview, 1989)

Niehaus was found guilty of being a member of the banned ANC, and
Lourens was found to be an active supporter of the ANC. According to
the prosecutor,

Niehaus identified the Johannesburg gasworks as a target for sabotage and provided the ANC with this information. He later took
photographs and made a drawing of the gasworks with a view to
sending it to the ANC. He was the first link in the chain of sabotage
and the sabotage could not take place without his efforts.
(The Star 24.11.1983)

Jansie admits that Karl was a powerful influence on her politically when
they met as students at Rand Afrikaans University (RAU):

I grew up in a very conventional Afrikaans home. But there were
always things I objected to. I argued with friends in 1976 who said,
'We mustn't give them schools because they just burn them down'.
I was in Standard 8 at that time. But certainly I had no real political
understanding and I was afraid of black people. This changed when
I got to know black people on an equal level. In 1980 I started going
to church in Alexandra. I was always a Christian and I objected to
how blacks were treated, from a Christian point of view. When I met
Karl my views were in place but I wasn't informed politically. I didn't
even read the newspapers. I developed an interest in politics through
and with Karl. We were both PFP supporters then. It was a time of
much discussion and argument.
    We left RAU in 1982 and I started teaching. I was living in a
communal house .... The house was raided at 4 a.m., but I was staying
with my parents at the time. I was fetched from school and taken to
John Vorster Square. I was in solitary for one month, when I had only
a bible. I had intensive interrogation for about a week. I was charged
and sentenced and altogether I spent four years and three months in
jail. It has strengthened my convictions. It gave me the experience of
being the underdog, of being stereotyped in a way that just isn't me.
People took away my responsibility completely. I think that as whites

we don't know what oppression is until we've gone through something like that .... In prison I also built up very good friendships with
the people I was with; people like Barbara Hogan. It was my first
experience of learning about solidarity. My fate was totally bound up
with the people I was with, so we could truly act in concert. Now I'm
not afraid of prison, but I am afraid of solitary confinement. Before
I found the thought of prison absolutely terrifying ... like a bottom-
less, black pit. But life goes on in prison. There are opportunities for
people to experience and to grow. Though it's not an easy growth.
(Interview, 1989)

The revolutionary commitment of women like Jansie Lourens is in-
sulted by the suggestion that, as women, they could not have been acting
autonomously. However, their status as white women also provided a
degree of camouflage. It has been suggested that

white women attract less attention than men and under the guise of
their femininity are able to travel more freely around the country
fulfilling vital roles in the underground war, a role which is likely to
expand in the near future.
(Major Craig Williamson in The Observer *31.3.1987)*

Another case where the South African state tried to undermine the
credibility of a woman revolutionary, this time by making allegations
of immorality, was that of Susan Donelly. Aged 24, Susan Donelly
pleaded guilty to ten charges of terrorism in the 'Broederstroom trial'
in June 1989. She was part of a highly-trained, all-white cell of Umkhonto we Sizwe. They considered themselves to be soldiers engaged in
a legitimate military struggle. Susan Donelly was subjected to sexual
harassment by the state prosecutor, Roets, in court. He referred to details
of her private life, including an allegation that she had had an abortion.
He asked her father if his daughter had ever had an affair with a black
man, or 'entertained a black caller' *(The Weekly Mail* 15.7.1989). This
was clearly an attempt to discredit her.

The politics of gender was also used by the media to query the
commitment of someone on the other side of the South African struggle
– the case of 27-year-old Odile Harrington, presently serving a 25-year
sentence in Zimbabwe for having attempted to infiltrate the ANC. She
was also portrayed as a failed woman,

a lonely girl who never recovered from her parents' shattered marriage. There were no parties, no boyfriends and no fun.
(Sunday Times 29.11.1987)

It was demonstrated in Chapter three how the politics of gender was used against men in the ECC. At an ECC demonstration a bystander was overheard to say contemptuously,

> Look, there's the moffie brigade.

One informant said,

> The reality is that most ECC men are wimps.
> *(Informant 35)*

But she went on to describe this as a

> good thing. We haven't accepted the values of our society. Our ECC men are not macho, they're more caring and sensitive.

Gender and the End Conscription Campaign

The ECC was an extremely important source of challenge to the militarization of South African society (see Chapter three). Started in 1984, it became a national coalition with 52 member organizations, branches in ten centres, and thousands of active members and supporters. It incorporated an extraordinary range of supporters of very different ideological persuasions. They were united by their opposition to conscription in the context of apartheid South Africa. Many of these supporters were white women,[5] who were an extremely important source of commitment and energy within this organization, right up to leadership level.

Many women who supported and led the ECC were moved by their maternal role – by their sense of responsibility to their children. It was often their role as mothers that generated their challenge to militarization. A letter to a local Johannesburg newspaper urged mothers to organize to demand better army treatment for their sons:

> The South African way of life allows a great many myths to exist in our society. One of the greatest of these is the one that goes 'the army will make a man of your son' … we allow the might of the army to swallow the boys we, as mothers, have spent eighteen years turning into civilized human beings, caring and considerate of others, and in two years turn them into efficient, largely unthinking, killing machines.
> *(Letter to* The Star *15.4.1986)*

These sentiments were amplified in 1989, when there was a nation-wide action from mothers against conscription and the increasing militarization of South African society. The background to this was the ECC's call for a change in the law to broaden the definition of a conscientious objector. Under the call 'Give our sons a choice', a petition signed by hundreds of women country-wide urged the government to give objectors 'a meaningful choice' of alternative national service. The petition urged

> constructive non-punitive alternatives to obligatory military service.

This was in part a response to the heavy jail terms meted out to objectors Ivan Toms, David Bruce, and Charles Bester. It came in the wake of the 1988 declaration by 143 conscripts that they would face jail rather than perform military service (see Chapter three). The greatest number of signatories came from around Johannesburg, where 371 women signed the petition. Some had sons in the army at the time, others had sons who had completed their service, and others had boys who faced military service in the years ahead. According to the press release, these diverse women speak out in confidence that many other mothers share their concern that:

> There should be forms of national service which enable young men to fulfil the values that they have learned in their homes, rather than deny these principles.
>
> There should be service options which defuse racial polarization and make meaningful contribution towards building a common, non-racial society.
>
> There should be options which will ensure that young people will contribute their talents wholeheartedly for the communal good, rather than abandon the country in which they were reared.
>
> There should be options so that families are not torn apart by exile or the spectre of jail.

The statement was described as

> a signal to our youth that we have not abandoned to them the entire question of war and peace in South Africa. And it is an appeal to women: the demand for a change in the law is a legitimate course of action. It can only be won by responsible and united action by those truly concerned. The signatories believe mothers have the capacity for such action and that their statement is just the first step in a process.

Limiting the action to mothers caused controversy. Some people commented,

> What about fathers? The call should have been to parents.

> Maybe mothers do care more.

> Does that mean mothers care more than other women?

> But if you have a son of call-up age, there's a particular urgency and pain in the issue of war and consciption.

> It's very anti-feminist. It's dividing women. It's inscribing women in the role of mothers. This is precisely what feminism is opposed to.

> It's privileging mothers over other women.

> All these 'Another mother for peace' T-shirts make me sick. I'd like to have one printed which said, 'Another childless spinster for peace'.

One of the organizers of the petitition responded,

> Limiting the signatures to mothers we thought would have an ideological appeal. We plan a later action around International Women's Day that will involve all women. The truth is that motherhood has a particular ideological pull in our society. It's not only here – there's the Mothers of the Plazo del Mayo for example.

One of the mothers participating was Judy Bester, mother of Charles Bester who was sentenced to six years' imprisonment (see Chapter three). In a press statement she described her role as 'the ultimate betrayal'.

> Because of his acceptance of my teaching, he refuses to espouse violent repression. Because I taught him that man is equal in the sight of God, and, therefore, has a right to a say in his own destiny, he is seen by the state to be as great a threat to society as the most hardened of criminals …. Who is responsible for his criminal status? Is it I, his mother? Or is it the school who encouraged independence of thought? Or is it President Botha who, as Minister of Defence, first enforced conscription on the young white South African male? As a young man President Botha decided not to fight when South Africa declared war on Germany in 1939. I assume the reason for his not participating in that war was because he, in his own heart, did not identify with the cause of the government of the day …. In 1939 President Botha availed himself of the option not to fight, yet he demands the blind obedience of today's young men to service in his Defence Force. Now

military service is deemed a sacred national duty, and not to take part is said to be unmanly, cowardly and morally decadent. There is a terrible inconsistency somewhere.
(Judy Bester statement issued in Johannesburg, 7.2.1989)

One of the key organizers of this anti-conscription action was 49 years old, the mother of two children, and describes herself as an activist and committed to non-violence:

Violence is not a means of achieving power or bringing about change. Much violence – especially that of the 1984-8 period – came out of frustration, defiance and anger. The young people were making demands; burning cars was a statement of defiance saying 'Listen to us'. I can't condemn necklacing because I understand the anger that provoked it. Also, most necklacing was spontaneous, and not thought through. I used to think a lot about the idea of using violence for change. I can understand the appeal and glamour and attractiveness of violence. Organizing is far less glamorous and exciting than throwing a bomb or burning a car. But a lot of it was a game. Little children got caught up in it. Even nine- and ten-year-olds were involved in putting up barricades and wires across the road in Tembisa [an African township] to catch cyclists going to work in defiance of the boycott .... No, I don't see us in a war, but during the 1984-6 uprising period the kids saw violence as the solution .... Violence is the easy option. It's glamorous and exciting to train as a soldier – it's the stuff of which spy stories are made. It's much more difficult to stay here and fight more creatively and constructively for the future through talking and organizing.

Men are allowed and encouraged to be violent ... for example there's a tolerance of punching on the rugby field. Much male violence is hidden, for example child abuse is only just beginning to surface. I've struggled in my relationships with men. I've been married and divorced twice. I've found women to be more reliable and caring. Men are incredibly egocentric. They're frightened to be seen as vulnerable in any way. I believe in the goodness of all people though. I think women are more resilient than men – especially township women. There are lots of heroines who survive that we don't know about. If we women can learn, and show more creative ways of dealing with problems and conflict, other than violence; if we can do this we can change things. If we mimic men then we're lost. I don't see Maggie Thatcher as a woman, but as a man. She's adopted manly ways of doing things.

I'm the mother of two children, but I've never felt motherish. Motherhood just happened to me. My life was never totally bound up with my children. It does involve restrictions though. I only felt free to involve myself politically when my daughter left school. My commitment to them came first .... Yes, I think women who don't have children have missed out. There's an amazing physical sensation with a baby growing in you and feeding on you.

I've spent 37 days in detention .... No, it wasn't expected, but I think I coped well. It was a strengthening period in many ways. I realized that I must have done something right for them to detain me. I worked from that basis. There's a challenge in coping on one's own without any of the usual comforts and supports. I kept it a day-to-day experience. I thought a lot about all the children who'd been detained – particularly one 11-year-old who came out bright and loving ... I read the Bible a lot. Christ was a very simple man, a man of the people. He lived among the people and had no possessions. Also the Moroka action was an amazingly powerful experience. ... we all felt very connected. It was very much a women's action.[6] We were refusing to accept male views and styles. I think that's why it was so threatening ....

I'm now proud to be a white South African. I used to feel guilty. Blacks are different. One doesn't want to be romantic about it, but they have a greater humanity – *ubuntu*. If you need something, you only have to ask and it's given. They're a lot less egocentric than we are ... they've got a lot of commitment to their families and their geographical communities.

(Informant 20)

Women and resistance

Women's resistance to militarization has often been rooted in their maternal roles.[7] However, as this last informant indicated, deeply-felt family obligations can also inhibit, set limits on participation and generate contradictory feelings. For many South African women as well as men, political commitment has meant a sacrifice of these other roles. It has often involved long and painful separation of family members. For example, in 1989 Ivy Gcina was released after three years in detention. The first thing she did was to visit the graves of her two sons, ANC guerrillas, who died in separate clashes with police while she was in detention (*New Nation* 19.5.1989). Ruth Mompati reluctantly left her two-and-a-half-year-old baby and her six-year-old son with her mother, her sister, and her sister's husband and went abroad in 1962. She writes movingly of meeting her son again as a sixteen-year-old:

> I can never explain the emotional suffering of this meeting. It is extremely painful for a mother to miss her children's childhood years. Right now I feel very bitter-sweet about being back here. The South African regime owes me, it owes me for forcing me to miss the childhood of my children. I was not a criminal.

She only saw her children again when they were smuggled out of the country to meet her in Botswana in 1972.

> I arrived one afternoon at the house I was staying in with friends and saw a couple of boys kicking a ball around nearby. My friend said to me, 'There are your sons'. I hadn't even seen photographs of them. I didn't know them. It was all right with the little one, I could still pick him up and cuddle him. But then I saw Pati. He was standing alone, very still, very quiet and so tall … I was a stranger to him. That was when my heart broke.
> *(Interview with Charlotte Bauer,* Daily Mail *3.7.1990)*

Ruth Mompati has been a key actor in the ANC for over 30 years, and a member of the NEC since 1985. She grew up in the small northern Cape town of Vryburg and trained as a primary school teacher. She moved to Johannesburg in 1952 and began working for Mandela and Tambo as a secretary in their law practice. In 1962 she was instructed to leave South Africa. Ruth Mompati thought she would return after a year, but in reality she could not return to South Africa for 28 years. She describes her exile as 'relative freedom' compared to the others who were imprisoned, tortured, and killed. She was one of the two women in the 35-person ANC delegation at the 1990 Groote Schuur talks. Now 64 years old, she says she has

> given my whole life to the struggle. I've done it for our children … we all want to create a better future for our children.
> *(Interview, Harare, May 1989)*

Ruth Mompati's story is exceptional in its courage. However, women in South Africa have displayed a wide repertoire of protest. The classic notion of a uniquely womanly non-violent resistance to militarization is 'the Lysistrata option' – the idea Aristophanes introduced to Athenians 2 400 years ago of women refusing to make love until men stopped

making war. There has been no Lysistrata option on the public terrain
of South African politics. However, women in South Africa have
participated in the struggle against apartheid in a great variety of ways.
Women constituted approximately 12 per cent of the 25 000 detainees
held in 1986-7 and 5 per cent of the 5 000 held in 1987-8 (Audrey
Coleman, cited by Russell, 1989c: 157). Sometimes women have been
treated worse than men because of their lesser numbers, as well as their
gender, for example the two women who at different times were alone
on Death Row in Pretoria – Theresa Ramashamola (Bernstein, 1988)
and Evelyn de Bruin (Cock and Vogelman, 1990).

Women political prisoners such as Thandi Modise have sometimes
reported sexual assault, and many women have experiences and fears
of sexual abuse and humiliation (Russell, 1989; Critical Health, 1989).
One security policeman has been named in civil actions brought by three
women detainees. The methods allegedly employed by this policeman

> included sexual advances and threats; putting himself forward as
> someone who had acted improperly towards female detainees in the
> past, breaking their resistance; and threatening that he and the detai-
> nee would be left alone where no-one would see what he did to her.
> *(*The Weekly Mail *5.10.1990).*

In 1989 a domestic worker from the Eastern Cape, Joyce Mbevu, was
awarded R5 500 in her court case against the Minister of Law and Order
and Sergeant Kim Botha. She told the court she was arrested in Port
Alfred on 5 September and locked up. At about 11 p.m. that night she
was taken by Sergeant Botha to a garage near the charge office. While
being questioned, she was suspended from the roofbeam for 'what
seemed like half an hour'. Sergeant Botha then drove her out of Port
Alfred. He stopped his vehicle and told her to take her clothes off. When
she was naked he made her urinate while facing the police vehicle's
headlights 'because he wanted to see the urine coming out while he felt
his private parts,' said Mbevu. The judge accepted that Mbevu was a
respectable women who had suffered 'an embarrassing, insulting and
humiliating experience' (*New Nation* 13.10.1988).

Sometimes the politics of gender has worked to protect women
activists. For example Koleka Nkwinti was detained and interrogated
about the stayaway of Port Alfred women in protest over the case of
Freddie Mavuso:

> The police asked me who was behind the stayaway. They couldn't

believe women organized it themselves. They detained the male
activists because they think men are behind everything women do.
(Quoted by Forest and Jochelson, 1986: 43)

While the politics of gender is often used to deny the validity of women's
independent, autonomous political action, paradoxically it also gives
them space for such action.[8] There is no white male equivalent of the
35-year-old white women's human rights organization, the Black Sash,
which in 1987 was nominated for the Nobel Peace Prize. Their silent
protest stands are reminiscent of the 'Mad Mothers' of the Plaza de
Mayo in Buenos Aires since 1976:

> The women of the Plazo de Mayo, having not been able to obtain any
> response to repeated requests for information about their relatives,
> found that only elderly women demonstrating in silence were not
> liable for immediate arrest; and thus became, with their white head-
> gear to identify their mute protest, the vanguard of public opposition
> to the Argentine government's policies .... They had found one
> loophole enabling them to act non-violently in a situation that
> blocked any legitimate expression of protest.
> *(McLean, 1982: 326)*

While this organization in the Argentine seems to have achieved a
diverse, heterogeneous class membership, the Black Sash has remained
more restricted. Its membership is extremely small – about 2 000
(Bishop, 1989: 19) – and largely English-speaking and middle-class in
its social composition. In the cases of both the Argentine women of the
Plaza de Mayo and the white women of the Black Sash, notions of
'motherhood' were real identities in which many women were deeply
invested, and not simply camouflage or a protective device. According
to Schirmer, none of the Argentinian women would 'hear of a feminist
interpretation of their actions' (Schirmer, 1989: 21). Similarly, many
Black Sash women reject feminism. The question of why there is no
male equivalent of the Black Sash is an interesting one. According to
Michelman,

> Possibly because women had more leisure to engage in the activities
> of steady harassment and continuing symbolic reminders to the
> government than men had, or possibly because these activities were
> more emotionally suited to women than to men, vigils for men were
> unsuccessful.
> *(Michelman, 1975: 49)*

Crapanzano writes that,

> In all these organizations (Black Sash, Kontak ...) women dominate.
> They are, so to speak, a daytime activity, when men are away at work.
> *(Crapanzano, 1985: 283-4)*

Clearly these statements raise more questions than answers.

In the case of the Black Sash and the organization formed to assist political detainees – the Detainees Parents Support committee (DPSC) – the state found itself confronting new forms of resistance based on notions of motherhood, parenthood, and the family. Many of the activists were not initially mobilized by ideology, but by the detention of a relative and the destruction of the family. In this sense the war politicized the traditional role of women within the family, and family relationships proved to be important in mobilizing women.

It is in this sense that 'Motherhood' was a mobilizing role. It was the connection between motherhood and powerlessness which seems to have led to support for radical political change and sometimes to support for revolutionary violence. The primary motive many ANC and ECC informants gave for their having joined their respective organizations was related to their socially assigned role as nurturing mothers; they could no longer stand by and watch the violence inflicted on their children by the apartheid regime.[9] However, it must be acknowledged that the same notion of 'patriotic motherhood' also surfaced in interviews with SADF women. The image generates not only revolutionary commitment and defiance, but also docile obedience and repressive violence to preserve the existing social order.

All of the women interviewed for this chapter chose to challenge that social order, but they chose significantly different ways in which to do so. What they shared was a vision of a non-racial, democratic, peaceful South Africa, and the willingness to make sacrifices to achieve it. If we are to be fair to the contributions of all these different women, we must expand the conventional definition of 'resistance'. Prevailing notions of resistance have tended to obscure women's contributions. [10] Research has been oriented towards those women in leadership positions or particularly colourful roles, or it has excluded women through a narrow focus on 'combat':

> Resistance is habitually equated with actual combat .... Definitions
> of resistance that emphasize combat ... tend to exclude women, since

few bore arms, although many provided the infrastructure that made combat possible.
(Schwartz, in Higonnet and Higonnet, 1987: 142-3)

Women have participated in numerous wars of resistance throughout Africa. For instance in the Zimbabwean struggle about 4 000 out of 66 000 combatants were women. Other women were an important source of supplies and intelligence (Harare conference statement). While to some the female guerrilla is an image of liberation, to others it is an image that evokes a sexist sneer. Caute wrote that in 1980:

> The female guerrillas here number 600 and are by no means to be regarded as camp-followers. The first two women who were officially listed as dead fighters rather than as 'women running with terrorists' died in November 1976. Throughout 1979 bulletins reported women 'terrorists' killed in combat. Strongly built, with big bottoms and large breasts, the women affirm their military status by greeting visitors to Delta with a fiercer disdain than do the men.
> *(Caute, 1983: 422)*

Women have often participated in wars of resistance throughout Africa in their traditional roles. Women who carried firewood in traditional society carried arms in the liberation struggle. But war alters social maps. To take an example from another part of Africa, Kikuyu women were traditionally keepers of the home, but in the Mau Mau rebellion women increasingly took on male roles (*Kanogo, in Macdonald, 1987*). It is sometimes claimed that participation in armed struggle is the key to achieving gender equality – that war empowers women and transforms gender relations. For example, Samora Machel maintained that the armed struggle in Mozambique had made the masses receptive to progressive ideas, such as the liberation of women, and that women's participation in armed struggle had transformed the consciousness of both men and women. Many revolutionary movements have included a commitment to women's rights and have provided a space for women to perform military roles.[11] On occasion guerrilla war has propelled women out of their traditional and subordinate positions into positions of combat and even of authority over men. For instance it has been claimed that women were fully incorporated into the actual fighting forces of the Sandinista Liberation Front in Nicaragua. They were active not only in transport, communication and logistics, but also in combat and positions of command (Chinchilla, 1983; Harris, 1988). It has also been claimed that in Uganda women were guerrilla fighters and commanders. However, these instances are the exceptions. Overall the pattern of women's participation in both liberation and conventional wars seems to involve an exclusion from direct combat and from any exercise of power that would put them in positions of authority over men.

Furthermore, the process of changing gender relations is not always irreversible in either conventional or revolutionary wars.[12] At the 'Women in the Struggle for Peace' conference in Harare in 1989, a former guerrilla told of her ambivalent treatment when she returned to her community. While the men of Zanla (Zimbabwe African National Liberation Army) were welcomed back as national heroes, many people were unsure how to respond to a woman guerrilla. Some of them had endured incredible hardships in seven years of fighting in 'the bush'. This woman's husband, who had fought alongside her for seven years, left her to marry a woman who had not been involved in the armed struggle. Many people in her community seemed to prefer women who fitted into the traditional image of a 'feminine' woman.

It has been suggested that Western feminists' disappointment in the return of women freedom fighters to the apparently traditional spheres of home and child-care, is based on an ethnocentric perspective (Kimble and Unterhalter, 1982). The family in the new social order, they maintain, is not an instrument of women's oppression. What happens in the new society is not that women are forced out of political roles, but that traditional female roles become political and are given increasing importance. They suggest that the crucial test is whether women also retain a presence and voice in public politics. But how does one secure this 'presence and voice'?

The process of relaxing women's exclusion from combat roles during revolutionary struggles against repressive regimes, but reasserting combat as male-exclusive once a stable state has emerged, could still signal the assertion of male domination. A previous chapter pointed to this process in both Israel and the USSR, and it also occurred in Guinea Bissau:

> Many women underwent guerrilla training, and fought alongside men in combat. But when the guerrilla militia was reorganized into the national army, women were no longer encouraged to go into combat.
> *(Urdang, 1984: 165)*

Urdang also provides a tantalizingly brief discussion of this issue in relation to women in Mozambique, where

> women's military actions tended more often to take the form of defence of the liberated zones rather than combat on the front ... and where women fighting in direct combat tended to be the exception rather than the rule.
>
> *(Ibid.: 166)*

This raises large questions: does equal rights mean equal responsibilities, including military service for women? Should such military service include combat roles? These are questions which are logically at the cutting edge of contemporary feminism, and which are discussed in the next chapter.

Notes

1. The following material was obtained from this interview and a profile of Thandi which was published in *The Weekly Mail* of 23.3.1989 and 31.3.1989.
2. Klaas de Jonge was eventually arrested. He managed to escape to the Dutch Embassy in Pretoria, where he spent two years before being deported in an international exchange of prisoners which included Wynand du Toit.
3. The important question of the relation between masculinity and militarism in traditional African cultures is not explored here. This – and the role of circumcision, which has been compared to conscription – urgently requires research.
4. Other white women who became ANC activists have met a fate worse than prison. Jeanette Curtis and Ruth First were both killed by parcel bombs sent by South African agents.
5. One woman ECC activist, Janet Cherry, was detained for two years.
6. The 'Moroka action' involved a protest march to the Moroka police station in Soweto, where it was believed some 300 children – some as young as 12 years old – were being detained.
7. Sometimes the content of that resistance has echoed and reinforced such roles. For example, the wording of the appeal from the International Women's Suffrage Alliance in 1914 to avoid war: 'In this terrible hour, when the fate of Europe depends on decisions which women have no power to shape, we, realizing our responsibilities as the mothers of the race, cannot stand passively by. Powerless though we are politically, we call upon the governments and powers of our several countries to avert the threatened unparalleled disaster,' (cited by Orr, 1983: 11)
8. Schirmer has written of this contradictory process in the repressive military societies of Latin America:
   'Paradoxically, ... the military in these societies preach traditional family values and valorize motherhood in an attempt to strengthen patriarchal rule in the home.

This insistence upon the women's sacrifice and obedience to the family and to her children has backfired on the military as women have demanded to know what has happened to their sons and daughters. The clandestine nature of forced disappearance has unintentionally politicized the family because of the state's refusal to acknowledge either death or life. As a result these women have launched actions of civil disobedience and placed themselves at risk at a time when there has been virtually no other visible protest against the regimes. This contradictory doctrine of at once valorizing and destroying the family has made their resistance possible: they have had to behave as mothers in order to survive (Schirmer, 1989: 6).

9. Beale *et al.* (1987) analysed the role of UDF mothers in the Durban struggle in the mid-1980s, where many women showed exceptional courage in support of their activist children in the face of police harassment. These authors conclude that the involvement of these women in the struggle falls within the boundaries of their traditional roles as mothers – supporting and protecting their children.

10. Conventional notions of resistance tend to exclude women generally. The outcome is that much of women's role in resistance is unknown. Despite Trotsky's admission, it is often forgotten that it was a strike by women textile workers that initiated the revolutionary events which brought down the Czarist government in Russia in 1917. Gandhi is famous for inspiring passive resistance, but Gandhi himself was inspired by the deeds of the suffrage militants in the formative years of his own programme of non-violent action.

11. Sometimes there has been an explicit revolutionary commitment to sexual equality. For example Marshal Tito had high praise for women in the ranks of his Yugoslav Partisans. Their presence 'confirmed the quest of women for emancipation' and 'inspired the men to heroism'. Often 'the women were braver than the men, perhaps because the very fact of joining the army and the revolution constituted a greater turning point for them, (quoted by Elshtain, 1987: 177).

12. For example the mobilization of Britain during World War Two and the way women's gains were eroded as the post-war social order was re-established along patriarchal lines.

6

The feminists and
the militarists

Questions about women's rights and responsibilities have a sharp
pertinency in contemporary South Africa. Does equal rights mean equal
responsibilities, including military service for women? Should such
military service include combat roles? Should women engage in military defence in a just society? Should women engage in violent resistance in an unjust society?

The extension of conscription to white women was seriously considered by the SADF in the 1970s. On the rare occasions that the issue
has been raised in public debate in the eighties, it has provoked controversy. For example the leader of the right-wing 'Kappie Kommando'
organization, Mrs Marie van Zyl, has expressed concern that young
white girl conscripts could be used as prostitutes. She issued a statement
challenging the then Prime Minister, Mr P.W. Botha, to guarantee that
if young girls were 'forced' to join a multiracial army, it would not be
'for the purpose of prostitution'. Her concern did not relate only to the
possibility of interracial sex. She has also been reported as saying that
'only lower class women' joined the Defence Force during World War
Two, and were 'used for prostitution' (*Rand Daily Mail* 24.3.1982).[1]

In 1990, introducing the debate on the defence vote in parliament,
the Minister of Defence suggested that it was time to give consideration
to drawing national servicemen from men and *even women* [my em-
phasis] from all population groups.

At present the ideological construction of defence force 'manpower'
in gender- and race-specific terms is being restructured. While the
commanding heights of the SADF are exclusively white, an increasing
number of blacks are being incorporated at the lowest ranks. There are
reports that more 'coloured' and Indian people are applying for voluntary service than the SADF can handle. A debate has begun about the
integration of the SADF and MK into a new South African army. There
has been no public mention of the place of women in this new army.
The experience of Namibia is disturbing in this respect. It has been

reported that no women who had served in Swapo's military wing (Plan) or in the South West African Territorial Force have been incorporated into the new integrated Namibian Defence Force (*The Namibian* 26.4.1990).

This chapter explores some of the different understandings of the issue that emerge firstly from a selection of feminist writing, and secondly from 50 interviews with different South African women, including soldiers in both the SADF and MK.

Theorizing feminism and militarism

> I am not going to advise women to turn their distaff into a musket, though I sincerely wish to see the bayonet converted into a pruning hook.
>
> *(Wollstonecraft, 1967: 219)*

In *A Vindication of the Rights of Woman* (1792), Mary Wollstonecraft raised a question that is logically at the cutting edge of contemporary feminism 200 years later. She argued for equal rights for women, but emphasized that this did not imply their equal right to bear arms. She assumed that the vocation of motherhood exempted women from arms-bearing.

> Militarism involves more than conscription and the practice of war. It has been defined as a set of attitudes and social practices which regards war and the preparation of war as a normal and desirable social activity. This is a broader definition than is common among scholars. It qualifies people other than John Wayne as militarists. But in an age when war threatens our survival it is as well to understand any behaviour, however mild in appearance, which makes war seem either natural or desirable.
>
> *(Mann, 1987: 35)*

The role of women in militarization has been largely obscured and mystified by two competing perspectives – those of sexism and feminism. Both analyses exclude women from war on the grounds that they are bearers of 'special qualities'. Sexism excludes women from the ranks of the military on the grounds of their physical inferiority and unsuitability for fighting. As the weaker sex, women must be 'protected' and 'defended'. One variant of feminism similarly excludes women, but on opposite grounds, that of their innate nurturing qualities, their creativity and pacifism. The outcome of both positions is that war is understood as a totally male affair, and the military as a patriarchal institution from which women are excluded and by whom women are often victimized. The military is viewed as the last bastion of male power, war as its last preserve.

The reality is that during this century women have increasingly been incorporated into the armed forces (see Chapter four). This trend is related to a number of factors, including the women's liberation movement. The ideology of this movement – feminism – is complex, varied, and contains contradictory perspectives. Analytically, a feminist perspective recognizes gender as a significant social relation which structures our social experience so that women have distinctive and specific experiences. Of course gender is not the only, or even the most significant, social relation which shapes the social world. In South Africa particularly, it is impossible to overlook the importance of class and race.

Politically feminism is splintered by deep divisions. The main line of cleavage is between liberal or equal rights feminists, who want equality for women with men within the existing order, and those who want an alternative order. The last category has generated an intense debate between radical feminists, who envisage this alternative order as based on 'female values', and Marxist and socialist feminists who see it as based on socialism.[2] Equal rights feminism stresses women's rights to achievement, power, and opportunity (within the world as it is presently constructed) – the rights to make both money and war. Equal rights implies equal obligations and responsibilities. In this sense, compulsory universal military service is tied to the concept of citizenship.[3] Consequently some liberal or equal rights feminists claim the right of women to serve in the armed forces. They maintain that the exclusion of women from war is linked to their exclusion from economic and political affairs. They deny any linkage of women with 'peace', asserting that women are no more or less peaceful and compassionate than men. They demand the reworking of gender roles, and call into question the traditional notion of 'femininity'. Equal rights feminists sometimes assert that women are as capable as men in combat roles. Access to combat roles demonstrates women's capacities for independence and action in the world.

In contrast to equal rights feminism, radical feminism asserts that women have 'special qualities'. Such qualities – rooted by some in biology, and by others in social practices – mean that women respond to war very differently to men. This 'special qualities' thesis was eloquently argued by Virginia Woolf. In the great text of pacifist feminism, *Three Guineas* (published in 1937), she argues that men and women are different. Men are more drawn to bellicosity. The emotions of aggressive pride and arrogant patriotism which in her view lead to war, do not take hold of women as deeply as they do men. This is rooted in women's exclusion from male-dominated institutions and values. The rallying cry to defend 'our country' does not have the same resonance among women, precisely because women have too little stake in the country's wealth and power to consider the sacrifice of lives to be justified.[4] Prevention of war, in Woolf's argument, would require the dismantling of the entire gender system, the desegregation of male and female spheres, and the depolarization of masculinity and femininity. Men would have to emancipate themselves from the notion that war was a necessary proving ground for 'manly qualities' (Woolf, 1938: 8). Her pacifist feminism sought equality beween the sexes not through admitting women to combat, but rather through liberating men from militarism. In Woolf's argument it is fundamentally sexism – women's exclusion from access to power and resources – that generates their 'special qualities'.

By contrast, the biological understanding of the 'special qualities' thesis is usually anchored in women's reproductive capacity. Women are viewed as 'the mothers of the race' and therefore 'the peace-loving sex'. There is believed to be a necessary link between mothering and a tendency towards peacefulness and responsibility to others; a natural caring for creatures whose well-being is at risk.Vera Brittain promulgated such an essentialist notion of natural female pacifism. (However, her diaries and letters of 1914-18 show she was torn between patriotism and pacifism.) Brittain endorsed Olive Schreiner's argument that, if women had political power, they would never let their children, whom they bear in anguish, go to war. She asserted that 'war violates a profound biological urge in women'. In her *Women and War*, Olive Schreiner argued that the mothers of the race have a special responsibility as well as a special power to oppose combat. She characterized a callousness toward life and death as 'instinctual' in men of certain cultures:

'It is a fine day, let us go out and kill something' cries the typical male of certain races, instinctively. 'There is a living thing, it will die if it is not cared for', says the average woman, almost equally instinctively.
(Schreiner, 1911: 176)

Men and women, in her view, put a different value on human life. She was suggesting a close linkage between being a woman and pacifism. Because women give birth to life, they have a special responsibility to help preserve it. Therefore there is an incompatibility between mothering and militarism.

This argument seems to imply that women have a greater sensitivity to human life and that this means a moral superiority. For example, Soper gives women a special authority on these grounds:

> by virtue of their role in human reproduction, their [women's] statements are given the authority of experience that men do not have. Some of these experiences match in their crude biological vitality the crude wreck of biology that would be the experience of nuclear war. The starkness of the contrast between the event of conception and the event which irradiates the womb, between the act of giving birth and the act which evaporates the child: this is something which women owe it to the world to talk about.
> *(Soper, in Thompson, 1983: 170-1)*

An irony in this kind of feminist thinking is that it may easily side with those men who would exclude women from militarism and war on the grounds of their biological capacity to 'stay home, have babies, and keep the home fires burning for the boys on the border'. This biological view posits women's child-bearing capacity as of overriding importance. Reproduction is women's incomparable and unique contribution as citizens to their state.

There is a biological reductionism at work in both the sexist and feminist arguments here that finds resonance in the dominant ideologies of masculinism. But there are other grounds on which much contemporary and historical feminism asserts that there is a necessary connection between feminism and anti-militarism. It has frequently been argued that militarism is the root cause of women's oppression.[5] 'Masculinity' is said to be associated with the patriarchal values of dominance, power, aggression, and violence. By contrast, feminist values are said to be peace, nurture, sensitivity, justice, and equality. These qualities are not 'natural', but a product of socialization. It was shown above that military training is a crucial agency of this socialization (see Chapter three). Men are socialized into a conception of masculinity that is violent:

> Military training is socialization into masculinity carried to extremes.
> *(Roberts, 1984: 197)*

The notion of 'combat' is the fulcrum of this process. 'Combat' is the key dimension in the development of the masculinity-militarism nexus. Combat is presented as fundamental to the development of manhood and male superiority (Enloe, 1983). Only in combat lies the ultimate test of a man's masculinity. The image of manhood inculcated through combat training hinges on aggression and dominance; it involves an emotional disconnection and an impacted sexuality (Eisenhart, 1975). Through combat the man affirms his role as protector and defender. In this sense the exclusion of women from combat roles is essential for maintaining the ideological structure of patriarchy. It has been documented how military combat training uses woman-hating as part of its method of turning men into soldiers, a process in which the individual must learn to dehumanize other people and make them into targets. Therefore there is said to be a necessary connection between feminism and anti-militarism.[6]

The experience of Nazi Germany is relevant to this debate about feminism and militarism. Recent scholarship suggests that women were not a major force against the militarization of German society. Koonz (1987) argues that there were elements of Nazi ideology that were attractive to some aspects of feminist sensibility. She demonstrates that in reality women contributed to the horrors of the Third Reich. Nazi women

> resolutely turned their heads away from assaults against socialists, Jews, religious dissenters, the handicapped, and 'degenerates'. They gazed instead at their own cradles, children and 'Aryan' families. Mother and wives ... made a vital contribution to Nazi power by preserving the illusion of love in an environment of hatred, just as men sustained the image of order in the utter disarray of conflicting bureaucratic and military priorities and commands.
> *(Koonz, 1987: 17)*

This is a crucial insight. Koonz's study means the loss of

> the idea that there is something about femaleness that can insulate us from Nazism and its like. For 200 years, one strain of feminism has emphasized the moral superiority of women. This is not necessarily a biologistic view; many modern feminists believe that women have been made different from men, but that these differences are nevertheless deep and thorough. Women have been acculturated, they argue, to be more nurturing, less violent, less aggressive, more co-operative than men. The history of Nazi women belies or at least

limits such views: there were many women responsible for substantial brutality, and many more enthusiastically supported men's brutality.
(Gordon, 1987: 100)

The debate about the relation between feminism and militarism must be informed by such historical evidence. Whether one's interest in this debate is to prevent war or to achieve gender equality, the question revolves around how to deconstruct masculinity; how to break the militarism-masculinity nexus. The answer hinges on two more concrete questions:

● Should women be conscripted?
● Should women serve in combat roles?

A number of contemporary feminists and anti-militarists have argued that women should be conscripted. For example Ruddick, writing as a feminist and an anti-militarist, proposes conscripting women in the interests of peace, partly to break the connection between masculinity and militarism. She views women as 'different', as having pacific qualities. Hence her argument hinges on the assumption that women soldiers would behave differently to men and would alter the nature of armies and wars. Similarly Reardon (1983) has argued that militarism in general is expressive of a masculine ideology. Therefore if women were included in the policy-making process, feminine notions of defence and national security could bring about a more peaceful and less militarized world. Also it is suggested that the presence of women in combat units blurs and decreases the harshness of military life. It perhaps lessens the brutalization of young men thrown into an all-male society for months on end. One could thus argue for women soldiers as an agency of degendering the military and loosening the militarism/masculinity connection. The function of the military and combat as a masculine proving ground will be eroded if women are fully integrated into the military. A man cannot prove he is a man by doing something that a woman can do.

The current global situation is that 75 countries world-wide practise conscription, including all Warsaw Pact and most Nato countries. Despite assertions of equality, women are conscripted in only three countries – Mali, Guinea, and Israel. Only five nations have no combat exclusion laws or policies – Canada, Denmark, Luxemburg, Norway, and Portugal. However, nowhere are women routinely utilized in combat roles.[7] Everywhere women are in the minority of armed forces:

> ... in no contemporary army, be it a liberation army, a national army or a professional army, do women participate in percentage terms to an extent even approaching that of men. In most cases women constitute no more than 5-7 percent of military personnel, often much less.
> *(Yuval-Davis, 1981: 33)*

Since Yuval-Davis wrote, the proportion of women in the US army has increased to 10 percent of an overall force of 2.1 million. (Elshtain, 1987: 241). The American experience is relevant here. It was described above how since 1972 women had been moved from their traditional confinement to health care and clerical jobs in the US army into all but 16 of the army's 377 military occupations. More and more jobs have been taken out of the 'direct combat' category so women could be used (Friedan, 1983: 177). The interpretation of this development by the leading exponent of equal rights feminism today, Betty Friedan, is interesting. Friedan defines feminism as

> a conscious campaign against sex discrimination culminating in a sex-role revolution, redefining the roles of men and women, that would lead to restructuring of work and home.
> *(Friedan, 1981: 298-9)*

According to her, the experience of integration of women at the bastion of militarist masculinity, West Point, has been positive:

> When the women entered West Point four years ago, there was a sense of ... outrage ... it was the ultimate threat to male superiority, the breaching of that last sacred fortress of masculinity. There was outrage, fear that women would lower the standards of courage, discipline and physical prowess that were the ethos of West Point ....
> *(Ibid.: 165)*

But the process has contributed, in Friedan's view, to the erosion of gender roles, and to

> the possibility of a new model of what it is to be a man, a new kind of male hero in America, as men begin to share the care of the children and home with their wives, as women share the burdens and responsibilities of earning – even the hardships and dangers and glories of military careers.
> *(Ibid.: 171)*

She suggested the initial

> hostility at women masked something more fundamental going on among the men themselves. After all, the image of what it is to be a man in America – all powerful, all dominant, superior to the whole world, tight-lipped, big-muscled, without fear or feeling, napalming the babies in Vietnam and Cambodia and the green leaves off the trees – had begun to change, after we lost the war in Vietnam.[8]
> *(Ibid.)*

Some erosion of gender roles does seems to have happened in the US Army. According to a West Point major,

> our own research shows the whole process of male identity is chan-ging – male bonding, the question of physical prowess is not so all-important.
> *(Ibid.: 180)*

Another officer said:

> There's a change in the male identity. Before women came here the way they solved this was the stereotype masks – stalwart, strapping, square-jawed John Wayne. Since the women came, the experience of male identity has become more heterogeneous; the men are not all giants roaming the plains any longer.
> *(Ibid.: 183)*

At the same time, Friedan reports that women at West Point are competent but feminine. They have not

> succumbed to the machismo role model. I came away from West Point feeling very good about those women cadets. No, they did not turn into imitation jocks, feeble or super-tough imitations of mach-ismo.
> *(Ibid.: 194)*

Instead they impressed Friedan as strong and healthy.

There are, paradoxically, elements of the radical feminist notion of women as the bearers of 'special qualities' in Friedan's argument. In her view, women soldiers would, as women, have more sensitive concern for life than do male soldiers, hence would be a force for caution and against brutality in any future war. Elshtain comments caustically that

such sentimentalism strains credulity. Women soldiers do not speak that way. They are soldiers. Period.
(Elshtain, 1987: 243)

Elshtain sees the increasing incorporation of women into the US army as

a male-forged identity being homogenized more widely. Yet in light of the fact that all too many women are still prepared to have men think and act politically on their behalf, the woman soldier, if that is the way the woman has defined herself, seems not the worst possible alternative among those now available to us ... I have reluctantly come to the position that women should be granted no automatic exemption from this feature of civil life (the draft). Involuntary, unreflective pacifism is no pacifism at all.
(Ibid.)

In 1981 the National Organization of Women (NOW) filed a legal brief as part of a challenge to all-male military registration. Beginning with the claim that compulsory, universal military service is central to the concept of citizenship in a democracy, Now supported an ideal of armed civic virtue: if women are to gain 'first-class citizenship', they too must have the right to fight. Laws excluding women from draft registration and combat duty perpetuate 'archaic notions' of women's capabilities; moreover, 'devastating long-term psychological and political repercussions' are visited upon women because of their exclusion from the military of their country (Elshtain, 1987: 239).

This is a controversial stand. According to one critic, Now's brand of equal-oppprtunity feminism functions to reinforce 'the military as an institution and militarism as an ideology' by perpetuating

the notion that the military is so central to the entire social order that it is only when women gain access to its core that they can hope to fulfil their hopes and aspirations.
(Ibid.: 239)

Both Friedan, and Woolf writing 50 years earlier, advocated the dismantling of the entire gender system and the desegregation of male and female spheres. Woolf wanted to prevent war and achieve equality between the sexes, not through admitting women to combat, but rather through liberating men from militarism. Friedan believes that female combatants are the best means of achieving this.

Feminism and militarism in South Africa

Woolf's and Friedan's ideas have a special relevance to us in South Africa. However, in our context the different understandings of the relation between feminism and militarism cannot be pegged very easily, for three main reasons. First, there is much ambivalence about the notion of feminism. There is here a widespread suspicion of feminism as bourgeois and divisive, as essentially concerned with entrenching and extending privilege. This is often true in a Third World context where issues of survival are paramount. As Kimble and Unterhalter write,

> Women of the ex-colonial world have seen much of the substance of [feminist] struggles as irrelevant to them. Women struggling to liberate themselves from the burden of oppression by imperialism – a burden which manifests itself in extreme ways through poverty, disease, genocide – appear to find little point of comparison between their own goals and the concerns of Western women. For them, Western women represent a privileged middle-class élite fighting for sectarian aims, while women in national liberation struggles are fighting on behalf of their whole people.[9]
> *(Kimble and Unterhalter, 1982: 12)*

But paradoxically, the notion of 'equal rights' for women has had an important place in many national liberation struggles. This is true of the South African struggle, and in our context 'equal rights for women' is a revolutionary call. It is revolutionary because it involves the transformation of the existing order. The idea is thus quite different to the liberal variant of feminism of advanced industrial societies, which is essentially conservative and concerned with equality between men and women within the existing order. In a Third World context this 'revolutionary feminism' is frequently militarist: it asserts women's equal right with men to take up arms against repression and injustice.

The third peculiar ingredient in the South African context is thus the militarization of the national liberation struggle since 1961. It was shown in the previous chapter how the armed struggle was launched in that year as a response to increasing state violence and the shrinking space for non-violent political activity by the ANC. MK included women as well as men, and they trained together. A commitment to 'equal rights for women', as well as the widespread acceptance of the legitimacy of the armed struggle and the notion of a 'just war,' means that the Western connection between feminism and pacifism is loosened in the South African context. In fact the female soldier, the MK guerrilla, is a popular mass image of the strong, liberated woman. No thread of strong, well-articulated pacifist-feminism emerged from the interviews for this study.[10]

In South Africa different positions on the relation between feminism and militarism depend on broader understandings of the nature of political conflict in South Africa. Attitudes towards conscription, armies and war are embedded in much larger constellations of beliefs and values. The debate thus taps deep-seated feelings on a wide range of issues. Different conceptions of 'war' and 'woman' were at the centre of the different understandings of the relation between feminism and militarism articulated by the women interviewed in this study:

Neither women nor war is a self-evident category.
(Elshtain, 1987: x)

'War' is our dominant symbol of violence. 'Woman' is our dominant symbol of home. 'Woman' is usually defined, even in very different cultural contexts, to embody values and virtues that are at variance with the violence of war. Different perceptions of 'women' and 'war' generated very different conceptions of 'feminism' and different positions on the conscription of women.

Different positions on the conscription of women

1. Women should be conscripted but treated differently to men.
This position advocates that the state should extend conscription to women but use them in different capacities to men.[11] In other words, men and women have equal rights but different responsibilities and duties. This includes the opinions that women should be utilized in non-combat roles in the SADF, and the view that women should be utilized in non-military service administered by the SADF. A minority of informants held this position. Among them was a high-ranking woman in the SADF:

Women should be conscripted into the SADF for one year. They could work as nurses and teachers and farm workers, as they did in Germany after Hitler. Women should get some training, and they could learn to serve …. Also our children don't learn community service at school. They are all for themselves … I don't feel for women's lib. Femininity is the most important thing for a woman to keep in any job. The SADF and the SAP attracted women with no

femininity and gave them authority. We had to be very careful when we interviewed. We had to watch out for lesbians, and this was a difficult thing. Lesbianism is not against the law. I'm not a feminist. Feminists look down on everything feminine. But I like an assertive, intellectual woman.
(Informant 14)

Another powerful, white, middle-class woman, who was a member of the President's Council when interviewed, said:

Women should do service in hospitals, crèches, and old age homes. They could learn how to treat their mothers-in-law and things like that that they need to know in later life. I punted the idea in government circles in the early 1970s and got an enormously positive response. Women leave school without being prepared for life. The government thought it was a good idea for white girls to perform some service to the community, but they also thought it was too expensive. Certainly girls can't be soldiers. There's nothing more ridiculous than women in the USA doing press-ups with the men. I value being a woman …. No, I'm not a feminist, though I've never felt anything but liberated. Those militant American women feminists frighten me. Germaine Greer is pathetic. And overall feminists frighten men. They don't achieve anything. My philosophy is not to work against power, but to work with it.
(Informant 25)

A white working-class woman informant said,

No, I don't think national service is necessary if we want equality with men. But I don't want to have to change the tyre on my car. I want the system to work for me. I like a lot of the role-playing …. No, I'm not a feminist. I don't particularly want to be a lumberjack.
(Informant 10)

2. Women should be conscripted and treated the same as men.
Again a minority of informants believed this. Informants' reasons for supporting this position varied enormously: for some, women's participation in the military was necessary for achieving gender equality; for others, it was necessary for changing the nature of war and eroding male violence; for others, universal military training could be an effective homogenizing agent in what they viewed as a dangerously diverse society – an exercise in nation-building – a means of overcoming both racism and sexism.

An African woman who had served an eight-year prison sentence for her role as an MK guerrilla believed that women should be conscripted and treated exactly the same as men:

People must know there's a war on. We have to fight. But I wouldn't call myself a feminist. I'm proud to be a woman. I can do most things a man can do. But I wouldn't go about burning my bras. Feminists really want to be men. Feminists are unfeminine. But it's true that men oppress women. Deep down all men think alike. They just see us women as objects they can amuse themselves with. One man said to me, 'I love your brain'. He wanted to put me on display. The African man is only a man if he can provide for his family. The bigger the family, the bigger the man. Today he can't do this, so he takes it out on his woman. But actually apartheid causes male violence. The solution is to end apartheid first and then to educate men.
(Informant 4)

The achievement this woman is most proud of is 'becoming a guerrilla' and the South Africans she most admires are Dorothy Nyembe and Albertina Sisulu.

Several informants asserted that equal rights meant identical responsibilities. One informant, who is a 20-year-old white university student, asserted this strongly:

Women as well as men should be conscripted, but they should have non-military alternatives. The army shouldn't distinguish between men and women. Women should have the choice of combat roles. The Israeli exclusion of women from combat roles is an expression of sexism. Sexism is acute in Israel [which she has visited twice]. However, there's no sexual harassment within the Israeli Defence Force. There's a huge respect for women. Yes, I'm a feminist in the sense that I believe in equal rights. But I shave under my arms. Fundamentally I'm a socialist ... this is a revolutionary thing. Working towards freedom and socialism is the centre of my life. Violence is necessary to achieve freedom. A revolution doesn't come about by passive reform. Armed struggle can help force people through fear into realizing the need to negotiate. But many more people will have to be killed. A revolution means innocent people being killed .... Yes, I could kill someone. Women are not less aggressive than men. Aggression is a socialized concept. There is no difference beween Israeli men and women in relation to their capacity for violence. To me, being a woman means being an equal.
(Informant 13)

Another informant, a middle-class white academic in her thirties who describes herself as a radical feminist, was also in favour of conscription for women, on the grounds that it would alter the nature of war. Both men and women soldiers would behave differently. Women would give more gentleness to the role of soldier, and the male soldier's role would be less violent:

> At the moment the macho image is very strong. It's unchallenged in the all-male environment of the army. There's a disproportionate emphasis on physical strength, and on women as the 'weaker sex'. Men are socialized into the idea of being protectors – of protecting the wife and kids – keeping the home fires safe. But what if the home fires come with you? The whole notion of the battlefield, of the boundaries between combat and support, would be redrawn.
> *(Informant 15)*

Another informant said,

> Yes, I believe in conscription for both men and women because I'm a feminist. Feminism means openness. Women and men shouldn't be trapped in stereotypes. Some form of military service has to be compulsory, but there should be space for objectors to do community service. This should apply to women as well. Women are capable of being combat soldiers. Men are more aggressive, but because they've been socialized into it. Society builds on the connection between being a soldier and being a man. It should be the ablest, strongest and healthiest members of our society who protect us – and that should include both men and women.
> *(Informant 12)*

A woman who left South Africa in 1980 to join the ANC because 'I felt I had no other option' said,

> Yes, women should be participants in armed struggle. Women should be used in combat roles. It's important for women to participate in all aspects of the struggle. Then they are one of the forces which create the new society. There should be an element of choice, but our army (MK) is a voluntary army. There's an element of democratic practice even in our army .... Being in the army is crucial for women's emancipation. There are two reasons why the issue of women's emancipation has to be tackled now: without it you won't tap the revolutionary energy of women, and women will continue to

be oppressed after the revolution. But then I'm a feminist. Most ANC people see feminism as divisive. Anti-feminism is pretty fixed position. Only three women out of 30 NEC members are women. The movement doesn't really take the issue seriously.
(Informant 6)

3. Women should not be conscripted into military service.

This was the dominant position held by 90 per cent of informants. According to one informant, who is a 37-year-old, white professor:

> Yes, I am a feminist if this means developing your abilities. No, women should not have to do military service. For women to penetrate military power would be too small an advancement. Women should rather focus on economic power. The American feminists were right to go after power and influence, but have almost parked their femininity. They have drawn too sharp a line between femininity and feminism. I am committed to knowledge and expertise as a power base.
> *(Informant 3)*

The South African this informant most admires is Harry Oppenheimer.

A woman who achieved exceptionally high rank within the SADF at the age of 37, listed three reasons why she was opposed to conscription for women:

> Firstly, it would be disastrous from a geographical point of view. There are enormous differences between South Africa and Israel. Israel is tiny – girls can visit their homes over weekends. Here girls hitch-hiking would be in danger of rape and so on. Secondly, it would be bad from a morale point of view. The situation would have to have deteriorated if women have to be forced to do military service. At the thought of it one can almost hear the waves breaking behind your back. It would almost be acknowledging defeat to have to resort to using women.
>
> Thirdly, it would create a lot of social problems. Israel has the highest rate of illegitimacy in the world … girls often fall pregnant to avoid military service. In Israel the detention barracks are full of girls who refuse to do military service. We have no detention barracks for women here ….
>
> P.W. Botha was keen on promoting women. There was a crisis in defence force manpower in South Africa at the end of the 1970s. Also women did so well. People felt that the experience and training at George was good for girls. It made them more mature and

responsibile. Many parents thought it was a good thing. Military training teaches you self-discipline, planning, time utilization.
(Informant 11)

This informant was keen to promote voluntary service in the SADF. However, she thought women should not normally serve in combat roles:

Our personnel philosophy within the SADF is not to utilize women in the eyes of the enemy. Now there are enough men to do the fighting. But if manpower shortages require, we women can fight and defend ourselves. Our history has proved that we can fight. I believe in equal rights and equal opportunities for women if it serves the ultimate aim. The ultimate aim of the SADF is to win the land battle. I'm not a women's libber in the sense that I want to prove women can achieve. But I am a women's libber in the sense that productivity and effectiveness count. I want the best person to be given the opportunity to get the job.
(Ibid.)

A very different woman, a 49-year-old white, middle-class anti-apartheid activist, who is divorced with two children, also believed that women should not be conscripted:

War is a male affair from which women are excluded. Women should speak out much more strongly against war. The trouble is that there's a glamorous side to war …. We women should be working for a society that doesn't have an army. National service accepts the male way of doing things. Women shouldn't have to do it to prove a point about equality …. Yes, I'm a feminist … I'm committed to changing attitudes and speaking out about things which appear to be abusive of women. I think feminism is about the right to choices, asserting better ways of doing things than the traditional male ways. Women mustn't just model men. We don't want to be mini-men or equal men. Feminism needs to be a total transformation.
(Informant 20)

A 48-year-old white, Afrikaans-speaking woman, who is a Nationalist Party member of parliament, was also opposed to conscription for women:

It would not be practical for women to do national service. What if they fall pregnant? And anyway we have more coloured and Indian volunteers for the SADF than we can cope with at present. There's certainly no need to conscript women.

(Informant 1)

However, she believes that women have an important role to play in support services:

Women should be, and are, in the majority of the welfare services. Men are at the top because women are afraid of taking responsibility.

(Ibid.)

This informant is unclear about whether to define herself as a feminist:

I have a problem with equal rights. You and I are equal in worthiness, but not in capabilities or in status. Equal rights and responsibilities have to be played off against individual differences. I'm not a woman's libber. The women's libbers are too aggressive and foolish. I'm thinking of the women who burned important pieces of clothing and thought that would liberate them. At my age I need that piece of clothing. The force of gravity works against me. I'm a people's libber. I believe in individual choice. Men and women are different. It's important for a girl to be pretty. Appearance is important. It's important to me to be feminine – it makes me feel normal ... Women look at things from a different angle. Women are more concerned with life and peace. Like a little kitten that you take in and save from drowning. But in black culture it's different.

(Ibid.)

A 'peace activist' was also opposed to conscription into military service for both men and women. However, she supported the idea of compulsory, non-military national service for everyone – men and women, white and black – in a post-apartheid South Africa:

On a day-to-day level men display more aggressive behaviour than women. But I don't believe that men are innately more aggressive than women; they are socialized into competitiveness and aggression. Their six weeks of basic training in the army plays an important part in this. Of course women are physically and psychologically capable of becoming combat soldiers. The Israeli women soldiers prove this. But the whole military system is wrong. Our politics is very male ... people are needing to own, possess and dominate.

I'm a pacifist, but I don't fall into any clear political model. I struggle to put myself in a box, but essentially I'm a socialist feminist.

I understand that to be a world-view that's concerned with freedom and justice for everyone. Actually I think it was my Christianity that catapulted me into feminism. As a feminist it alarms me to see how women co-operate with the system. There are more and more women in the power structure. But they act like men. That's the one problem. The other problem is that most women (even progressive ones) think it is part of men's responsibility to protect and defend them. They demand a defending role from men. I'm a physically strong person. I can beat many men at arm wrestling .... I can change a car tyre and bake a cake ...

In a post-apartheid South Africa we should have a small professional army and a system of national service. Compulsory national service for everyone would teach people responsibility, and a sense of national pride. As a patriot I think that's important.
(Informant 35)

A black South African who left the country in 1980, spent a year in MK training camps in Angola, and is now in a senior position in the ANC's diplomatic mission, is strongly committed to equality for women and opposed to conscription:

War and armies discriminate by excluding women. In the new South Africa, if we are to have an army, women must be part of it. They must be volunteers, not conscripts. The ANC is against conscription. Women should be in combat roles .... We can still retain our femininity. That's important to me .... But no, equal rights does mean equal responsibilities. We can't have the one without the other .... Within a volunteer, professional army, women should be used in combat roles. Within MK, men and women are treated equally.
(Informant 5)

A similar viewpoint was expressed by another member of the ANC, who believed that

it is sexist to exclude women from combat roles. MK is very sexist in its deployment of women.
(Informant 48)

A very different woman, who was a high-ranking officer in the SADF, head of the SADF college for women at George for ten years, and part of the delegation to Israel to investigate the possibility of conscripting white women into the SADF, was also opposed to conscription for women:

Women are only any good if they volunteer. What do you do to punish a woman? Men do press-ups. What do you do with girls? People who are forced will do more harm than good, even in hospitals. I don't think conscientious objectors should be in the army, even in hospitals.

The question of volunteers is quite different. At the SADF women's college at George, the girls developed, but then the kind of girl who applied was a very superior kind of girl. For example Ruda Landman was head girl. About 900 applied every year from which we selected only 220. The girls who were chosen were very good at sport, study, and had leadership qualities. But they also learned leadership qualities through their training. The training was tough ....
However, women should not be used in combat roles. Having to go out and kill is not good. I've seen what it's done to my youngest son – it's made him a split personality. I'd hate to see women split in that way. Killing causes psychological problems. Women are gentler – their whole social upbringing is towards that.

I believe in equal rights but you shouldn't put women and men together. The problem of sexuality won't go away. Yes, equal rights, does mean equal responsibilities, but not killing. I'm not an ardent feminist, but I do think women should not be discriminated against in the workplace, or harassed because of their sex, and helped in the home.
(Informant 7)

This informant confessed that she had experienced a lot of problems with men within the SADF who 'didn't want to accept my rank'.

An informant who had attended the George Army College during this woman's principalship was also opposed to conscription for women:

No, I'm strongly against conscription for girls. While I was at the George Army College my best friend there had a nervous breakdown. She had a very serious depression, she developed a stutter and became overweight. She had to be taken to a mental hospital. The army did nothing good for her, in fact it was really damaging. That's why I'm against conscription for girls. Girls are too fragile.
(Informant 16)

A white grandmother in her sixties was opposed to conscription for women and described herself as a pacifist:

I've always been a pacifist. I resolved at the age of 20 that I wouldn't let my sons go into the army. My two sons left South Africa because

they wouldn't go into SADF, and my main reason for emigrating to Australia next year is to be nearer my children. I also feel very ineffectual here. No, I don't see any connection between being a soldier and being a man. The slogan 'Let the army make a man of you' reflects a kind of brainwashing. If you have to prove your manhood through killing, it's a pretty sad state of affairs. War is about power, and people have to be taught aggression. Killing is not natural. People have to be made to feel that the enemy is not human, but evil and needing to be punished, or raped or killed.
(Informant 8)

A well-known Afrikaner women, who has published four books of essays and is 'a leader of my people', believes women should not be conscripted:

Women should have equal rights and that does mean equal responsibilities, but women shouldn't be conscripted. Women can't be sent to the battlefield. But women could be used as volunteers in the intelligence part. If you put a woman in a uniform and give her a gun and tell her to kill, that's wrong. Woman was created to give life, not to take life. Women have mother instincts. Women were born to have children. Women are less violent than men, but violent women shame the men. During 1984-6, black women were very violent. But black people have a different outlook to whites, and different attitudes to violence. They've always fought. They use knives a lot; they don't stop; they're much more violent than the white race. Blacks are a different race. We have totally different cultures; there are many things we don't understand about each other. Integration will never work here. In no African country are whites treated equally. There's corruption in all those governments. Black men cannot handle power. They're not responsible enough for power.

... No, there's no such thing as right-wing violence; violence comes from the mad ones. Afrikaners value freedom above everything. Everything we've done in our history was for freedom. Now we acknowledge the need for change, but we want to govern ourselves; we want our own country. We are no terrorists, but we are prepared to fight for our own country. We will declare a war in a decent way. There's definitely no such thing as right-wing violence ....
(Informant 17)

This informant believes in 'the Boshoff option'. Professor Boshoff, a son-in-law of Dr Verwoed, hopes to establish an Afrikaner homeland in an isolated desert region around Upington.

The Karel Boshoff option is the one which I prefer. We want the Orange River and the Karoo ... we want to include the Orange River development. The trouble is that we Afrikaners are divided about what we want. There's the CP, the Boshoff option and the Boerestaat option. But on one thing we are all united. We want our own country and our own freedom. That's our bottom line. We'll die for that. We're like the Zulus and the Xhosas – they will also want to have their own country ... I cannot see peace in the next ten years. The greatest danger is that the big powers will intervene ...

I'm not a feminist – they're too militarist. I don't have to fight men to show that I'm equal. My husband and I share decisions and money. But in most Afrikaner homes men have the power and authority ... I didn't grow up feeling that I was inferior. I was orphaned when I was ten, but I went on to become a teacher. I wanted to become a learned person. We Afrikaners were brought up believing we had to study because of the black people – because of their great numbers. We had to be their intellectual masters. Also there was the attempt to Anglicize us after the Boer War.
(Ibid.)

One informant who is a political prisoner was also opposed to conscription for women, though she thought equal rights does mean equal responsibilities for military service:

With the present level of technology I do not believe that physical strength is a determining criterion for being a combatant. Within the armed forces men and women may be better suited to different kinds of work, but I feel a lot of the supposed 'physical inability' of women is because from childhood we are pampered and 'protected' from physical strain (barring childbirth of course) ... I don't think men are particularly psychologically capable of being combat soldiers – they are socialized to be such. Aggression, and defence of self and of group are basic animal instincts, and I do not believe that aggression is a *male* instinct .... Both men and women are capable of aggression, compassion, sensitivity, caring. We are socialized to either develop or suppress these different aspects, resulting in what we superficially define as 'male characteristics' and 'female characteristics'. I hope that the new man and the new woman of the future will have the personal freedom to develop both sides of their personalities – and that society will have progressed to a stage of peace in which the aggressive, militaristic side of life is diminished ...

The apparent connection between war and masculinity is a product of the history of societies and the way in which the dominant ideologies have entrenched a particular image of men and a particular image of war. It's not an automatic, inherent or natural connection .... No, I'm not a feminist. I am a Marxist-Leninist committed to participatory democracy, women's emancipation and an end to exploitation, all of which are only fully realizable under socialism.

... I think there should be some kind of system for expanding the standing army in times of war – a volunteer procedure or a ballot draft. I am tempted to suggest that in a post-apartheid South Africa there should be some form of national service – democratically decided on of course. And by national service I do not mean military service. I mean some form of service that would train citizens to fulfil civil responsibilities – be it development projects, disaster relief work, work in community programmes – and I think this should include some basic defence training. Whether this is compulsory or voluntary is basically for the people to decide. However, with the amount of reconstruction work that faces this nation, I would call for people to make it compulsory ... I, as a woman citizen of a democratic South Africa in an international war situation, would volunteer for the armed forces and would be prepared to sacrifice my life if necessary. More than that, I would do what I could to rally women, to maximize women's involvement in the war effort without stipulating what specifically women or men should do. War must cease to be seen as a 'male affair'; it should become an unpleasant necessity for a nation to defend itself.

(Informant 49)

The last two quotations reflect the vastly different ideologies to which informants subscribed. This diversity clearly reflects the informants' different understandings and experiences of war and the military. The relation between feminism and militarization is a complex one, and one about which many women feel an acute ambivalence. The dominant position expressed by informants was that women should not be conscripted. This position was adopted by extremely diverse women, ranging from SADF colonels to MK cadres. It was paradoxically informed both by a commitment to equal rights (in the Betty Friedan tradition) and by a notion of women as 'different', as having 'special qualities' (in the tradition of Olive Schreiner).

No strong thread of pacifist feminism emerged from the interviews. Only one informant described herself as a pacifist, and none mentioned

Emily Hobhouse. A woman political prisoner implied that pacifism was a self-indulgent avoidance of reality:

> Pacifism is a refusal to particpate in war. It's a belief that I cannot identify with at all. Until society has developed to a level of civilization where world peace is realizable, war is a fact of life, and to say 'I will not participate in a war' is to avoid dealing with the harsh reality of life.
> *(Informant 49)*

There are several paradoxical themes at work here. For example there is a rejection of the *label* of 'feminism' in the case of both the SADF colonel and the MK cadre, but not its *content*. Furthermore, 'feminism' is sometimes claimed as the reason for both supporting and opposing conscription for women:

> Yes, I believe in conscription for both men and women because I'm a feminist.
> *(Informant 12)*

> It's because I'm a feminist that I'm against conscription for women. We women don't want to identify with men. Nor do we want to compete with them. Equality with men must stem from an acceptance and respect for the ways in which we're different from men.
> *(Informant 9)*

Conclusion

This chapter has argued that militarization is a feminist issue. All that has been attempted here is to peg out the field, to identify some of the different understandings of the issue that emerged from interviews with diverse South African women. All that is asserted is that we have to confront some difficult questions:

- Will the conscription of women serve the cause of peace by loosening the connection between militarism and masculinity?
- Will the conscription of women serve the cause of equal rights by demonstrating women's strength and competence?
- Will the conscription of women mean that a male-forged identity and violent style is spread more widely and thus cements both militarist and patriarchal relations?

There is the possibility that even posing these questions reinforces the conception of the military as a social institution which is central to the entire society. There have been sociologists – notably Max Weber – who argued that the military influences all other major social institutions, including the state, the organization of work, the labour process and the family (Weber, 1968: 1153, 1155). If this is the case, then perhaps it is the military – rather than war – which is the central problem.

The experience of women in the two South African armies that were – according to their own definition – at 'war' in the 1980s is especially relevant to this debate. The SADF and MK reflect all the myriad differences between a conventional army and a guerrilla one. However, in both armies there are significant similarities in the position of women. In both the SADF and MK there was a dramatic increase in the numbers of women soldiers between 1976 and 1989. However, despite this process of increasing incorporation, in both armies women are under-represented in positions of leadership and authority, and are excluded from combat roles. This exclusion from combat may be significant, given that the experience and tradition of actual combat with the enemy is an important ingredient in MK's prestige.

Military actions are frequently eulogized by ANC as well as SADF leaders. The ANC position is evident in the NEC's statement delivered by Comrade Commander-in-Chief Oliver Tambo on Heroes' Day, 16 December 1986, on the occasion of the 25th anniversary of MK. This statement laments that

> our people had been deliberately deprived of the skills of modern warfare and denied access to weaponry.
> (Dawn, Journal of *Umkhonto we Sizwe, Souvenir Issue)*

Women have been subject to the same process of 'deprivation'. The key question is whether these 'skills' are desirable; whether this 'access' is a necessary part of equality. This question taps deep into the different hopes and aspirations of feminists. But our answer must be anchored in the understanding that modern warfare involves a level of destruction that reduces us all to victims.

Notes

1. According to the National President of the Ex-servicewomen's League in South Africa, her comments were an insult to the 28 000 South African women who took part in the war (*Rand Daily Mail*, 24.3.1982).
2. Within pacifism there is a similar division between those who accept the *status*

quo and those who do not (Stephenson, 1983). The division is between those who conceive of peace primarily as the absence of war and direct violence (Boulding, 1978; Scruton, 1988), and those who fuse peace with social justice (Galtung, 1969; 1971). In the latter conception of peace there is an absence not simply of direct violence, but of indirect, structural violence, i.e. violence which is inherent in the structures of racism, sexism and other forms of exploitation. These contrasting conceptions are sometimes termed 'negative' and 'positive' peace.

3. The connection between conscription and citizenship is still relevant. For example it surfaced in the House of Commons debate on the British Nationality Bill as late as February 1981, when Enoch Powell claimed that nationality should be transferred only through men, because 'nationality, in the last resort, is tested by fighting. A man's nationality is the nation for which he will fight.' (Cited by Gould in Higonnet and Higonnet, 1987: 125)

4. *Three Guineas* sounded a dire warning about the importance of seeing the connections between patriarchy and militarism, the identification of man with warrior. Both Hitler and Mussolini repeatedly insisted that it was 'the essence of manhood to fight', 'the nature of womanhood to heal the wounds of the fighter' (Woolf, 1966: 186). For Woolf, the 'picture of evil was the man in uniform claiming to be Man himself, the quintessence of virility' (Woolf, 1966: 142-3). That man posed the threat of war.

5. An eloquent historical statment of this causal connection is Ogden and Florence, 1915. A modern radical feminist variant is given by Russell, 1989

6. For example, 'One of the purposes of the Campaign (against militarism) is to examine the psychology of those who believe that war is worthwhile because it gives the winner power and status, increased authority, territory and security. All these are an integral part of a political and social system loaded against women and are synonymous with characteristics traditionally defined as 'masculine', such as aggression and competition. In order to hold on to this kind of power, a "male dominated" state has a military force backing it up. So in wanting to free themselves from men's oppression, women must oppose this military force too. That this military force is essentially masculine in character is acknowledged in the advertising which the armed forces use for recruiting purposes – "let the Army make a man of you"' (Orr, 1983: 5.)

Another argument is that 'feminism as a value system is the antithesis of militarism .... The non-coercive, non-hierarchical organization models being developed by feminist groups offer the most promising alternatives to militarism and other patriarchal structures (Reardon, 1983: 8, cited by Roberts, 1984: 198).

Stephenson suggests that the linkage between feminism and pacifism is central to each movement: 'This is the linkage of these feminists who reject the 'male value system', with its emphasis on dominance and power, i.e. power over or against, with those pacifists for whom non-violence includes a rejection of both direct and structural violence. The central commonality between feminists and pacifists is their opposition to oppression, whether that oppression be sexism, racism or any other oppression. In both cases this opposition to oppression is based on the empowerment of the individual, on power which is constructive rather than destructive.'

7. There is no straightforward relation between attitudes towards equal rights and women's conscription. For example a national survey in Switzerland found that Swiss women were strongly opposed to mandatory participation of women in the Swiss army. (Military service is mandatory for men, and an equal rights amendment was passed in Switzerland in 1981.) While 83.7 per cent of all women in the national survey were against any mandatory military service for women, so were 77 per cent of all men. Almost half (41.6 per cent) of the entire sample believed that participation in the military should be voluntary for both men and women.

There is also no straightforward relation between equal rights and women's position within the military. In reality the commitment to equal rights has very different outcomes for the position of women in different armies. For example in Denmark equality of the sexes does not extend to national service. All young men must serve for a year, but there is no women's draft.

On the other hand, in 1988 it was decided that women could fulfil combat roles in the Royal Danish Navy, Army, and Air Force, making Denmark the first Nato country to introduce such equality between the sexes. The decision means that they will be able to drive tanks and become parachutists, as well as commando and infantry soldiers

8. According to Ehrenreich, American men's revolt against the masculine role-model began in the 1950s (Ehrenreich, 1983).

9. In South Africa, as in other Third World contexts, not only are issues such as lesbian rights often dismissed as irrelevant, but they are sometimes the grounds on which feminism is rejected. For example in an interview Dr Ellen Khuzwayo said she did not see herself as a feminist 'because there are connotations I don't agree with – like lesbianism' (*The Star* 13.12.1990).

10. Nationalist militarism can be dangerous for women. '… militarization puts a premium on communal unity in the name of national survival, a priority which can silence women critical of patriarchal practices and attitudes; in doing so nationalist militarization can privilege men' (Enloe, 1983: 58).

11. Attitudes towards male conscripts who serve in the SADF varied very widely, and were frequently coloured by different conceptions of 'loyalty'. The issue of conscription has clearly generated conflict, particularly for mothers. One study reported 'the dilemma experienced as a result of the mothers' opposition towards conscription and their simultaneous feelings that, as mothers, they should be committed to supporting their sons' (Feinstein, 1986: 77). It is significant that in this study, 'the issue of conscription was hardly discussed by the families. Discussion between mother and son on the issue of conscription was almost non-existent. All mothers felt that their sons should be informed, but distanced themselves from the process' (*Ibid.: p.76*).

7

The victims

Lena does not know her age, but at the time she made the following sworn statement she was estimated to be in her seventies. She has eight children and 'many' grandchildren who are in high school.

I live with my husband at 71 Mazoiwe Street, Lingelihle, [the African township] in Craddock. On Saturday 3 August 1985 I saw two vehicles patrolling the streets around my house. I think they are called Hippos. In the late evening I walked to a relative's home. I was alone. A Hippo drove up behind me and stopped. Two white soldiers jumped out. One said, 'Here walks a bitch, alone at night, probably looking for a man. We'll help her.' The words were spoken in Afrikaans. One soldier lifted me by my shoulders and one by my ankles. I struggled and said, 'Where are you taking me?' The same soldier said, 'You'll see.' There were other soldiers in the Hippo, but I don't know how many. The Hippo drove to the national road and went towards Port Elizabeth. The soldiers did not speak or interfere with me, but the same two held me. A few kilometres away the Hippo stopped. The one soldier jumped out and the other pushed me out. The two soldiers lifted me over the fence and climbed over. The Hippo drove in the same direction. I can identify the spot. The two soldiers were very young. The one held my arms while the other lifted my dress and removed my slip and panties. I said, 'What are you doing children?' The one replied, 'Ons gaan jou naai. As jy nie wil, gaan ons jou doodmaak.' [We are going to fuck you. If you don't we'll kill you.] They then pushed me down with my hips on a big stone. The one soldier held my arms over my head on the ground. The other soldier [who had done all the talking] raped me. He was very rough and I was bleeding when he finished. The other said, 'Maak gou. Ek is haastig. Ek wil ook naai.' [Hurry up. I'm in a hurry. I also want to fuck.] The two men switched positions. The one held my hands over my head. The other raped me. He was also rough. The two soldiers then walked away towards the road, but more towards Port Elizabeth than direct. The first soldier asked me, 'Sal jy vir ons ken?' [Will you recognize us?] I said, 'Ek sal nie vir julle ken.' [I will not know you.] I pulled my dress down, left my slip and panties and walked to Michalsdal.

On the following Monday this woman went to the police station:

> I saw one coloured and one black security policeman together, and told them the story in Xhosa. They recorded the facts and asked questions. I was not asked to sign anything. They asked if I knew the soldiers or the Hippo number. They said they would contact me and have not done so.
> *(Sworn statement made to Brian Bishop, 1985)*

There are a number of accounts of rape by South African security forces. Some of these have occurred in Namibia.

Sarah Nhenda was asleep in her hut with her two young daughters, when she heard a hammering at the door. 'It is us, the soldiers. We want to sleep with you,' the men outside the door said. 'Open up or we will break down the door.' Nhenda said,

> They forced their way in and began talking to me. They said they wanted to sleep with me. I said to them, 'My daughters are here, you cannot do this thing,' and they told my daughters to leave. Then they beat my head against the wall. I fell down. Then the one soldier grabbed my arms and forced me down on the bed and the other soldier began raping me …. They both raped me.

Nhenda reported this incident to the Human Rights Centre in Owamboland.

Many human rights violations reported to this centre involved rape. According to a doctor in northern Oshakati state hospital, approximately ten rapes per month, allegedly perpetrated by members of the South African security forces, were reported at the hospital in 1988. A local attorney said that in his view there was a 'virtual state of lawlessness' in northern Namibia – an area where more than half of the territory's population lives (*New Nation*, 10.11.1988). Some of these rapes involved children. For example, in 1988 Namibian police arrested two SADF soldiers following an investigation into the alleged rape of two Namibian girls aged eight and ten (ibid.).

Rape is common in wartime and is the most obvious form of distinctive victimization of women by war.[1] The explanation for this lies in the connection between militarism and masculinity. Men's insecurity in relation to their masculinity may become exacerbated by the physical danger of combat. In these situations rape may be used to try and improve morale.[2]

The most obvious victims of war are its casualties – the 'final sacrifice' paid by young South African men killed in action far from home. The very different figures quoted make it difficult to write with any confidence about the scale on which these deaths occurred. For example in Angola (which South African troops first invaded in 1975), the SADF acknowledged that 28 of its soldiers died in the last three months of 1987. But the Angolan government claimed that during the same period 230 South African soldiers had died there. Professor Green of the Institute for Development Studies in Sussex has estimated that as a proportion of the white population, the number of white South African men who lost their lives fighting Swapo was more than three times the number of American lives lost in Vietnam.

But the casualties of war go far beyond those killed or raped. Many of the young boys conscripted into the SADF who survived physically intact were emotionally damaged. Much has been written of the 'post-traumatic stress disorder' experienced by Vietnam veterans. Much has been said – both in print and film – of the fear and loneliness of American boys far from home in Vietnam. Many South African conscripts suffered the same emotions in Angola and Namibia. Also there was often a sense of confusion – amplified for those conscripts in the townships who had no clear conception of what they were doing there (see Chapter three). Some of the emotional damage inflicted by war is more obscure. 'Edward' was the young Harare man used by Olivia Forsyth to obtain access to people in the ANC. He describes himself as 'a victim of deception':

> I was shattered when my ANC contact told me she was a lieutenant in the security police .... The experience undermined my self-confidence. I came to lack confidence in my own judgement. I'm terrified to let anyone come close to me. I think the experience skewed the prospect, the possibility, of developing healthy relationships with women. It's made me almost schizoid in my relationships. I feel very close and intimate and loving, and then nothing. My current lover says it's like dealing with two people .... When Olivia was taken by the ANC from Harare to Lusaka, I was instructed to go into hiding. I spent two months listening to music. I thought of her all the time. I was in touch with a rage I never knew I was capable of. I had no focus for my anger ... nothing. There was nothing I could do. When I heard she was in Angola I told someone

they should take her up in a helicopter and drop her in the sea ... let the sharks get her. I think the experience was a contributing factor to the shattering of the relationship I was in at the time – a relationship that was deeply valuable to me. Both my sexual infidelity and my poor judgement diminished me in her eyes.
(Interview, 1989)

These are some of the victims of the South African war. Others have lost their lives or loved ones, their property, or their limbs. But all of us have lost something of our humanity. In the final analysis it is difficult to privilege different people's experience of loss. Not all the victims made political choices; not everyone chose to put him or herself at risk. However, it is arguable that the worst victims of the war in South Africa in the eighties were people who *did* make political choices, who *did* choose to place themselves at risk, but they were people whose choice and commitment was totally inappropriate to their age – our children.

If South Africa in the decade of the 1980s was a society at war, this war was fought mainly by children – boy children. The major protagonists were the white youths conscripted into the SADF to defend 'apartheid', and the black youths who were challenging it. They were extremely unequal opponents. During the 1984-6 period especially, in scenes of violent confrontation in black townships almost every day, the police and soldiers met sticks and stones with armoured cars, tear-gas and bullets from automatic weapons.

While these black and white children grow up in totally different social worlds, they both grow up believing that war and violence are inevitable. Most white children grow up to believe that state violence is necessary to maintain order. Most black children grow up believing that resistance violence is necessary to achieve justice. The actors in violent conflict are frequently acclaimed by their respective parties in heroic masculine terms – 'the young lions' in the case of blacks, or 'our boys on the border' in the case of whites. In both cases the pattern of socialization is connected to gender identity, and the outcome is a masculinist militarism. However, the paths of this socialization into militarism or war culture are different.

In Johannesburg there is a piece of wasteland with trees and ruined buildings that is a popular venue for white children – a vast majority of them boys – at weekends. They pay an entrance fee and hire guns with pellets which explode on impact and mark their target with a red dye 'just like blood'. Their targets are other children. They may choose the battlefield on which to play these 'tactical war games'. The battlefields are named Angola, Vietnam, Lebanon, and Soweto. Thus to many of these white children Soweto means a battlefield, a site of violent conflict against an enemy force, rather than a place where almost two million black South Africans live. However, few of them have been into a black township or know any black people other than the 'girls' and 'boys' employed by their parents as domestic workers and gardeners. Many of them know other whites who went into Soweto as soldiers during the 1984-6 occupation of the townships by the soldiers of the SADF. Some of the children playing Tactical War Games on a rainy Saturday in April, 1989, understood the connection. One commented,

> Yes, I am learning to become a good shot. This will help me when I go into the army to do my national service.

Tactical War Games is a highly profitable enterprise run by a former officer in the SADF. It is one of the ways described in Chapter three in which white boys are socialized into becoming soldiers in the SADF.

Black children are similarly socialized into a war culture through games and toys. A black boy, spending the school holidays in Pietermaritzburg with his mother, a domestic worker in the city, says he is familiar with war and with torture. Thousands of people have died in the area in violent political conflict. He was interviewed while engrossed in a video game called *Vigilante*:

> Ten-year-old Mkhululi grips the knobs of the video machine with excitement and becomes engrossed in the game. Mkhululi comes from Mpophomeni. He says, 'In Mpophomeni we fight. Here in the game there is only one person against the entire mob, but in Mpophomeni there are many of us. Those who die, die, and those who live, live,' he says while delivering a series of punches and karate kicks to the thugs that appear on the screen. He keeps losing the game to a particularly tough guy and fetching another 20c to play again. He says the tough guy reminds him of a very fierce vigilante in Mpophomeni. 'In Mpophomeni small children fought big men,' he says. The hero of the screen is a little chap in blue jeans who takes on all the heavies in town. Mkhululi returns to the machine. As he knocks down each of his opponents, words flash onto the screen: 'Law and order has failed. But the vigilantes have won. Vigilantes now rule the city.'
> (The Weekly Mail *30.7.1989*)

The perception that South Africa is a society at war was expressed by all the young white schoolboys interviewed for this chapter. Their identification of the main protagonists in this war variously included 'the state', 'Swapo', 'the people', 'the ANC', 'the revolutionary on-slaught', 'the powers of evil', 'Afrikaans nationalism', 'African nation-alism', 'ANC terrorists' and 'the communists'. This perception was also expressed by all the young black boys interviewed.[3] They are also caught up in a war culture. However this revolves around violent resistance to white minority rule, rather than its violent defence:

> It's a war. It's not a picnic. The whites must realize that the sweet life is over. We are prepared to die, to be shot or hanged from Death Row. We will win this war.
> *(Informant 90)*

> There's a war between the Boers and the black people.
> *(Informant 93)*

> There is a war going on to eradicate racial domination and economic exploitation. The war is between those who are committed to apart-heid and those who are committed to a non-racial, non-sexist, demo-cratic society.
> *(Informant 95)*

During the decade of the eighties, many young black children have come to have a militant spirit.

> I would ask them – these very young fellows – 'What is the struggle?' and they would say ... 'The struggle is fighting.' It is shocking the extent to which children turned into daredevils. Soldier meant only tear-gas to them, policemen only enemy target. There was such a great contrast with the young whites, still playing with toys and pestering their mothers for popcorn and ice-cream.
> *(Youth leader, Dan Motsisi, cited by Johnson, 1988: 113)*

Motsisi neglects the extent to which these young whites are also being socialized into a war culture. However, the content and style of the war games and toys involved are very different to those of whites. Most black children grow up in poverty. They improvise toys and games, for example playing 'chicken' around used tear-gas cannisters or parading with wooden models of AK47s (the rifles used by ANC soldiers). Whereas the black child cited above is fortunate (and unusual as the son of a domestic worker) to have 20c pieces to play with, the white children who visit 'Tactical War Games' in Johannesburg pay a R25 entrance fee, and often spend a further R25 on an additional tube of pellets. Many of the regular players own their own pellet guns – some costing as much as R1 500. Clearly these children come from affluent homes. The black children interviewed for this study all come from Soweto, the black township outside Johannesburg, where the average household income is about R800 a month.

The social contexts of these black and white children are very different in material terms. Soweto has been described as 'one of the most violent regions on earth' (Hirson, 1979: 4). It is the largest urban black community in South Africa, with a population of about two million spread over a geographical area of about 40 square miles. It exhibits many of the characteristics of disadvantage and deprivation that are typical of South Africa's black urban townships. It is marked by poverty, overcrowding, a lack of community and recreational facilities, and criminal violence. This criminal violence must be understood partly as a reaction to oppressive social conditions.

> Life here is fast. Two people living near me were stabbed in a fight over a dog. Life here is too fast. It is because people are squeezed. The violence in Soweto is because of poverty. Apartheid is to blame. It creates poverty and crime. People are angry with whites, but they can't rob and kill whites. Whites live far away and are more protected by security. It's high risk to attack whites. It's easy here. With poorly lighted streets people are easy targets. The white man's laws create poverty. Poverty creates this crime. People are not employed or educated. They resort to crime in order to survive.
> *(Informant 85)*

The outcome is that many black children from Soweto grow up in a culture of violence; a context in which violent behaviour is routine, everyday experience. The denial of opportunities for either employment or education are further ingredients which create a heady mix of anger against the existing order. Whereas the white child is socialized into a war culture of repression partly through the militarist content of white schooling, many black children are denied access to schooling, and this exclusion contributes towards a political commitment to change the system of apartheid and white minority rule. In other cases, black schools have become centres of a war culture of resistance. Johnson describes them as

> laboratories and fortresses of resistance, providing raw political education to the pupils passing through them, and deeply influencing the youth outside.
> *(Johnson, 1988: 96)*

Black students' attempts to organize protests and demonstrations around the inferior quality of black education have frequently been broken up by the SADF and the SAP. For the white child, the SADF is an ideological presence; for many black children the SADF is a physical presence. It is a physical presence which symbolizes oppression and white minority rule. The most famous such protest was that of 16 June 1976, when around 10 000 students in Soweto protested against official attempts to introduce Afrikaans as a medium of instruction in African schools. The police responded with tear gas and bullets, and almost 1 000 African children died from police violence as the riots spread. One informant, who is now a quadraplegic and confined to a wheelchair for life, said,

> I was shot during the riots in 1976. I was sixteen at the time. It was just an acccident. Police were shooting up and down and I was just passing. After I was shot I had to lie there for about two hours before I was taken to hospital by the very same police. I should have laid a charge against the police. But I think my parents were stupid and I was still young and confused. I didn't know what had happened to my life.
> *(Informant 86)*

It was after the Soweto riot that thousands of black children left South Africa to undergo military training with the ANC in exile, in its Umkhonto we Sizwe (Spear of the Nation) armed wing. Umkhonto we Sizwe (MK) soldiers are frequently 'heroized' by township youth.

> Armed struggle is a defensive strategy against a violent government. The attacks by MK are one way of weakening the state power and fighting back. A lot of the people who join MK have been involved in peaceful struggle, but they have seen that peaceful means do not bring about change. These people are frustrated by the slow pace of peaceful struggle and they have seen that the only way the government can be brought down is by using violence and joining MK.
> *(Informant 87)*

> I don't see the planting of bombs by MK combatants as a form of violence. It is a defence mechanism for the right to exist. MK defends our right to life.
> *(Informant 88)*

> MK is the army of the people which truly fights the enemy.
> *(Informant 89)*

A popular song captures the extent to which many black youths revel in the escalation of ANC sabotage activity:

> There is Sasolburg, the Supreme Court, Warmbaths,
> Koeberg, Pitoli, going up in flames.
> We are going there, the Umkhonto *boys* have arrived.
> We are going there. Hayi, Hayi. We are going forward.
> Don't be worried, the *boys* know their job.
> Let Africa return.

A pattern has also emerged in which civilians have been the targets of some bomb attacks. White right-wingers, or ANC cadres operating in defiance of ANC discipline, have been suggested as the culprits. Informants had different responses to these incidents in which 'ordinary' white people have been killed:

> I personally don't think that there are ordinary white people in this country. This country is involved in a civil war. The battle lines are drawn. People are either in the people's camp or the enemy camp. The white voters wield a lot of power. For the mere fact that they vote the government to power it is important that they get hit, and very hard too.
> *(Informant 88)*

> I think it is unfortunate that ordinary whites are killed, but as one knows, in a war situation there have to be casualties. We cannot deny that there is a war in this country, and in a war people have to be killed.
> *(Informant 87)*

> These bombs have been planted by enemy agents in order to confuse our masses and to discredit the ANC in the face of the white community. It is against ANC policy to attack civilian targets.
> *(Informant 81)*

> The bombs may be out of order because they kill innocent people, but in one way or another they may be helpful to show those 'innocents' that there is a war going on in South Africa.
> *(Informant 80)*

The 'comrades', who call themselves 'the young lions' have been the 'shock troops' of black resistance in the last four years. Boys as young as ten years old have been involved in violent confrontations with the SADF and the SAP. They are socialized into violence through a particularly militarist conception of masculinity. This is reinforced by a gender-defined sense of social solidarity, a brotherhood of combatants. The comrades, the 'Amabuthu', of the Eastern Cape have been described by Swilling as made up primarily of boys between 12 and 16 years old, with at best only a few years of primary schooling:

> They are unemployed, virtually illiterate, the offspring of broken or scattered families, living in packs 100 or 200 strong in what they call 'bases' on the fringes of the poorer squatter camps. They have little knowledge of the intricacies of formal political organization. Instead, they have fashioned their own military structure. Emerging independently from other township associations, the Amabuthu declare their allegiance to the ANC. For them, the ANC and its imprisoned leader, Nelson Mandela, are the liberators, but otherwise their ideology is limited to a few basic slogans. They may not have a programme, but some of them do have guns and grenades to complement the petrol bombs, some of which were captured initially from the SADF.
> *(Swilling and Lodge, 1988: 6)*

Their consciousness has been described as 'militarist':

> ... the Amabuthu groups brought with them a lexicon and set of symbols that glorifed the armed struggle and Umkhonto we Sizwe. The toyi-toyi, the commonly worn black beret, the petrol bomb and wooden AK 47s, were all manifestations of a militaristic sub-culture that became part of township life and political meetings. To be an Amabuthu amongst township youth involved a raw masculine pride. The most common Amabuthu songs were
>
> The Boer is oppressing us.
> The SADF is shooting us like animals.
> Kill the boer.
>
> and
>
> We won't abandon Umkhonto we Sizwe.
> These Boer blood-suckers won't get us.
> We won't abandon Umkhonto we Sizwe.
> *(Ibid.)*

Swilling cites the first verse of a well known poem called *Run guerrilla run*:

> Run guerrilla run,
> Chase them for the fun.
> Get Botha and Malan,
> Destroy mother, father and son.
> Till they say to you Number One,
> Run, guerrilla run.
> *(Ibid.: 8)*

One Amabuthu told Swilling,

> I don't want to go to school or work. I want to fight for freedom. We will go to school and work after we have won our freedom.
> *(Ibid.: 12)*

Another told him,

> We are prepared to talk to them [the government], but if they kill, we are also going to kill them.
> *(Ibid.)*

More organized groupings include student organizations and the youth congresses established to organize the youth excluded from schools. In March 1987 the South African Youth Congress (SAYCO) was formed to co-ordinate youth congress activity at a national level. Before it was banned, it claimed a membership of 500 000 – 700 000, and its slogan was 'Freedom or death; victory is certain'. Many also state their willingness to die in the struggle for liberation:

> I know many who have already died and many others who are prepared to die fighting against apartheid.
> *(Informant 89)*

An ex-Sayco activist said,

> We are prepared to die and to kill. From a moralistic point of view it is wrong to kill, but from a South African point of view it is not always wrong to kill people. If the state has been using violence against the people, it is not wrong for the people to counter the violence of the state. It is not wrong to kill people who defend apartheid.
> *(Informant 87)*

Several observers have commented on this 'kamikaze pilot' phenomenon:

> We've got a new breed of children. They believe that they are going to die ... and the frightening thing is that they actually don't care.
> *(Archbishop Desmond Tutu, quoted in* The Star *18.4.1986, cited by Johnson, 1988: 122)*

Another priest warned whites that

> what had emerged was a youth revolution ... a civil war in the townships, with soldiers patrolling the streets while young people control the community .... The elderly people may be confused, but the youngsters know what they want: liberation has entered their minds and they are obsessed to be liberated. They will die for it if they must.
> *(The Star 18.6.1986)*

There is a reckless heroism in this generation of boy 'comrades', guerrillas and Amabuthu. After the SADF were sent into the townships in 1984,

> hundreds died or were injured in clashes with police and soldiers, and thousands of young blacks – exhibiting extraordinary courage – began to employ 'guerrilla-style' tactics, improvising petrol bombs, ambushes and roadblocks, and learning to communicate and convene meetings clandestinely.
> *(Johnson, 1988: 115)*

But there is also a level of brutalization:

> I went into Lindile's yard and observed what was happening. I saw that the people were attacking a man I knew as Peti. I saw that he was full of blood. I saw him fall. The people who were attacking him were the comrades. Mtutu was hitting the deceased with a sword, so was Lunga Petrol. Boy-Boy had a small knife; he was stabbing the deceased. After a while it was obvious that the deceased would not be getting up again. The comrades then left. We also went into one house and I had breakfast.
> *(Court document quoted by Riordaan, 1988)*

Some young people have clearly perpetrated cruel acts of political violence in the name of the liberation struggle. These acts have included the 'necklacing', burning and stoning to death of suspected informers and 'collaborators'. 'Necklacing' is a weapon of terror that involves placing a car tyre around the neck of a victim, filling it with petrol and setting it alight. Different views on this practice were expressed by the black youths interviewed:

> I think necklacing is not wrong because it is the revolutionary discipline which came during the revolution and I can say people were showing their anger against those who betrayed them.
> *(Informant 80)*

Necklacing is very frightening and I don't like it, but if we think of the ways the enemy tortures people in detention, and if I remember how I was tortured in detention, I don't blame people who use necklacing against spies and collaborators and all enemy people.
(Informant 89)

Necklacing may be justified, or it may not be justified. It all depends on the context. Necklacing came about during the height of the struggles of 1984-5 and was used to eliminate government agents. It has been effective in eliminating the so-called informers – all those who aligned themselves with the government. But it was a gruesome weapon to use against these people.
(Informant 87)

One must understand the anger and frustration that has built up within people over the years of oppression, and necklacing becomes one of the ways of expressing this anger. I agree with Mrs Winnie Mandela that you have to be violent in order to get what you want in South Africa. We had to necklace those who betrayed us. They don't deserve to live. They must die. Even Mrs Mandela said that 'with our boxes of matches and necklaces we will liberate the country'. She also believes that our violence will bring about changes. Necklacing is a necessary discipline. It shows others not to be traitors. It is cruel, but we blacks are fighting for democracy and others are betraying us. They have to be eliminated. They encourage this bad system of apartheid.
(Informant 56)

In South Africa black and white youths grow up in sealed social worlds. There is no social contact between the two, and little common understanding. Only one of the youths interviewed for this study claimed to have friends of a different race group. Many of them were caught up in racist stereotypes. A black youth described whites as 'selfish and greedy' (informant 88), while a white youth said,

Much black violence has a genetic base. Think about dogs. A bull terrier is much more aggressive than a German shepherd. They're different but come from the same species. It's the same with blacks and whites. Blacks are more aggressive.
(Informant 77)

The totally divergent political understandings of the two groups emerged from their dramatically different definitions of 'terrorists' and 'terrorism'. The white children asociated terrorism with the ANC and bombs, while the black children linked it to the state:

> The SADF is a terrorist institution, precisely because it has terrorized people over the years. MK was formed to defend the people (the oppressed masses, that is) against the terrorists. For me terrorists are the state and all their machinery which is terrorizing us every day.
> *(Informant 87)*

None of the black children defined ANC people as 'terrorists'.

Both white and black children are products of social dislocation. In the case of blacks, this is the outcome of the disruption of family life that the migrant labour system has involved. Only two of the ten black youths interviewed lived with both their parents. In the case of whites, the divorce rate in the Johannesburg area is now two out of every three marriages. Only three of the ten white youths interviewed lived with both their parents. All the black children reported a generation gap that centred on political differences with their parents:

> I only talk to my mother about politics. We disagree strongly about the armed struggle. We are braver than our parents. After the horrors of the Sharpeville Massacre, most of our elders withdrew from active politics. Now the youth are leading the struggle. We are prepared to fight up to the last drop of our blood and we are also prepared to kill in the process.
> *(Informant 81)*

> I don't talk politics with either of my parents any more so I don't really know their views.
> *(Informant 76)*

> My parents are very difficult to talk to on politics because they think I am not clear on why I am in the struggle. But we do talk sometimes, when a stay-away is called, because then my mother does not have to go to work. I think we agree that apartheid is wrong and that it should go, but they think we rush things by the violence which goes on in the township.
> *(Informant 89)*

All South Africans are caught up in a spiralling pattern of repressive and revolutionary violence. In this process violence has come to be accepted as a legitimate solution to conflict, The violence is often embedded in a particular conception of gender identity – a militarist masculinism.

Black and white boys are central actors in this brutal and brutalizing conflict. The outcome is that all South Africa's boy children are robbed of their childhood:

> The children of South Africa, particularly black children, are denied their rights to be children. Children are violently forced by the conditions in the country to be adults before their time. They are put into a situation where they have to make decisions which are normally made by adults. They are forced to make choices which they should not make at their age. They are made to fight battles they should not be fighting as children.
>
> *(Rev. Frank Chikane, cited in the* New Nation *2.6.1989)*

Only the future will tell whether these children have been brutalized to the extent that they have lost their humanity. For clearly what Johnson terms this 'children's crusade of sorts' will have long-term consequences:

> If it is true that a people's wealth is its children, then South Africa is bitterly, tragically poor. If it is true that a nation's future is its children, we have no future and deserve none .... We are a nation at war with its future .... For we have turned our children into a generation of fighters, battle-hardened soldiers who will never know the carefree joy of childhood. What we are witnessing is the growth of a generation which has the courage to reject the cowardice of its parents ... to fight for what should be theirs, by right of birth. There is a dark, terrible beauty in that courage. It is also a source of great pride – pride that we, who have lived under apartheid, can produce children who refuse to do so. But it is also a source of great shame ... that this is our heritage to our children: the knowledge of how to die and how to kill.
>
> *(Percy Qoboza,* City Press *20.4.1986)*

Mr Qoboza wrote these words as the father of black children. However, the words are true for many white children as well. In the war decade boys were the main protagonists; they fought as 'patriots', but the form and content of how they did so was shaped and coloured by their gender identity.

Notes

1. Brownmiller maintains that 'War provides men with the perfect psychological backdrop to give vent to their contempt for women. The very maleness of the military – the brute power of weaponry exclusive to their hands, the spiritual bonding of men at arms, the manly discipline of orders given and orders obeyed, the simple logic of the hierarchical command – confirms for men what they long suspect, that women are peripheral, irrelevant to the world that counts, passive spectators to the action in the centre ring …. In the name of victory and the power of the gun, war provides men with a tacit licence to rape. In the act and in the excuse, rape in war reveals the male psyche in its boldest form, without the veneer of "chivalry" or "civilization"' (Brownmiller, 1975: 33).

2. For example, 'In 1966 an American patrol held a 19-year-old Vietnamese girl captive for several days, taking turns at raping her, and finally murdering her. The sergeant planned the crime in advance, telling the soldiers during the missions briefing that the girl would improve their "morale". When one soldier refused to take part in the rape, the sergeant called him 'queer' and 'chicken'; another testified later that he joined in the assault to avoid such insults' (Komisar, cited by Vogelman, 1990: 144). The contempt for women in some of this violence is illustrated by an American marine's comment, 'If she's old enough to bleed, she's old enough to be butchered' (cited by Higonnet and Higonnet, 1987: 42)

3. In retrospect, limiting the interviews to a selection of male 'comrades' identified by my field worker was a mistake. I was interested in the connection between masculinity and militarism, but this kind of limitation reinforces the exclusion of young girls from our understanding of militant township political activity.

Conclusion

We are at a critical time in South Africa's history. We are engaged in creating an entirely new and different society. Nadine Gordimer has called this

> one of the most extraordinary events in world social history – the complete reversal of everything that for centuries has ordered the lives of all our people.
>
> *(From address given at The Weekly Mail Book Week, 1990)*

Violence was always involved in this ordering, but it peaked in the decade of the eighties, a period that many people defined and experienced as a 'war'. In this spiralling process of repression and revolutionary violence, violence comes to be accepted as a legitimate solution to conflict. This acceptance threatens to destroy our humanity; to erode our capacity for humane responses. A prominent 'specialist in violence' (as an American sociologist described military men) and a previous head of the SADF, General C.J. Viljoen, said,

> South Africans must be prepared to accept certain levels of discomfort, disruption and even violence in their everyday lives.
>
> *(Viljoen, quoted by Hough, 1984: 6)*

There is a very real danger that all South Africans will come to feel overwhelmed by the violence in our society and withdraw into a kind of survival mentality. This involves an emotional anaesthesia, a disengagement from others, a retreat from social involvement into a private defensive core. In South Africa the normalization of violence and atrocity threatens to blunt our human sensibilities.

This retreat into passivity is illustrated by the public's lack of response to two items which appeared in a Sunday newspaper in November 1990. On one page there was a full account of Patrick Lawrence's horrifying book on the death squads. This book documents meticulously the relation between political assassinations and the CCB, a special unit of the SADF. In the same newspaper, there was an account of the installation of General Kat Liebenberg as chief of the SADF. This is the man who, the Harms Commission was told, had authorized operations of the CCB against the ANC. This is the man who, as head of the SADF Special Forces in the mid-1980s, was intimately involved in the SADF strategy of destabilization and cross-border raids. According to this same newspaper report, General Liebenberg was one of the SADF officers who planned to subvert the Nkomati Accord in 1984 by continuing to supply Renamo, the movement fighting the Frelimo government in Mozambique. The fact that the juxtaposition of these two newspaper reports provoked no public outrage or protest action speaks for itself.

It is widely believed that South Africa is moving away from militarization. Indicators of this are the halving of the period of initial military service from two years to one, reductions in the programmes and personnel of the SADF and Armscor, and the dismantling of the national security management system. A book published in 1990 stated:

> We are a country virtually at war, therefore you should be armed.
> *(Hamann, 1990: 740)*

Private gun ownership is increasing dramatically. The period since F.W. de Klerk's 2 February 1990 speech has been marked by violent conflict in which thousands have died.[1] Most of this violence has been perpetrated by men using not only guns but also 'traditional' or 'cultural' weapons which are legitimated as symbols of masculinity. A number of leaders have warned that there may be a 'third force' made up of elements within the security forces who are operating in the conflict, and who are intent on weakening the ANC and disrupting the negotiation process. In reality we still have the largest and most powerful army and police force in Africa. This is the same force, with the same leaders, that operated the eighties' policy of violent repression. It is not clear to me that the SADF or the SAP can be trusted to maintain peace.

The only solution to the escalating spiral of violence and war is finding the courage to deal with its causes. The starting point must be to eliminate the material inequalities and injustices upon which South African society is structured. This extreme inequality has been conceptualized as a form of violence:

> Violence is present when human beings are being influenced so that their actual somatic and mental realizations are below their potential realizations.
> *(Galtung, 1969: 168)*

This 'structural violence' is equated with injustice and discrimination:

The violence is built into the structure and shows up as unequal power and consequently unequal life chances.
(Ibid.: 171)

Two indicators point to the extent of this inequality in South Africa: income distribution and infant mortality rates. Breaking the chain of political violence involves eradicating this structural violence on which apartheid is based. In concrete terms this means improving the mass of South Africa's people's access to well-paid jobs, adequate pensions and social services, decent housing, health services, education, proper sanitation and clean water. This can only be achieved by a massive redistribution of power and resources within a new political dispensation – a non-racial democracy.

However, the problem of violence and war goes beyond this. We have to dismantle the ideology of militarism – the notion that violence is a legitimate solution to conflict. And we have to loosen the connection between militarism and masculinity; to eradicate the notion that aggression and violence are acceptable forms of manly behaviour. This means that we have to recast the present pattern of gender relations. This book has tried to show why; it has tried to demonstrate that South Africa in the eighties was a society at war and that there was a gender dynamic involved. Through interviews with diverse South Africans it has tried to map out some of the roles through which men and women were incorporated into the process of war and militarization.

Women's role in militarization has been largely obscured and mystified by two competing perspectives: sexism and feminism. Both analyses exclude women from war on the grounds that they are bearers of 'special qualities'. Sexism excludes women from the ranks of the military on the grounds of their physical inferiority and unsuitability for combat roles. One variant of feminism similarly excludes women,but on opposite grounds – women's innate nurturing qualities, their creativity and pacifism. Another variant of feminism excludes women on the grounds that men have a monopoly on power. This last perspective emphasizes that war and militarization are initiated, directed, and controlled by men; that this male dominance is implicit in all the attempts to conceptualize the power of the military, from 'the military-industrial complex' to the 'garrison state'. The 'garrison state' is an extension of the 'barracks community'; it is structured on the principles and practices of male bonding. Therefore a militarized society reflects not only the power of the military, but the power of men. All these positions suggest that war is predominantly a male affair, and the military a patriarchal institution from which women are often excluded and by whom women are often victimized:

> Women are victims in all wars. Men plan them, they train for them and they conduct them.
> *(As, 1982: 355)*

This book has tried to unsettle this view. It has tried to demonstrate how in South Africa in the 1980s women were more than victims; more than passive objects to be 'protected' and 'defended'. They did far more than simply acquiesce to war and the mobilization of resources for war. Even without direct coercion into the SADF in the form of conscription, many white women contributed both directly and indirectly, both materially and ideologically, to the militarization of South African society. In a number of different senses they did, in the words of the chief of the SADF, 'keep the fires burning'. They fed the flames of violent conflict partly through socializing boys into a strong, aggressive masculinity, and policing conformity to that role. Thus they maintained the popular notions of masculinity and femininity with their polarization of human characteristics. In the process they elaborated an ideology of gender roles which linked masculinity to militarism. Some white women also contributed to militarization through their work in support organizations such as the Southern Cross Fund, in armaments production, and – increasingly since the late 1970s – through their direct incorporation into the SADF.

The increasing incorporation of white women directly into the SADF (as with other armies) threatened to breach the ideological construction of gender; to contaminate or dilute the ideological construct of 'femininity'. But this construct is crucial as a source of legitimation for the connection between masculinity and militarism. The identification of manhood with soldiering is of such ideological importance that it may not be easily breached. Therefore considerable efforts were made to avoid this breach and to elaborate a traditional but expanded notion of femininity for women within the SADF. White women's increasing participation in the SADF did not finally challenge the system of gender relations which keeps women subordinate. Most of the women in the SADF are confined to subordinate positions which reflect the sexual division of labour in the wider society. Within the SADF, as in the wider society, there are very few women in the top levels of policy- and decision-making. This sexual division of labour is reinforced by the elaborate cultivation of femininity and a 'superwoman' image whereby

SADF women are encouraged to combine their jobs with their traditional domestic responsibilities as wives and mothers. The dominant form of masculinity is unchallenged.

On the contrary, definitions of masculinity are mobilized in military training to turn men into soldiers. Many men in the SADF were coerced into fighting. Many went to war in Angola, Namibia, and the townships to defend an image of social order that was symbolized by 'women'. In reality, what men in the SADF were protecting and defending was 'the survival of a dying order'.[2] Thus the SADF reflected and reinforced both the racial and sexual inequalities on which South African society is structured.

This book has tried to sketch some of the ways in which gender relations shaped both incorporation in and resistance to those inequalities. The 'resistance' focus was on two organizations which, in the decade of the eighties, presented significant (albeit very different) challenges to the militarization of the South African state – the ECC and MK. The ECC was committed to non-violence; MK was an army structured around a reluctant acceptance of violence.

MK and the SADF reflect all the myriad differences between a conventional and a guerrilla army. However, it has been shown that in both armies there are significant similarities in the position of women. In both there has been a progressive incorporation of women in recent years, but in both armies women are excluded from power and authority. There are important questions behind these apparently contradictory processes of incorporation and exclusion. Does equal rights mean equal responsibilities, including military service for women? Should such military service include combat roles? These are significant questions; they are logically at the cutting edge of contemporary feminism. If these questions become more openly and publicly debated in South Africa, this book will have achieved its purpose.

The book leaves many questions unanswered. The role of women in MK; the many differences between MK and the SADF; the shape of a future defence policy; the linkages between masculinity and militarism in traditional African cultures – these are all questions which are only touched on here. It is hoped that this book will stimulate research and debate on these issues. Debate is urgent, as the current ideological construction of defence force 'manpower' in gender- and race-specific terms is being reworked.

In South Africa and elsewhere, men and women relate to war very differently. War does not challenge women to prove that they are women, whereas war has always been the great touchstone of 'manliness'. The concept of war as this proving ground of manliness has centred on the notion of combat. Combat is understood to be the ultimate test of masculinity, and thus crucial to the ideological structure of patriarchy. But modern military technology has transformed the nature of war. Warfare has become distant and impersonal; 'combat' has become increasingly ambiguous and difficult to define. It does not provide the same unproblematic validation of masculinity. But 'the myth of combat dies hard' (Enloe, 1983: 13).

In her *Thoughts on Peace in an Air-raid*, Virginia Woolf posed the question:

> Mustn't our next task be the emancipation of men? How can we alter the crest and spur of the fighting cock?
> *(Woolf, 1942, cited by Oldfield, 1989: 123)*

She argued that women in the future must try to help men to emancipate themselves from their need to identify masculinity with aggression and domination:

> We must compensate the man for the loss of his gun ... we must give him access to the creative feelings ... we must free him from the machine.
> *(Ibid.: 126)*

But in order to do this women must also free themselves from gender stereotypes:

> If we could free ourselves from slavery we could free men from tyranny. Hitlers are bred by slaves.
> *(Ibid.: 125)*

At present gender stereotypes link femininity with nurture. But the differences between men and women in nurture and other forms of behaviour are not innate and fixed. They are primarily the result of social conditioning:

> ... the fact is that everyone has the capacity to nurture. That women have been socialized to do so is a reality, and it's an asset we have going for us.
> *(Warnock, 1989: 191)*

The core of the problem is our gender identities – 'womanliness' and 'manliness' – 'both so hateful', as Virginia Woolf expressed it. What really mattered to Virginia Woolf was that we should rework these identities; that we should all bring 'the unconscious Hitlerism' – the desire to dominate and be dominated – within ourselves up to the level of consciousness. The drives for domination and for subservience are 'the two great destroyers', and are encoded in our gender identities. Thus, in her view, war can be abolished only if men and women free themselves of their gender roles and their subconscious drives to dominate and be dominated.

Virginia Woolf did not pay attention to the military as a social institution. This book has asserted that the answer to the question of why individuals fight wars involves analysing the military and its power in society; understanding the military involves analysing gender relations. South African individuals' experiences of the war in the 1980s were shaped not only by race, class, ethnicity, and ideology, but also by gender relations.

This linkage between war and gender is a crucial and hidden relation. War both uses and maintains the ideological construction of gender in the definitions of 'masculinity' and 'femininity'. Soldiers usually go to war to defend an image of social order which is symbolized by 'woman'. Women are widely cast in the role of 'the protected' and 'the defended', often excluded from military service, and the almost always – whether in guerrilla or conventional armies – excluded from combat. Dividing the protector from the protected, defender from the defended, is crucial to both sexism and militarism.

For this reason, in the final analysis, changing gender relations is necessary to reduce the risks of war. There are other necessary tasks – the conversion of the arms industry to civilian purposes; the dismantling of the military-industrial complex; the subordination of the military to civilian control in a democratic state; the teaching of political tolerance and non-violent forms of conflict resolution; the fostering of international co-operation, and much more. But the recasting of gender relations is an urgent task. We must do all this because, in the words of that remarkable woman war correspondent, Martha Gellhorn,

> war is a malignant disease, an idiocy, a prison, and the pain it causes is beyond telling or imagining.

Notes

1. Part of what this step created was a highly volatile atmosphere in which heightened political expectations were harnessed to continuing structural violence and oppression. The outcome is increased levels of criminal as well as

political violence. An ironic theme is that much of the criminal violence involves AK47 assault rifles obtained from Mozambique, where they were supplied to the Renamo rebels by the SADF. Roland Hunter went to prison for five years for passing information to the ANC about the shipment of thousands of AK47 assault rifles to Renamo.

2. 'The enemy forces are being compelled to recognize that the only cause that they have to defend is the survival of a dying order; that even in death they can only die for the past and not for the future – they therefore only defend a cause already lost, whose path is increasing demoralization.' (Statement of the NEC by President Tambo on Heroes' Day, 16 December 1986, on the occasion of the 25th anniversary of MK. Quoted in *Dawn*, Souvenir Issue.)

Bibliography

Adam, H. 1988. *Modernising Racial Domination*. Lawrenceville: Princeton University Press.

Adams, D. and Bernstein, S. 1988. 'Conscription in South Africa'. Unpublished paper.

Archer, D. and Gartner, R. 1978. 'Legal homicide and its consequences', in Kutash, I. (ed.), *Perspectives on Murder and Aggression*. San Francisco/London: Jossey Bass Publishers, pp. 219-32.

Arendt, H. 1970. *On Violence*. London: Allen Lane.

As, B. 1982. 'A feminist perspective on war', in *Women's Studies International Forum*, vol. 5, no. 314.

Bahro, R. 1982. *Socialism and Survival*, introduced by Thompson, E. P. London: Heretic Books.

Barrell, H. 1990. *MK: The ANC's Armed Struggle*. Johannesburg: Penguin.

Baynham, S. 1987. 'Political violence and the security response', in Blumenfeld, J. (ed.), *South Africa in Crisis*. London: Croom Helm/Royal Institute of International Affairs.

Beale, J., Friedman, M., Hassim, S., Rosel, R., Stiebel, L., and Todes, A., 1987. 'African women in the Durban struggle 1985-6', in Moss, G. and Obeng, J. (eds), *South African Review* 4. Johannesburg: Ravan Press.

Beckett, D. 1982. 'Family planning', in *Frontline*, August.

Bennett, M. and Quin, D. 1988. 'Political conflict in South Africa', in *Indicator*, vol. 13, December.

Bernstein, H. 1988. 'Who will sing for Theresa?' in *Feminist Review*, no. 29, May.

Bird, A. 1985. 'Organizing women workers', in *South African Labour Bulletin*, vol. 10, no. 8, pp. 77-91.

Bishop, D. 1989. 'Years of championing rights – the successes and failures of the Black Sash', in *Sash*, March, pp. 17-21.

Black Sash, 1989. 'Inside South Africa's death factory'. Unpublished research report.

Boulding, K. E. 1978. *Stable Peace*. Austin: University of Texas Press.

Brownmiller, S. 1975. *Against our Will: Men, Women and Rape*. New York: Simon and Schuster; London: Secker & Warburg.

Budlender, D. 1990. 'Women and the economy'. Unpublished paper.

Burman, S. 1990. 'The family in a South African context'. Paper delivered at the Lawyers for Human Rights International Conference, 'Putting Women on the Agenda'. Johannesburg, November.

Callan, H. and Ardener, S. (eds) 1984. *The Incorporated Wife*. London: Croom Helm in association with the Centre for Cross-Cultural Research on Women.

Campbell, C. 1990. 'The township family and women's struggles', in *Agenda*, no. 6, pp. 1-22.

Catholic Institute for International Relations, 1988. *Now Everyone is Afraid: The Changing Face of Policing in South Africa*. London: CIIR.

Caute, D. 1983. *Under the Skin*. London: Allen Lane; Harmondsworth: Penguin Books.

Chapkis, W. (ed.) 1981. *Loaded Questions: Women in the Military*. Amsterdam: Transnational Institute.

Chinchilla, N. Stoltz, 1983. *The Case of Nicaragua*. Working Paper, no. 27, Michigan State University.

Cock, J. 1980. *Maids and Madams: A Study in the Politics of Exploitation*. Johannesburg: Ravan Press; London: The Women's Press (1989).

Cock, J. 1987. 'Trapped workers: constraints and contradictions experienced by black women in contemporary South Africa', in *Women's Studies International Forum*, vol. 10, no. 2, pp. 133-40.

Cock, J. 1989. 'Introduction' in Cock, J. and Nathan, L. (eds), *War and Society: The Militarization of South Africa*. Cape Town: David Philip; New York: St Martin's Press.

Cock, J., Emden, E., and Klugman, B. 1983. 'Child care and the working mother: a sociological investigation of a sample of urban African women in South Africa'. Second Carnegie Inquiry into Poverty and Development in Southern Africa. Cape Town: Southern African Labour and Development Research Unit (SALDRU).

Cock, J. and Vogelman, L. 1990. 'Alone on death row: The case of Evelyn de Bruin', in *Feminist Forum, Women's Studies International Forum Newsletter*.

Cole, J. 1987. *Crossroads*. Johannesburg: Ravan Press.

Cooper, C. 1988. Chapter on 'Political developments', in *Race Relations Survey 1987/88*. Johannesburg: South African Institute for Race Relations (SAIRR), pp. 19-64.

Costello, J. 1985. *Love, Sex and War: Changing Values 1939 -1945*. London: William Collins.

Crapanzano, V. 1985. *Waiting: The Whites of South Africa*. New York: Random House; London: Granada.

Critical Health, 1989. 'Women and detention', in *Critical Health*, no. 26, May.

Davey, D. 1988. 'A phenomenological explication of problems in intimacy experienced by the returned conscript as a result of military experiences in the SADF'. Rhodes University, Psychology Honours dissertation.

Davis, A. 1982. *Women, Race and Class*. London: The Women's Press.

Davis, S. 1987. *Apartheid's Rebels: Inside South Africa's Hidden War*. New Haven: Yale University Press.

Detainees' Parents' Support Committee, 1987. 'A year of emergency, a year of repression', in *Review of African Political Economy*, no. 40, December, pp. 96-103.

Driver, D. 1989. 'Women and language in the ANC constitutional guidelines'. *IDASA Occasional Papers* no. 26, *Towards a Non-sexist Constitution: Women's Perspectives*. Cape Town: IDASA.

Ebersohn, W. 1987. 'Ring of fire', in *Leadership*, South Africa, vol. 6, no. 1, pp. 39-42.

Ehrenreich, B. 1983. *The Hearts of Men*. London: Pluto Press.

Eide, A. and Thee, M. (eds) 1980. *Problems of Contemporary Militarism*. London: St Martin's Press.

Eisenhart, R. 1964, in Jourand, S., *The Transparent Self*. Lawrenceville: Princeton University Press; New York: D. Van Nostrand (1971), p. 26.

Eisenhart, R. 1975. 'You can't hack it little girl: A discussion of the covert psychological agenda of modern combat training', in *Journal of Social Issues*, vol. 31, no. 4.

Elshtain, J. 1987. *Women and War*. New York: Basic Books; Brighton: Harvester Press.

Enloe, C. 1983. *Does Khaki Become You? The Militarization of Women's Lives*. Boston: South End Press; London: Pluto.

Evans, G. 1983. 'The role of the military in education in South Africa'. University of Cape Town, Honours dissertation.

Fanon, F. 1963. *The Wretched of the Earth*. New York: Grove Press; London: McGibbon & Kee, (1965).

Feinstein, A. 1986. 'Some attitudes towards conscription in South Africa', in *Psychology in Society*, no. 5, pp. 66-80.

Figes, E. 1970. *Patriarchal Attitudes: Women in Society*. London: Faber & Faber.

Flisher, A. 1987. 'Some psychological aspects of commencing national service in South Africa', in *Psychology in Society*, no. 7, pp. 36-53.

Forest, C. and Jochelson, K. 1986. 'Writing against rape', in *Work in Progress*, no. 43, pp. 25-8.

Foster, D. and Chandler, D. 1987. *Detention and Torture in South Africa*. Cape Town: David Philip; London: James Currey.

Frankel, P. 1984. *Pretoria's Praetorians: Civil-Military Relations in South Africa*. Cambridge: Cambridge University Press.

Frederikse, J. 1986. *South Africa: A Different Kind of War*. Johannesburg: Ravan Press; London: James Currey.

Friedan, B. 1981. *The Second Stage*. New York: Summit; London: Michael Joseph (1982).

Gaitskell, D. and Unterhalter, E. 1989. 'Mothers of the nation: A comparative analysis of nation, race and motherhood in Afrikaner nationalism and the African National Congress', in Yuval-Davis and Anthias.

Galtung, J. 1969. 'Violence, peace and peace research', in *Journal of Peace Research*, vol. 6, no. 3, pp. 167-91.

Gellhorn, M. 1959. *The Face of War*. London: Rupert Hart-Davis; London: Virago Press (1986).

Glaser, B. G. and Strauss, A. L. 1967. *The Discovery of Grounded Theory: Strategies for Qualitative Research*. Chicago: Aldine.

Gordon, L. 1987. 'Nazi feminists?' in *Feminist Review*, no. 27, September.

Grundy, K. 1983. *Soldiers without Politics: Blacks in the South African Armed Forces*. Berkeley: University of California Press.

Grundy, K. 1987. *The Militarization of South African Politics*. Oxford: Oxford University Press.

Gwagwa, N. 1989. 'The family and women's emancipation in South Africa'. Unpublished paper.

Hall, P. and Roux, M. 1988. 'Life after detention', in Sash, vol. 31, no. 1, June, pp. 44-5.

Hamann, M. 1990. *The Gun and You.* Johannesburg: Ashanti.

Harris, H. 1988. 'Women and war: The case of Nicaragua', in Isaksson, E., *Women and the Military System.* New York: Harvester Press.

Haysom, N. 1989. 'Vigilantes and militarization', in Cock, J. and Nathan, L. (eds) 1989. *War and Society: The Militarization of South Africa.* Cape Town: David Philip; New York: St Martin's Press.

Higonnet, M. and Higonnet, F. (eds), 1987. *Behind the Lines: Gender and Two World Wars.* London: Macmillan; New Haven: Yale University Press.

Hirson, B. 1979. *Year of Fire, Year of Ash: The Soweto Revolt: Roots of Revolution.* London: Zed Press.

Horne, A. 1977. *A Savage War of Peace.* London: Macmillan.

Horowitz, I. L. 1973. 'Political terrorism and state power', in *Journal of Political and Military Sociology*, vol. 1, pp. 147-57.

Hough, M. 1984. *Institute for Strategic Studies August Review.* Pretoria: Institute for Strategic Studies.

Human Awareness Programme, 1986. *Militarism Dossier.* Johannesburg: Human Awareness Programme.

Human Rights Commission, 1988. 'A free choice: Memorandum on repression and the municipal elections'. Special Report SR-1, October.

Huston, N. 1982. 'Tales of war and tears of women', in *Women's Studies International Forum*, vol. 3, no. 4. Oxford.

Johnson, P. and Martin, D. 1989. *Apartheid Terrorism: The Destabilisation Report.* London: James Currey.

Johnson, S. 1988. 'The soldiers of Luthuli: Youth in the politics of resistance in South Africa', in Johnson, S. (ed.) *South Africa: No Turning Back.* London: Macmillan, pp. 95-151.

Jourard, S. 1971. *The Transparent Self.* New York: D. Van Nostrand Co.

Kaldor, M. 1981. *The Baroque Arsenal.* New York: Hill & Wang; London: Deutsch (1982).

Kaldor, M. 1982. 'Warfare and capitalism', in New Left Review (eds), *Exterminism and Cold War.* London: Verso.

242 Women & war in South Africa

Keegan, J. 1976. *The Face of Battle: A Study of Agincourt, Waterloo and the Somme.* New York: Viking/Penguin; London: Jonathan Cape.

Keegan, J. and Holmes, R. 1985. *Soldiers – A History of Man in Battle.* London: Hamish Hamilton.

Kidron, M. and Smith, D. 1983. *The War Atlas.* London: Pan Books.

Kimble, J. and Unterhalter, E. 1982. 'ANC women's struggles 1912-1982', in *Feminist Review*, vol. 19.

Kimmel, M. 1987. 'The contemporary "crisis" of masculinity', in Brod, H. (ed.) *The Making of Masculinity.* Englewood Cliffs: Prentice Hall.

Klugman, B. 1988. 'Decision-making on contraception amongst a sample of urban African working women.' Masters dissertation, University of the Witwatersrand.

Koonz, C. 1987. *Mothers in the Fatherland: Women, the Family and Nazi Politics.* New York: St Martin's Press; London: Jonathan Cape.

Laqueur, W. 1987. *The Age of Terrorism.* London: Weidenfeld & Nicolson.

Lasch, C. 1985. *The Minimal Self: Psychic Survival in Troubled Times.* London: Pan Books.

Laswell, H. 1941. 'The garrison state', in *The American Journal of Sociology*, vol. 46, pp. 455-68.

Laurence, P. 1990. *Death Squads: Apartheid's Secret Weapon.* Johannesburg: Penguin Books.

Law, L., Lund, C. and Winkler, H. 1987. 'Conscientious objection: The church against apartheid's violence', in Villa-Vicencio, C. (ed.) *Theology and Violence: The South African Debate.* Johannesburg: Skotaville.

Lawson, L. 1985. *Working Women.* Johannesburg: Ravan Press.

Levin, R. 1987. 'Class struggle, popular democratic struggle and the South African state', in *Review of African Political Economy*, no. 40, pp. 7-21.

Lifton, R. 1973. *Home from the War: Vietnam Veterans; Neither Victims nor Executioners.* New York: Simon & Schuster.

Linn, R. 1986. 'Conscientious objection in Israel during the war in Lebanon', in *Armed Forces and Society*, vol. 12, no. 4, pp. 489-511.

Lodge, T. 1983. *Black Politics in South Africa Since 1945.* London: Longman.

Lowy, M. and Sader, E. 1985. 'The militarization of the state in Latin America', in *Latin American Perspectives*, vol. 12, no. 4, pp. 7-40.

Macdonald, S. 1987. 'Drawing the lines – gender, peace and war: An introduction', in Macdonald, S. *et al.* (eds), *Images of Women in Peace and War: Cross-cultural and Historical Perspectives*. Basingstoke: Macmillan Education in association with Oxford Women's Studies Committee, pp. 1-26.

Maconachie, M. 1985. 'Looking for patterns of women's employment and educational achievements in the 1985 census', in *Agenda*, no. 5.

Mann, M. 1987. 'The roots and contradictions of modern militarism', in *New Left Review*, no. 126, March/April, pp. 35-51.

Mason, T. 1976. 'Women in Germany, 1925-1940: Family, welfare and work, part 1', in *History Workshop Journal*, no. 6, pp. 74-113.

Mattelart, A. 1979. 'Notes on the ideology of the military state', in Mattelart, A. and Siegelaub, S. *Communication and Class Struggle, Vol. 1: Capitalism and Imperialism*. London: Verso; New York: International General; Bagnolet: IMMRC.

McCuen, J. 1966. *The Art of Counter-revolutionary War: The Strategy of Counter-insurgency*. London: Faber & Faber.

Merryfinch, L. 1981. 'Militarization/civilianization', in Chapkis, 1981.

Michelman, C. 1975. *The Black Sash of South Africa: A Case Study in Liberalism*. Oxford: Oxford University Press.

Moll, P. 1986. 'Conscientious objectors under renewed attack', in *South African Outlook*, October, pp. 113-15.

Moore-King, B. 1988. *White Man Black War*. Harare: Baobab Books; London: Penguin (1989).

Moss, G. 1988. 'Politics with a price on its head', in *Work in Progress*, no. 53, April, pp. 24-7.

Nathan, L. 1987. 'Resistance to militarization: Three years of the End Conscription Campaign'. *South African Review* 4. Johannesburg: Ravan Press.

Ogden, C. K. and Florence, M. 1915. *Militarism versus Feminism*. London: Allen and Unwin.

Oldfield, S. 1989. *Women Against the Iron Fist: Alternatives to Militarism 1900-1989*. Oxford: Basil Blackwell.

Orkin, M. 1989. *State versus Zwane and Three Others*, evidence in mitigation. Case no. 41/1017/89.

Orr, R. 1983. *Women, Militarism and Non-violence*. London: Peace Pledge Union.

Parker, T. 1985. *Soldier, Soldier*. London: Heinemann.

Petras, J. 1987. 'The anatomy of state terror: Chile, El Salvador and Brazil', in *Science and Society*, vol. 51, no. 3, pp. 314-38.

Phillips, M. 1989. 'The nuts and bolts of military power: The structure of the SADF', in Cock, J. and Nathan, L. *War and Society: The Militarization of South Africa*. Cape Town: David Philip; New York: St. Martin's Press.

Pillay, P. 1988. 'Women in employment in South Africa: Some important trends and issues', in *Social Dynamics*, vol.11, no. 2, pp. 20-36.

Prekel, T. 1980. 'Why a special look at women?' in *South African Journal of Business Management*, vol. 11, no. 2.

Ramphele, M. 1989. 'The dynamics of gender politics in the hostels of Cape Town: Another legacy of the South African migrant labour system', in *Journal of South African Studies*, vol. 18, no. 3, pp. 393-414.

Randle, M. 1981. 'Militarism and repression', in *Alternatives*, no. 7, pp. 61-144.

Ratcliffe, S. 1983. 'Forced relations: The State, crisis and the rise of militarism in South Africa.' Unpublished Honours dissertation, University of the Witwatersrand.

Rich, A. 1978. *The Dream of a Common Language: Poems 1974-1977*. New York: W. W. Norton.

Rich, P. 1984. 'Insurgency, terrorism and the apartheid system in South Africa', in *Political Studies*, no. 32, pp. 68-85.

Riordaan, R. 1988. 'Murder by proxy – the modernization of South Africa's security juggernaut'. Paper delivered at Michigan State University, conference on State Terrorism.

Ritter, R. 1989. 'Bringing war home: Vets who have battered'. Unpublished paper. Fort Wayne: Veterans' Centre.

Roberts, B. 1984. 'The death of the machothink: Feminist research and the transformation of peace studies', in *Women's Studies International Forum*, vol. 7, no. 4, pp. 195-200.

Russell, D. (ed.) 1989a. *Exposing Nuclear Phallacies*. New York: The Pergamon Press.

Russell, D. 1989b. 'Life in a police state: A black South African woman speaks out', in *Women's Studies International Forum*, vol. 12, no. 2. pp. 157-66.

Russell, D. 1989c. *Lives of Courage: Women for a New South Africa.* New York: Basic Books.

Said, E. 1988. 'Identity, negation and violence', in *New Left Review*, no. 171, October, pp. 46-60.

Saul, J. 1987. 'Killing the dream: The role of the counter-revolutionary guerrilla in the militarization of the Third World'. Paper presented at Queens University, conference on 'Militarization in the Third World: the Caribbean Basin and Southern Africa', January.

Saywell, S. 1985. *Women in War.* Toronto: Penguin Books.

Schirmer, J. 1989. 'Those who die for life cannot be called dead: Women and human rights protest in Latin America', in *Feminist Review*, no. 32, Summer, pp. 3-29.

Schreiner, O. 1911. *Women and Labour.* London: Unwin.

Schweik, S. 1987. 'Writing war poetry like a woman', in *Critical Inquiry*, vol. 13, Spring, pp. 532-56.

Scruton, R. 1987. 'Notes on the sociology of war', in *British Journal of Sociology*, vol. 38, no. 3.

Scruton, R. 1988. 'Left and right: War and peace', in *British Journal of Sociology*, vol. 39, no. 2, pp. 281-5.

Shaw, M. 1988. *Dialectics of War.* London: Pluto Press.

Simkins, C. 1986. 'Household composition and structure in South Africa', in Burman, S. and Reynolds, P. (eds), *Growing Up in a Divided Society.* Johannesburg: Ravan Press.

Soule, A. 1987. *The Wynand du Toit Story.* Johannesburg: Hans Strydom Publishers.

South African Institute of Race Relations (SAIRR) 1986. 'Conscription and race relations', in *Race Relations News*, March/April.

Stiehm, J. H. 1983. 'Women and men's wars', in *Women's Studies International Forum*, vol. 5, no. 314.

Strange, P. 1989. 'It'll make a man of you: A feminist view of the arms race', in Russell, D. 1989a.

Summer, A. 1975. *Damned Whores and God's Police.* Sydney: Penguin Books.

Swilling, M. 1989a. In Frankel, P. *et al.* (eds), *State, Resistance and Change in South Africa.* London: Croom Helm.

Swilling, M. 1989b. 'Can war be stopped by those who are meant to wage it?' in *Sash*, March.

Swilling, M. and Lodge, T. 1988. 'Run guerrilla run: South Africa's children's war'. Unpublished paper.

Tambo, O. R. 1986. Statement on Heroes' Day, 16 December 1986. Published in *Dawn*, Souvenir Issue on the 25th anniversary of Umkhonto we Sizwe, Lusaka.

Terkel, S. 1984. *World War II*. Harmondsworth: Penguin Books.

Thompson, D. 1983. *Over Our Dead Bodies*. London: Virago.

Thompson, E.P. 1982. 'Notes on exterminism, the last stage of civilization', in New Left Review (eds), *Exterminism and Cold War*. London: Verso.

Tomaselli, R. 1988. 'Social construction of the "enemy": SABC and the demonization of the ANC terrorist', in Graaf, M. (ed.), *Hawks and Doves: The Pro and Anti-conscription Press in South Africa*. Durban: Contemporary Cultural Studies Unit.

Unterhalter, E. 1987. 'Women soldiers and white unity in apartheid South Africa', in Macdonald, S. *et al.* (eds), 1987, *Images of Women in Peace and War: Cross-cultural and Historical Perspectives*. Basingstoke: Macmillan Education in association with Oxford Women's Studies Committee, pp. 100-21.

Urdang, S. 1984. 'Women in national liberation movements', in Hay, M. and Stichter, S., *African Women South of the Sahara*. London: Longman.

Van der Vyver, A. D. 1988. 'State sponsored terror violence', in *South African Journal on Human Rights*, vol. 4, part 1, March.

Van Eyk, J. 1989. *Eyewitness to Unrest*. Johannesburg: Taurus.

Venter, M. 1983. *Vrou en die Soldaat*. Pretoria: Kopiereg.

Vogelman, L. 1990. *The Sexual Face of Violence: Rapists on Rape*. Johannesburg: Ravan Press.

Von Holdt, K. 1988. 'Vigilantes versus defence committees', in *South African Labour Bulletin*, vol. 13, no. 2, February, pp. 16-27.

Walliman, I. 1987. 'Sex roles and participation in military and defence: Outlining Swiss women's attitudes and values towards militarism, conflict resolution and peace', in *International Journal of Sociology and Social Policy*, vol. 7, no. 2, pp. 68-79.

Walther, E. 1969. *Terror and Resistance: A Study of Political Violence*. Oxford and New York: Oxford University Press.

Walzer, M. 1987. *Just and Unjust Wars*. London: Allen Lane.

Warnock, D. 1989. Interview in Russell, D. (ed.), 1989a.

Weber, M. 1968. *Economy and Society*. New York: Bedminster Press.

Williams, R. 1983. *Towards 2000*. London: The Hogarth Press.

Wilson, F. and Ramphele, M. 1989. *Uprooting Poverty*. Cape Town: David Philip.

Wollstonecraft, M. 1792. *A Vindication of the Rights of Woman*. References to the 1967 Penguin edition.

Woolf, V. 1938. *Three Guineas*. London: The Hogarth Press.

Young, N. 1986. 'War resistance, state and society', in Shaw, M. (ed.), *War, State and Society*. London: Macmillan, pp. 95-118.

Yuval-Davis, N. 1981. 'The Israel example', in Chapkis, W. (ed.), 1981.

Yuval-Davis, N. 1985. 'Front and rear: The sexual division of labour in the Israeli army', in *Feminist Studies*, vol. 2, no.3, pp. 649-76.

Yuval-Davis, N. and Anthias, F. 1989. *Women-nation-state*. London: Macmillan.

Zille, H. 1986. 'Beginning life in an apartheid society', in Burman, S. and Reynolds, P. (eds), *Growing Up in a Divided Society*. Johannesburg: Ravan Press.

Index